THE GOLDEN GENERATION

THE GOLDEN GENERATION

HOW CANADA BECAME A BASKETBALL POWERHOUSE

OREN WEISFELD

ECW

Published by ECW Press
665 Gerrard Street East
Toronto, Ontario, Canada M4M 1Y2
416-694-3348 / info@ecwpress.com

Editor for the Press: Michael Holmes
Copy Editor: Carrie Gleason
Cover Design: Moya Garrison-Msingwana and Jess Albert
Cover Image: Aurora Shields

LIBRARY AND ARCHIVES CANADA CATALOGUING IN PUBLICATION

Title: The golden generation : how Canada became a basketball powerhouse / Oren Weisfeld.

Names: Weisfeld, Oren, author.

Description: Includes bibliographical references.

Identifiers: Canadiana (print) 2025025266X | Canadiana (ebook) 20250252708

ISBN 978-1-77041-799-1 (softcover)
ISBN 978-1-77852-484-4 (ePub)
ISBN 978-1-77852-485-1 (PDF)

Subjects: LCSH: Basketball—Canada—History. | LCSH: Basketball players—Canada.

Classification: LCC GV885.8.C3 W45 2025 | DDC 796.323/640971—dc23

This book is funded in part by the Government of Canada. *Ce livre est financé en partie par le gouvernement du Canada.* We also acknowledge the support of the Government of Ontario through the Ontario Book Publishing Tax Credit, and through Ontario Creates. This book was also funded in part by the Marian Hebb Research Grant from the Saskatchewan Arts Board Access Copyright Foundation.

PRINTED AND BOUND IN CANADA

PRINTING: MARQUIS 5 4 3 2 1

For my parents,
Harvey and Ariela

"Not only is there more to life than basketball, there's a lot more to basketball than basketball."

— THIRTEEN-TIME NBA CHAMPION PHIL JACKSON

NOTE TO READERS

Quotes from individuals in this book come from a variety of news sources (past tense) as well as from the author's own interviews (present tense). A detailed source section is provided on page 266.

The Golden Generation is in no way affiliated with Canada Basketball and is not an official biography of Team Canada or its players.

CONTENTS

INTRO

OPENING A PANDORA'S BOX

Canada's national basketball federation was desperate for help.

With a $1.3-million deficit that stemmed from a federal government that has historically been hesitant to fund team sports, costly mistakes made by previous regimes, and the banks no longer willing to lend it any more money, it was the summer of 2007 when Canada Basketball needed an injection of cash to survive. "Things were incredibly grim," CEO Wayne Parrish said. "We didn't know if we could meet payroll or pay rent. Every day was day-to-day."

Parrish walked into the offices of Maple Leaf Sports and Entertainment (MLSE) on 50 Bay Street in downtown Toronto to meet with Bryan Colangelo, the president of basketball operations for the Toronto Raptors. MLSE and Canada Basketball had a relationship dating back to 1994, when the two organizations worked together to host the FIBA World Championship in Toronto. They understood that what was best for the long-term success of each business was to put their minds and resources together to help grow basketball across the country.

"You know, it's a terrible way to start off a relationship" Parish recalls saying. "But is there any way you could provide some help?" And he walked out of the meeting with a cheque for $300,000. "My experience in those early months, in the first couple of years certainly, was that so many people just wanted to help make it work," he says.

Halfway through the meeting, Colangelo asked if someone could join them, and in walked a short Italian man with a strong accent named Maurizio Gherardini — the assistant general manager of the Raptors who was better known for managing some of Europe's best clubs since 1975. "I don't think Maurizio said a word in the conversation," Parrish says. "He just listened." But at the end, Colangelo asked Gherardini if he wouldn't mind working with Canada Basketball going forward, bringing his knowledge of international basketball and network of connections to the Canadian federation. Gherardini accepted, but not without giving the organization a healthy reality check.

During his first meeting with the board of directors a couple weeks later, Gherardini walked to the front of the board room, took out a black marker, and wrote one word on the whiteboard: Revolution.

After digging into the Canadian basketball landscape, Gherardini understood that Canada was bursting with potential. He saw the liberal immigration policy leading to an increasingly diverse population; he saw the passion and inspiration that the Raptors were beginning to have on young kids following Vince Carter's tenure with the team; and he saw the school teachers and coaches working to develop the next generation of players at the grassroots level.

But he also knew that it was going to take nothing short of a revolution for Canada to reach its potential. Despite placing seventh at the Olympics a few years prior in 2000, Canada's basketball scene appeared to be regressing, with a splintered infrastructure that included school, club, and provincial teams all playing under different rule sets and pulling kids in different directions. Meanwhile, the national program couldn't even recruit its best players, let alone fund a top-tier program.

"Keep in mind, at that time Canada had in the NBA one icon named Steve Nash, and a guy named Joel Anthony," Gherardini says. "That was it. There was no other Canadian talent; no other Canadian players in any European top competition."

But thanks to the work of countless Canadian basketball players, coaches, parents, and businesspeople who invested time and resources into the expansion of grassroots basketball, Canada is now a basketball powerhouse.

During the 2024–25 season, Canada had a record 28 NBA players, the most of any country outside the United States for 11 straight seasons. Andrew Wiggins, Jamal Murray, and RJ Barrett are household names, while Shai Gilgeous-Alexander just cemented himself as the best player in the world after winning the NBA MVP award and leading the Oklahoma City Thunder to the 2025 Championship.

Meanwhile, the Canadian basketball passport had become one of the most attractive on Earth, with a record number of Canadians playing in top professional leagues across Asia, South America, and Europe, including in the EuroCup and EuroLeague. Team Canada is ranked fifth in the world after winning bronze at the 2023 FIBA World Cup and participating in its first Olympic Games since 2000 at Paris 2024.

Canada now has a comprehensive prep school ecosystem, some of the best club teams in the world, and a FIBA-sanctioned domestic league that is growing at an unprecedented rate. At the youth level, participation rates have doubled since 2010, with more than 700 officially registered clubs and 100,000 registered participants across the country (not including school, Amateur Athletic Union, or house league). In fact, basketball is among the fastest growing sports in Canada, especially among young people and immigrants, who make up 23 percent of the population.

"The system, the approach changed, and it looks like we opened up a Pandora's box," Gherardini says. "This is the game today. But we should go back and see the whole process."

By now it is well-known that Vince Carter's dunks inspired a generation of Canadians before Kyle Lowry, DeMar DeRozan, and Kawhi Leonard poured fuel on the fire by helping the Raptors win its first NBA Championship in 2019. But inspiration is one thing, and development is another. And for a long time, Canada lacked the resources and imagination to send its best players to the pros.

However, as one generation learned from their experiences and mistakes, they passed down tribal knowledge to their sons and daughters, nieces and nephews — former athletes who lacked the developmental tools to play professionally but taught their children how to shoot on Fisher-Price nets before driving them to practices all across the provinces; coaches who grew up in dangerous, impoverished neighbourhoods and volunteered countless hours in the gym to improve their communities by providing a refuge for inner-city kids; and club programs that learned from our neighbours to the south and understood that in order to be the best, you had to go down to America and beat them.

This book tells the story of the trailblazers that took their hits in order to lay the foundation for the current Golden Generation of Canadian players to thrive: coaches like Ro Russell and Mike George who helped countless kids get NCAA Division I basketball scholarships; parents like Charmaine Gilgeous and Roger Murray who passed down the lessons they learned growing up to their sons; and players like Junior Cadougan,

Cory Joseph, and Andrew Wiggins who were guinea pigs for the wild world of American basketball, creating a pathway for the next generation to follow.

Of course, the role Canada Basketball has played in identifying and developing the nation's best players and coaches cannot be overlooked. From players like Steve Nash inspiring a generation of kids to dream during his magical run at the 2000 Olympics to coaches like Jay Triano and Leo Rautins giving players the opportunity to wear the red and white to executives like Parrish and Michael Bartlett bringing money into the program to give the athletes the treatment they deserve, this growth would not have been possible without Canada's national federation keeping the lights on despite the obstacles.

(While the Canadian women's program has had more success than the men in recent years, going to four straight Olympics and producing a record number of WNBA players, it's clear that the best is yet to come. With the third-ranked girls' program in the world, a pipeline of exciting young prospects currently entering college, and a WNBA team coming to Toronto in 2026, it didn't feel right to include their stories at this time.)

After interviewing more than 100 of the most influential figures in the modern history of Canadian men's basketball, this book aims to tell the never-before-told story of how Canada became a basketball powerhouse, going from the bottom of the international basketball rankings to the top. By jumping back and forth between developments within the Canadian men's national team, innovations in the grassroots community, and profiles of Canada's top players, the book aims to answer questions like: How did a cold-weather, hockey-crazed country of 40 million produce the best player in the world, and 28 NBA players in 2025? How did the Canadian national team, once a laughingstock of the international basketball community, win its first ever medal at the 2023 FIBA World Cup? And why does the developmental infrastructure in place suggest that what we are seeing now is just the beginning?

Sure, a "revolution" that opened up a "Pandora's box" sounds extreme. But when it comes to the history of Canadian basketball, the truth really is stranger than fiction.

PART 1

TRIBAL KNOWLEDGE

CHAPTER 1

CAPTAIN CANADA

JOHN NASH

Steve Nash dribbles at Santa Clara University, the lone NCAA school to offer him a basketball scholarship.

"If every basketball player worked as hard as I did, I'd be out of a job."
— STEVE NASH

Steve Nash was born in Johannesburg, South Africa, in 1974 to John and Jean Nash, Brits who lived there briefly before fleeing the racial apartheid for sunnier pastures. The family settled in Victoria, the capital city of British Columbia, located on the southeastern tip of Vancouver Island on the Pacific coast.

"Really it was the best thing we could have done," John says. "Wonderful place to bring up children." The island was safe from crime, and as Canada's lone snow-free capital, their three kids, Steve, Martin, and Joann, could bike around freely and play outdoor sports year-round.

John was a professional soccer player back in South Africa and England, where he met Jean. He wasn't particularly big or physical, but he was skilled and known for his playmaking instincts, with a knack for setting up teammates from anywhere on the pitch. As soon as his kids were old enough to walk, he taught them the right, selfless way to play in the backyard of their home. "If they played a one-two around me, even if it was a bad one-two, and they passed the ball around me, I would let them get away with it," he says. "If they tried to fake it and dribble, I'd tackle them."

Steve took to soccer immediately, with his first word being "goal." But he excelled in everything from baseball to hockey to box lacrosse to rugby to chess, making 10 of 10 place kicks in his first high school rugby match, scoring seven goals in a juvenile lacrosse game, and winning three elementary school chess titles. In high school, he became the only player in the history of British Columbia to win the province's most valuable player in soccer, basketball, and rugby. "I think he would have been a pro in at least three, maybe four sports," his college basketball coach, Dick Davey, says.

And he might have been a professional soccer player like his younger brother, Martin, if it wasn't for the fact that Victoria was going through a basketball renaissance in the 1980s, right when Nash was coming of age.

The best university team in the country, the University of Victoria Vikes, won seven straight national championships between 1980 and 1986 behind head coach Ken Shields and starting point guard Eli Pasquale. Shields grew up in Haida Gwaii, BC, and fell in love with the game playing with the local Indigenous kids before moving to the mainland and coaching at Laurentian University for six years. There, he met a local high schooler named Pasquale, who followed Shields to U Vic in 1980 and became the best player in the country, dominating Canadian university basketball (U Sports) alongside a group of local islanders — several of whom went on to play for Team Canada.

"I think for many of them it was an inspiration," Nash's high school coach, Ian Hyde-Lay, says of the Vikes' impact on the teenagers he was coaching. "McKinnon Gym was packed every night. It was a big ticket . . . With no pro sports teams in the town, it was one of the events to go to."

Nash was already a multi-sport athlete who spent his weekends taking a ferry back and forth from Metro Vancouver for rep soccer and hockey tournaments. He had a keen sense of footwork, hand-eye coordination, spacing and angle concepts, and problem-solving skills that turned out to be transferable to basketball, which he excelled in after discovering the sport in eighth grade.

In fact, after participating in his first pick up basketball game, Nash ran home to his father bursting with excitement. "Dad, it's like cheating," John recalls his son saying. "You can use your hands!"

■

Dave Thomson was the physical education teacher at Arbutus Junior High School, where Nash went from grades 8 to 10. He would open the gym for Nash and his friends to play at all hours, spending entire evenings and weekends there, only pausing briefly to run across the street to Mark Kennedy's house for lunch.

"It was kind of crazy," Thomson says. "But they loved it so much. And they loved being together so much that it seemed to work for them."

Nash fell in love with the game once he started playing regularly with his new friends Kennedy, Mike Schaeffer, Al Whitley, and Adam Miller at Arbutus. "I wanted to be with my friends playing basketball," he says, getting tired of returning from Vancouver every weekend and hearing stories about how much fun they had. "I didn't want to miss that. So, I stopped soccer and hockey after that season so that I could be with my friends playing basketball."

Nash had developed such an elite feel for the game by grade 9 that the boys won the junior high school provincial championships. At the same time, basketball was becoming a more popular sport worldwide, as the red and white Air Jordan 1s hit the market with Spike Lee joining Michael Jordan in the commercials. And Nash took to it with a religious fervour, jumping over his backyard fence to practise his jump shot at the Hillcrest Elementary School playground, 50 metres away, whenever he had time to spare. "Steven would get out there and he would grind," John says. "If he even thought about not shooting, say, 100 threes — if he got halfway through and saw that — he had the determination to say, 'I'm gonna start again at zero to punish myself for thinking that I should give up on a project.'"

When he wasn't shooting, Nash would carry a basketball around with him, distracting neighbours with the sound of him dribbling and practising crossovers, pass fakes, and shoulder shakes, visualizing moves that he would then use in a game. "I think the bottom line is, for whatever reason, however — nature, nurture — I can get obsessed," Nash said. "I got obsessed with trying to be the best I could be.

"So, I put in that time. I constantly was trying to get better."

Nash transferred to St. Michaels University School (SMUS) in November of grade 11 after having academic issues at his first high school, Mount Douglas Secondary. Unfortunately, because of Canada's archaic high school transfer rules that disable mid-year transfers from playing sports during the same season, Nash became a "redshirt" basketball player who was only allowed to participate in practices and exhibition games — a tough pill to swallow for a kid who was beginning to set his sights on obtaining a scholarship to play Division I basketball in America's National Collegiate Athletic Association (NCAA).

Still, his new coach Hyde-Lay connected him with Ken Shields, who let him come to U Vic and play pickup ball with the university team. "It was a really amazing opportunity to kind of feel the level and feel what it's like to play against men," Nash says.

His real breakthrough came that summer, between grades 11 and 12, after Shields had begun coaching the Canadian senior men's national team. The training camps were held in Victoria, where Nash got to train with Canada's best players. "He had such a tremendous skill set," Hyde-Lay says, "that when he moved to the next level, he could adapt."

In fact, it quickly became apparent that Nash was skilled enough to hold his own against grown men despite giving up several inches and tens of pounds, using his speed and advanced handle to drive into the lane without fear before using the defensive attention to set up his teammates for easy baskets. One day, a group of coaches were watching the team scrimmage from the sideline when Shields turned to them: "You see that little skinny kid out there?" Shields recalls saying. "He's gonna play in the NBA."

Nash spent the second half of the summer of 1991 practising with Canada's junior national team in Lethbridge, Alberta, where they were preparing for the upcoming Under-19 World Cup. But after already establishing a core group of players through previous competitions, head coach Ken Olynyk cut the 17-year-old Nash, who gave up a lot of size and strength to the 19-year-olds he was competing against. Nash was named an alternate who only played exhibition games, including one against Long Beach State that went so well for Nash that the school's coaching staff surrounded him after the game and expressed their interest in recruiting him. "And then I never heard from them again," Nash says.

He began his grade 12 basketball season at SMUS with a chip on his shoulder. After redshirting the prior season and getting cut from the junior national team that summer, Nash had one final chance to land an NCAA scholarship. And everything came together as he averaged 21 points, 11 assists, and 9 rebounds a game for the dominant SMUS team, showcasing a fast, creative style of play that kept fans on the edge of their seats as he dribbled through a sea of bigger opponents, while anticipating how the defense was going to react . Nash wasn't yet the elite three-point shooter that he would become or tall enough to consistently finish at the rim, but everyone enjoyed playing with him because he understood the art of setting up his teammates — just like his father taught him in the backyard when he was a boy.

"That's what made him happy," Nash said. "So, when my dad told me he liked a pass, I wanted to recreate it and get that positive reinforcement — that love from my father."

Despite the gaudy statistics, Nash wasn't getting any attention from NCAA schools. Victoria was just 20 kilometres from the US border but there was no history of basketball players coming out of the province, which might as well have been Siberia as far as the NCAA was concerned. So, Hyde-Lay had Nash draft a list of 30 American basketball programs that might be in need of a freshman point guard, and his coach wrote to all the schools and said, "I really believe there's a very special player here. A diamond in the rough. You really should follow through on this guy."

"And most — almost all of them — just blew it off," said Hyde-Lay.

Nash was a short, skinny white kid from Victoria who had yet to begin lifting weights and whose only competition were other short, skinny white kids, making it nearly impossible for coaches to determine how his game would translate to the next level. "The lack of response hurt me, because I thought I was good enough that people would come knocking on my door," Nash said. "It was like I was trapped in an elevator and I'm screaming, but nobody could hear me."

Fortunately, one school heard him. And that was all he needed.

■

Santa Clara University sits on the hills surrounding the Jesuit Mission Santa Clara de Asís in Santa Clara, California. And in the spring of 1992, the men's basketball team was in desperate need of a point guard.

Scott Gradin, the restricted earning coach at the time, was put in charge of helping them find a new recruit. Only he wasn't allowed to leave campus as part of his job, so he scoured the database for any leads. Nash was one of them.

The previous summer, there had been a big Amateur Athletic Union (AAU) exposure tournament in Las Vegas, Nevada, where the best American teams went to play in front of NCAA coaches. And after getting cut from the junior national team, Nash joined Team BC for the Under-17 national championship, which used the AAU tournament as a tune-up for Canadian nationals.

Team BC was excited to match up against California high school standout Jason Kidd's team in the big gym in front of hundreds of college coaches, but they lost their previous game and were relegated to a small, nearly empty gym instead. Still, sitting in the bleachers was an assistant coach from Saint Mary's University, which played in the West Coast Conference (WCC) with Santa Clara. And the coach took note of the small, heady point guard, mentioning his name to Santa Clara assistant coach Larry Hauser, who put Nash in the database. He simply noted that his friend liked Steve. "And so that was enough for me," Gradin says. "I put him on the recruiting list."

The first thing Gradin did was call Nash and introduce himself, explaining that he was a coach at Santa Clara. The two of them got to talking basketball, and it was clear to Gradin that he understood the game at a high level. "He was really articulate, and I'm thinking right away this kid is already heads and tails, mentally way ahead," Gradin says.

The only problem was that Nash didn't have any game film. Instead, all Nash could do was offer up a hit that the local news station did on the impressive SMUS team, which showed Nash toying with his opponents. "Steve was so good with the ball and he could get guys off balance, change direction, and they would fall down," Gradin says about what became dubbed the Grainy Cult Film. "Everybody asked me, 'What are you laughing about?' I said, 'It's this guy from Canada, man. He makes people fall down.'"

Still, nobody on the staff believed that there were any good players in Canada, let alone in Victoria of all places. It took some time to convince Dick Davey, the associate head coach at the time, to go see Nash in person. But after getting eliminated in the second round of the WCC tournament in Portland in 1992, Davey continued on to watch Nash play at the senior boys' provincial championship weekend in front of 5,000 people at the Agrodome in Vancouver.

Davey was impressed before the game even started. After watching Nash go through his detailed warmup routine, where he went through dribbling drills, practised layups with both hands, and barely missed a shot, Davey called Gradin. "I think he could help us next year," Gradin recalls him saying. "He might be a guy that could go a whole year and not miss a free throw. He's that good of a shooter."

Davey met with Nash after the game and immediately told him that he was one of the worst defenders he had ever seen. "But I'll give you a scholarship right now if you'll take it," Nash says. It was his only Division I scholarship offer despite being the best high school player in Canada, going on to help SMUS win its first ever provincial championship a few days later, with Nash winning tournament MVP. But due to a lack of exposure or connections to American coaches, Nash almost slipped through the cracks like many great Canadians before him. As he put it, "In the recruiting process it took extra long to get attention because I was Canadian."

But despite the obstacles, his small hometown offered some unique advantages. Before departing for university, Nash learned an important lesson from Pasquale, who by then had led U Vic to five consecutive national championships as the university's all-time leading scorer. Like many players of his era, Pasquale only ever wanted to play for Team Canada growing up, as the NBA seemed too unrealistic. And while he played 73 games for Canada — the second most games by any player (official game and point records can be found on page 264) — he realized too late that he was good enough to play in the NBA.

Not wanting Nash to make the same mistake, Pasquale offered him some advice during a car ride home from one of his basketball camps. "He said to me, 'You know, if you want to play in the NBA, you should decide right now,'" Nash said. "What he was trying to say was that it's important to declare your intentions . . . it's the first step to holding yourself accountable and making a tangible path to realizing your goals and your dreams."

And with that, Nash was off to America.

•

By the time Nash arrived in Santa Clara in 1992, the history of Canadians making it to the NBA was scarce, and the ones who had made it bore little resemblance to the 6'3" Nash. Mike Smrek, Jim Zoet, and Ron Crevier all played in the NBA in the 1980s. But they were all seven-footers who could command an NCAA scout to cross the border.

As was Bill Wennington, who grew up in Montreal but moved to the United States during high school, similar to Canadian citizens Stewart Granger and Ernie Vandeweghe, who all had the unique advantage of developing their games in the United States.

As soon as Nash arrived in Santa Clara, he realized how important that development was, as the transition to living alone in a different environment and playing against American competition several years older than him proved challenging. Davey took over as head coach just before the season started and was old school, immediately clashing with Nash over things like one-handed passes, which he thought were too risky.

Davey was especially tough on his six-player freshman class. After one exhibition loss to Nevada Reno, in Reno — which sits at an altitude of 4,400 feet — Davey looked at his team and told them, "It's my fault, guys, it's my fault. I'm sorry," fellow freshman Phil Von Buchwaldt says. "But I can tell you one thing: when we get back to Santa Clara, we will become the best conditioned team in America."

The bus ride home was silent, because everybody knew that the next day's practice was going to be an epic shit show. And they were right, as Davey sent the players into a frenzy, making them run up and down the court so much that guys were puking all over the place.

Nash also had to go up against John Woolery in practice every day: a defense-first guard with a strong build, long wingspan, and penchant for getting steals. Woolery made things tough on the freshman point guard by picking him up full-court and not letting Nash dribble past him. Woolery would steal the ball at half court, score a layup, and repeat. At one point during an early season practice, the whistle blew and Coach Davey walked up to where Woolery kept stealing the ball from Nash. "I can see Steve is starting to get upset, teary-eyed," Von Buchwaldt says.

Davey slammed the ball into Nash's stomach a few feet away from half court and said, "Can you take it from here?"

Nash was so down on himself during the early days that he would call his parents and say he wanted to go home. "There's a lot of guys who would have quit," Von Buchwaldt says. "But not Steve. Steve was like, 'Okay, what do I need to do for this to stop happening?'" And the answer was to develop one of the best handles in the history of basketball, thanks in part to Woolery. "He was a tough-minded son of a gun," Davey said. "A three-hour practice wasn't enough for him. He wanted to be as good as he could possibly be."

Nash struggled early in his freshman year, but that only made him work harder and become more obsessed with improvement, remaining confident in his abilities despite the obstacles. A month into his freshman season, Nash and Von Buchwaldt sat in the campus library studying when Nash looked up from his papers to declare that he would play in the NBA one day.

"I'm like, 'Yeah, okay, sure. That's a good one,'" Von Buchwaldt says, thinking that he could make some extra cash off the least-known recruit in Santa Clara's six-man freshman class. So, they made a bet that if Nash ever dribbled a ball in the NBA, he would give him $100.

But a couple weeks later, Von Buchwaldt realized that Nash might not be so dumb after all. He woke up at 7:45 a.m., rolled out of bed, and jogged to a Theology of Marriage class at 8:00, saving a seat for his teammate. A few minutes later, Nash walked in drenched in sweat, basketball on his arm, backpack on his back, having woken up at 6:30 a.m. to put up 200 shots before class. "And I remember thinking if that's what it takes, I don't have it," Von Buchwaldt says. "I can't do that. Not at that age, not at 19 years old. I didn't have the maturity to do something like that. . . . I also don't think that I had the willpower to do that.

"I don't think anybody else did. He did that by himself."

This is the same Nash who didn't feel right or sleep well if he didn't train that day; whose advice during his Naismith Basketball Hall of Fame speech was to find something you love, become obsessed with it, and find balance later. And who famously said, "If every basketball player worked as hard as I did, I'd be out of a job."

Nash made his mark during the WCC tournament at the end of the year, becoming the first freshman MVP in WCC tournament history as he helped Santa Clara win the conference and receive an automatic bid into its first NCAA tournament since 1987.

He improved each season, averaging 17 points and 6 assists in his senior year while hitting over 40 percent of his threes and 86 percent of his free throws across his four seasons as a Bronco. He finished his career as Santa Clara's all-time leader in assists (510), free throw percentage (86.7), and three-pointers made (263), becoming the first student-athlete to have his jersey retired at the school.

After graduating with a degree in sociology, Nash declared for the 1996 NBA Draft, and Santa Clara's entire six-person freshman class showed up to support him. Von Buchwaldt put the $100 he owed Nash towards a plane ticket.

Nash was selected 15th overall by the Phoenix Suns. Despite his success at Santa Clara, the selection elicited a hail of boos from bewildered fans who still hadn't heard of the small white point guard from Canada. "I don't look like I'm going to be a tremendous basketball player on appearance," Nash said. "I probably would've booed myself too."

During his 18-year NBA career, Nash became the first Canadian All-Star and MVP, revolutionizing the game by ushering in a fast-paced, freewheeling, three-point-happy style of play — one that led to 5 of the 10 best offenses in NBA history.

More importantly, Nash pushed basketball forward in a cold-weather, hockey-crazed country that was finally ready to embrace it.

CHAPTER 2

THE DARK CLOUD, PART 1

CANADA BASKETBALL

The 2024 Canadian Olympic team surrounded by members of the program's previous five Olympic teams (1976, 1980, 1984, 1988, and 2000).

"We talked about it all the time: We were better known around the world than we were in our own country."

— JAY TRIANO

The 1994 FIBA World Championship was originally set to be played in Belgrade, Serbia, until a civil war broke out in Yugoslavia in 1991. The International Basketball Federation (FIBA) had to reluctantly reopen the bidding competition for a new host. Boris Stankovic, the head of FIBA, called Canadian businessman John Bitove and asked if Canada would consider hosting.

Bitove understood that the only way it would be worth hosting an event of that magnitude was if NBA players were allowed to participate, bringing with them the marketing cache and fan interest that could put butts in seats coming off the heels of the 1992 Summer Olympics in Barcelona, Spain. The Barcelona Games were the first Olympics that allowed professional players to participate in the basketball competition, enabling Jordan, Magic Johnson, Larry Bird, and Charles Barkley to come together and form the US "Dream Team," dominating the storylines on and off the court. The Dream Team won the gold medal with an average margin of victory of 43.8 points, opening up the world to basketball's incredible potential.

Bitove called NBA commissioner David Stern to ask for his blessing. "[Stern] said, 'Listen, young man, I don't know you, but I do know Canada, and I know Toronto,'" Bitove says. "'And the only way we would allow the pros to play in the World Championship is if it's in North America.'"

With that, a committee co-chaired by Bitove and Canada Basketball CEO Rick Traer raised $13 million and won the bid to host the 11-day tournament held in Toronto's SkyDome and Maple Leaf Gardens and Hamilton's Copps Coliseum.

They sold a World Championship–record 332,334 tickets, including a gold medal game with a record 32,000 fans at the SkyDome. After breaking even on the massive investment weeks before the games began, Canada Basketball got 40 percent of the profits, which helped keep an organization on the brink of collapse afloat.

One year later, in 1993, Bitove leveraged the contacts he'd made hosting the World Championship into becoming the owner of Toronto's first NBA franchise, the Toronto Raptors. "Without the '94 Worlds," he says, "I wouldn't have had the NBA team."

The 1994 World Championship was Nash's international coming-out party. In his first tournament with Canada's senior team, a 20-year-old Nash averaged 7 points, 3 assists, 3 rebounds, and 2 steals in 23 minutes per game as the team's youngest player. "We spent all of our time trying to get [Canada's lone NBA player] Rick Fox freed up to play," Bitove says. "Lo and behold, Steve Nash stole the show."

Despite Nash beginning to capture the country's attention with his flashy play, the Canadian team disappointed, finishing seventh in the 16-team tournament and second last in their group after losing key games to Russia and Greece. Team USA's "Dream Team II" won the tournament behind an MVP performance from Shaquille O'Neal, with its closest margin of victory being a 15-point win over Spain.

"They weren't good enough to win the Worlds that year, but to have at least gone to the finals," *Victoria Times Colonist* sports reporter Cleve Dheensaw says. "Canada was eliminated and got a lot of bad press for it, to sit out the quarter-final stage at home."

And the bad press didn't end there. Even though the building was full every time Canada played, it quickly became apparent that most fans were not there to support Canada, but it's opponents. In fact, one key game between Canada and Greece saw far more blue flags than red ones, eliciting a rant from *Hockey Night in Canada*'s Don Cherry. "Back then basketball was a little bit more of a niche sport," Nash says. "Fans from those nations were coming out to support the countries against Canada."

It was symbolic of the massive immigrant population in metropolitan cities in Central Canada like Toronto, Montreal, and Hamilton in those days, giving testimony to an intense patriotism and basketball fandom that many Canadians could not comprehend. "It was one of the most embarrassing sports events I've ever been at," Doug Smith, a basketball reporter for the *Toronto Star*, says. "There was no excitement around that, not a lot of buzz about Canada Basketball."

It wasn't the first time Canadian basketball players felt a lack of support in their home country, as the sport lacked mainstream appeal prior to the arrival of the Toronto Raptors and Vancouver Grizzlies in 1995. "Nobody ever saw us play," former Team Canada captain Leo Rautins said.

Jay Triano and Eli Pasquale talked about it all the time. They would walk down the streets of Madrid, Spain, during the 1986 FIBA World Championship and people would chant their names and follow them into stores. Meanwhile, in training camp back home in Ottawa weeks prior, the team tried to get into a bar and the bouncer turned them down, not relenting after they explained that they were national team athletes.

"We were better known around the world than we were in our own country," Triano says.

■

There would soon be much more pressing concerns for Canada Basketball than the lack of fan interest. Despite having an NBA player in Rick Fox, overseas pros like Greg Wiltjer, Martin Keane, Joey Vickery, and Dwight Walton, as well as a young Steve Nash, the team couldn't compete against the best in the world. And they played a slow, methodical brand of basketball that wasn't very exciting to watch.

However, that was what head coach Ken Shields knew, primarily rostering former U Sports athletes who came from the West Coast, including several Vikes — better known for their fitness and execution than for their speed and skill — and just five Black players. "Let's be honest: the national teams were white teams," former Team Canada assistant coach Eddie Pomykala says.

Upon taking over as head coach in 1989, Shields centralized the national team in his hometown of Victoria, using his connections in the city to strike deals with a hotel, apparel company, and Thrifty Foods to ensure that a select group of amateur players could train there year-round. "Ken Shields had a program that was unlike anything else in the world," says Joey Vickery, whose father, Norm, coached Shields in high school. "It was like an experiment. He was like, 'Guys, I don't know what this is. But we're going to be training all year. And maybe one of you might make the team next year.'"

And that experiment paid off, with several of the players improving to the point that they got pro contracts, while four of them even made the Canadian team in 1994.

But it didn't work for everyone, as the balance of basketball power was shifting from west to east in Canada, specifically towards diverse, metropolitan cities like Toronto and Montreal which were receiving an influx of immigrants from the West Indies. As a result, Toronto- and Montreal-based high school and provincial teams had become dominant, regularly sending athletes to the NCAA and the pros for the first time in the country's history.

And because these athletes learned the game by playing pickup on outdoor blacktops in their inner-city neighbourhoods, East Coast ballers played a different brand of basketball that was more individualistic, improvisational, fast, rambunctious, creative, rough, and generally played above the rim.

"This city game is quick, it's upbeat," John Petruschak, the legendary coach of the Runnymede Redmen, said. "It comes from streetball. The teams from Metro Toronto are all like that."

Ken Shields's teams were not. In fact, Shields dominated Canadian university basketbell with an inside-out, John Wooden–inspired offense with two big men stationed in the paint and players meticulously cutting around them in the half court. But when it came to the national team, that style didn't fully take advantage of the speed, athleticism, and instincts of a lot of Canada's best Black players. In fact, inner-city kids from Toronto and Montreal believed that their chances of making the national team were marginalized because Shields's system favoured West Coast–based players who practised together for months. And Victoria wasn't the most friendly or comfortable environment for Black players, either.

"When you grew up in British Columbia, we don't have a big West Indian community," Nash says. "We don't have as much exposure to that culture and community to how they feel about the national team."

Back then, the organization was also full of traditionalists who only knew one way to play. "They didn't want the flash," says Brian Cooper, who was a board member back then and became chair of Canada Basketball in 2020. "They didn't want the on-court creativity. They didn't want the iso, one-on-one. They didn't want any of the celebration."

It was hard not to wonder if Canada was really putting its best team forward at the 1994 World Championship when, less than 10 days after the tournament wrapped up, Canada's leading newspaper, *The Globe and Mail*, published a story entitled "Toronto Blacks Assail Basketball Canada." It claimed that "Basketball Canada has turned its back on . . . countless other black basketball players from Toronto."

•

Cordell Llewellyn and Wayne Yearwood were considered two of the best players in the country by the mid '90s. They developed a reputation as high school stars in Toronto and Montreal, respectively, before going on to play in the NCAA. They even played for Canada at the previous summer's FIBA Americas tournament before being cut ahead of the '94 World Championship, which they believed was racially motivated.

"They have a preconceived opinion of black players," Llewellyn, who averaged 13 points a game at Rhode Island in 1994–95, told the *Globe*. "They say you've got attitude. It's not my game that got me cut, it's because they think if you have Canada written across your chest, you have to be white, because to them, Canada's white, and they'd rather lose than have too many blacks on the team."

Yearwood, meanwhile, was a member of Canada's 1988 Olympic team and had a successful pro career in Greece and Switzerland before rejoining Canada that summer in hopes of landing a new pro contract. He was a veteran leader throughout training camp, helping younger players assimilate to the team. But two weeks before the competition, Shields told Yearwood that he would be an alternate. "I was pissed. And I said to him, 'You don't even understand your team,'" Yearwood says. "He didn't put the best talent on the floor."

"I think he has a cultural problem, and perceives the black guys in a different way," Yearwood told the *Globe*. "It's more ignorance than racism. He's got us typecast. White players are assertive, black players have attitude. White guys are good players, Black guys are good athletes."

Freelance journalist Laura Robinson was originally tipped off about the story by an assistant basketball coach at Toronto's Eastern Commerce Collegiate Institute named Harry Baird, who explained to her that no matter how many stars Toronto sends to NCAA Division I schools, they're not making the national team. And after interviewing more than 20 players on the record, Robinson concluded that Canada Basketball had a problem of systemic racism stemming from the way it structured its training camps in BC and a style of play that favoured West Coast U Sports athletes.

As a result of the *Globe* story, Canada Basketball sought an external review of its practices conducted by Sport Canada and chaired by Caribbean-Canadian diplomat Cal Best, with Shields saying that if the review found him to be racist, he would step down from the job. After interviewing 60 people inside and outside the organization, the report found that "race played no role in the selection of Canada's national basketball team," adding that "No one with whom the committee met, talked to or heard from suggested that racial considerations played any part in selecting and coaching the national team."

Shields also sued *The Globe and Mail*, which settled out of court and issued a retraction in the paper the next day. "The process (allegations of racial prejudice) is not something I'd recommend anyone go through," Shields said. "The whole thing was very painful."

However, the 20-page report did make 11 recommendations for the men's program, including splitting the job of program director and head coach, attracting more minority coaches to participate in the national coaching certification program, and expanding the open tryout system to more Canadian cities.

It turned out to be neither the first nor the last allegation of racism made against Canada Basketball. Enabled by a white media cohort and covered up by board members who were out of touch with inner-city communities, it's a dark side of the country's basketball history that has never been told. "Nobody speaks about the real issues that existed back then, and nobody has because it's hard to put yourself out there," Llewellyn says. "People of colour, that's how we get up every morning knowing that you have to be careful with what you say, how you say it, because it's going to jeopardize — you don't know who is going to read it.

"So, it's scary."

But it's also a part of our history. And while the program has changed to the point where there are now Black executives in positions of power and the 12 best players are selected regardless of race or geography, its reputation as a racially biased entity lingered well into the 21st century. In fact, some of today's best players grew up with preconceived notions about the national team — ones that set Canada Basketball back decades.

CHAPTER 3

THE DARK CLOUD, PART 2

STEVE KONCHALSKI

Coaches Jack Donohue, Steve Konchalski, and Doc Ryan at the 1983 World University Games in Edmonton, where Team Canada won its first ever gold medal.

"We had lots of people in this city at that time that thought we should make our own national team, because there was no colour at all on that team for many, many years."
— NORMAN CLARKE

To fully understand the unequal power dynamics that existed within Canada's government-funded basketball federation by the 1990s, it helps to go all the way back to the sport's invention.

James Naismith was born in Almonte, Ontario, near Ottawa, to a long line of Scottish immigrants in 1861. At the age of nine, he lost both parents to typhoid fever, and he and his two siblings moved in with their uncle in nearby Bennie's Corners.

By the time 21-year-old Naismith enrolled at McGill University in Montreal, he was a standout athlete who competed in lacrosse, football, rugby, soccer, and gymnastics, eventually named the top athlete of his graduating class. It was there that he realized that his calling was not in the seminary as his family originally planned, but in ministering young men through sport.

Naismith taught physical education at McGill before moving to Springfield, Massachusetts, in 1890, where he got a job as an instructor at the local Young Men's Christian Association (YMCA). The YMCA began in 1844 as a bible study primarily servicing poor immigrant men trying to escape the hard realities of urbanization and industrialization in cities, and it eventually started the first organized sports programs in North America.

Naismith was tasked with handling a class of hard-to-please students nicknamed the "incorrigibles." These rugby and football players were restless and unimpressed with the winter gym activities suggested by two previous teachers, who quit in frustration. But Naismith had an idea. One of his favourite outdoor childhood games in the Ottawa area was "duck on a rock," where kids would try to knock down a large rock sitting on a stone by throwing smaller rocks at it from about 15 feet away, the length of a free throw. The strategy was to toss a high-arching shot out of the reach of a designated guard, who stood in front of the larger rock to protect it. The game originated in 19th-century Scotland, where the targets were real ducks.

Inspired by "duck on a rock," Naismith nailed two peach baskets to a board 10 feet off the gym floor, found a large round ball, and, on December 21, 1891, put his group of incorrigibles through the first ever game of "basket ball."

Four of the original 18 students at the YMCA in Springfield were Canadian, and they helped establish the new sport across the country. By 1900, basketball was being played in Canada by both men and women at local YMCAs and YWCAs, with a championship between YMCA affiliates beginning in 1907. Basketball had become one of the most popular winter sports in Canada by the start of the First World War in 1914.

Soon, Canadian businesspeople started sponsoring amateur traveling teams to boost their brand visibility. And after the creation of the Canadian Amateur Basketball Association (CABA), a national senior championship was launched in 1923.

The winner almost always came from one of Canada's original dual basketball hubs: Windsor in the east and Victoria in the west. But the 1936 Canadian Basketball Championship between the Windsor Ford V8s and Victoria Blue Ribbons had an extra incentive: not only would the winners hoist the Montreal Cup, given to each year's winner, but they would also be representing Canada in the first ever Olympic basketball tournament later that year. Basketball had become so popular in Europe that the International Federation of Basketball (the forerunner to FIBA) was founded in 1932, and basketball was invited to make its Olympic debut four years later at the highly anticipated Berlin Games — also known as Hitler's Olympics.

Windsor's team won the championship, and an amalgamation of players from the two teams went to represent Canada at the Olympics. Canada dominated the early stages of the tournament before matching up against North American rival Team USA in the final. But the weather did not cooperate, with steady wind and rain turning the outdoor court into a muddy mess, disabling any dribbling or long shots. Plus, before they thought about cutting holes out of the bottom of the peach baskets, there was a jump ball after every made basket, giving the taller Americans a significant possession advantage. Team USA won gold after beating Canada 19–8.

That silver medal remains the closest Canada has ever come to Olympic glory.

▪

CABA was originally focused on national championships and regulatory matters, giving little time or money to its other mandate of fielding Olympic teams, which continued to be represented by the national champions. While Canada qualified for five of eight Olympics between 1936 and 1972, it never came close to winning another medal.

In 1971, however, Canadian Parliament approved an act to create several sports organizations housed in a national office in Ottawa, including Basketball Canada (which later became Canada Basketball). And after missing out on qualifying for two consecutive Olympics for the first time in its history, in 1968 and 1972, Canadian basketball needed a shot in the arm if there was to be any hope of not only qualifying for the upcoming 1976 Games in Montreal, but medaling on home soil.

The new national body had the power to host tryouts and the money to bring in a top-flight coach and try to build a winner. And after receiving nearly 200 resumés, they hired John Patrick "Jack" Donohue in 1972. The heavily accented Irish New Yorker was a coaching lifer who quickly rose up the New York City high school basketball ranks, sandwiched between a brief stint with the US military. He eventually landed a job at Power Memorial Academy, an all-boys Catholic school in Manhattan.

He built Power Memorial into a force even before ninth-grader Kareem Abdul-Jabbar joined the varsity squad, sprung up to 7'2", and became the best player in America with his patented sky hook. Power Memorial won 71 games in a row and three Catholic city titles, earning the title "Team of the Century" in a vote by American sportswriters.

When Donohue arrived in Canada, however, the extent of the country's basketball problems became astonishingly clear. It wasn't so much a lack of players, but a lack of passion and confidence that set Canada back. "There wasn't a bad attitude; there wasn't any attitude at all," Donohue said. "If you like Jack Donohue, fine. If you didn't like Jack Donohue, fine. But if you don't care about Jack Donohue, that's awful."

To that end, Donohue set about on a national tour to sell the game of basketball to fans and to make as many friends in the coaching fraternity as he could, extending an open invitation to every coach in the country to attend his training camps.

■

Eddie Pomykala was a 21-year-old assistant coach of McGill University's men's basketball team when he walked into a Team Canada training camp and was handed a whistle and a pen. "Jack Donohue had the ability to make you feel like you were the most important person in the world," Pomykala says. "He had just such a special quality about him."

Donahue understood that while the public may think of basketball as an overwhelmingly physical game where huge, uncovered bodies run and jump towards each other at breakneck speeds, it's really a mental game — one where decision-making, chemistry, comradery, and discipline are needed to perform when the pressure reaches its peak. And that was even more true in international basketball, which always came down to one game that you either won and qualified for the Olympics, or you lost and waited four more years.

Donohue's teams always found a way to win that crucial game because he understood the human condition, connecting with players and coaches to form genuine relationships on and off the court. "He was like a second father to me," says Doc Ryan, who played for the national team in the '70s before joining Donohue's staff as an assistant coach, reminiscing about the times Donohue would bail him out of a bad situation or give him life advice.

It led to a core group of players including Ryan, Triano, Rautins, Pasquale, Gordon Herbert, Howard Kelsey, Ross Quakenbush, Jim Zoet, and Gerald Kazanowski who kept coming back year after year to represent the country. "They stayed with the program because of the relationships he built and how he motivated people and made the game fun," says Steve Konchalski, an assistant coach with Donohue for 16 years.

Donohue tried to create a light familial atmosphere for his teams with the annual softball tournament at the SkyDome and his regular "joke of the day" before each practice. But the best example of how well he understood his players came in 1988, when the Canadians had a crucial game against Uruguay at the FIBA Americas Championship in Uruguay, where the winner was going to the Olympics and the loser was going home.

Instead of going through scouting reports or walking through scenarios that might happen in Canada's most important game in four years, Donohue used Canada's final practice to play shooting games and other sports. "He knew what had to happen to lighten the guys up," Konchalski says. "That's a master motivator."

That night, the players wrote notes to the coaching staff about how much they loved playing for Canada, leaving the staff in tears. And the next day, Canada came out of the tunnel in the infamous "El Cylindro" arena, known for its cement foundation, freezing temperatures, and wild fans, to see smoke covering the floor from the barbecues grilling meat and the fireworks going off from section to section. When the game started and the riot police stepped away from Canada's bench, the Uruguayan fans starting whipping coins and bolts towards the players, hitting Canadian forward John Hatch square on the forehead before the jump ball.

But in the days before Magic Johnson's AIDS diagnosis and blood protocol, Hatch simply smeared the blood up and down his face and jumped for the ball, letting the Uruguayans know that he and the rest of the Canadians would go to war for their country. "We were up 20 and the biggest challenge we had after halftime was to keep our coats over our heads so the coins and all the different objects that we were being thrown from the stands wouldn't hit us," sports psychologist Cal Botterill says.

That same spirit led to the "Miracle on Hardwood" at the 1983 World University Games in Edmonton, Alberta — Canada's biggest achievement in the history of the sport, when a team led by Pasquale, Triano, and Bill Wennington beat Charles Barkley and Karl Malone's Team USA in the semifinal. Then, in the final against the reigning Olympic champions Yugoslavia — of whom it was said that while America invented the game (not technically true), Yugoslavia perfected it — Canada shut down star guard Drazen Petrovic and won gold in front of a sold-out home crowd.

"I've won three [NBA] championships," says Wennington, who played with Michael Jordan and the Bulls in the 1990s. "To stand on a podium and receive a gold medal and hear the national anthem — my national anthem — played, there's nothing like that."

A favourite saying of Donohue was to "dream big dreams." And Team Canada certainly did throughout his 16-year tenure as head coach, qualifying for every World Championship and Olympic Games from 1972 through to his retirement in 1988, when he became the longest tenured coach in amateur Canadian sports history. Canada finished fourth at the Montreal Olympics in 1976, a standing that hasn't been surpassed since. It also finished fourth at the 1984 Games and sixth in 1988.

But Donohue was by no means perfect. Abdul-Jabbar claimed that the coach called him the N-word in a poor attempt to motivate him during a halftime speech towards the end of their time at Power Memorial. Meanwhile, after Barry Howsen became the first Black player to represent Canada at the 1964 Olympics, it took more than a decade of Donohue being the coach — and two decades altogether — before another Black player wore the red and white at an international competition in 1982. And it's not like they got a lot of playing time when they did make the teams.

"It's like a bitter and a sweet taste, right?" said Tony Simms, who guarded Petrovic in the 1983 final, winning MVP of the gold medal game and representing Canada at the Olympics a year later. "Because I had made the Olympic team and they know I was a dominant player, they know I was better than [some of the white players], and they were playing before me. And I just didn't understand that."

There were complaints made against Donohue and the program from Black players in Toronto and Montreal during that time — ones Canada Basketball swept under the rug. And there was a common line of thought among the inner-city basketball communities that the national team had a quota for how many Black players they would take to represent the country.

"We had lots of people in [Toronto] at that time that thought we should make our own national team because there was no colour at all on that team for many, many years," said Norman Clarke, one of three Black players on the Canadian team at the 1988 Olympics. "Until they had a token in Tony Simms, and they had a second token in Norman Clarke."

•

The experiences that some of these players had on the national team are harrowing and emblematic of the barriers that Canada Basketball put up in incorporating players of different cultures into the historically white federation.

Clarke grew up in the west end of Toronto attending Oakwood Collegiate Institute when it was on its way to becoming a high school basketball powerhouse, taking advantage of the tiny blue and yellow court with a smothering defense that forced backcourt violations and out-of-bounds calls. He was named the most improved player there, invited to a camp at Niagara University, and made the junior national team at 18 before being recruited to St. Bonaventure on a basketball scholarship.

After years of being treated like a practice player, being invited to training camps, cut, and brought back too many times to count, Clarke finally made the Canadian senior B team in 1984. That's when one of the coaches took him aside and told him in no uncertain terms how bad he was, explaining that he couldn't shoot, play defense, pass, or dribble. "I had no idea what to take from that," Clarke says. Instead of giving a young kid constructive criticism, "it was basically a denouncement of me as a person, of my ability, my efforts.

"That is where the racism hit me in the face."

And it wasn't just the coaches, either. After winning a medal one year with the junior national team, a teammate jumped Clarke and tried to beat him up. Another time, some of his teammates broke into his room and poured cold water over him while he slept. But Clarke never made a formal complaint "because had I gone to the coach and said anything," he says, "I'd be the guy going home."

After sticking it out, Clarke finally achieved his dream and made the 1988 Olympic team. But at the Seoul Games, he never got on the floor during a crucial loss to Team USA despite being one of the few players there with experience playing against the Americans from his time in the NCAA. "We weren't allowed to play our game," Clarke says. "We had to fit a mould that restricted us and our ability and our determination . . . Otherwise you weren't even going to be on that team.

"You couldn't be who you are based on your culture, your personality, your creativity — that was all put on the back burner. You couldn't do the things you were born to do."

Dwight Walton, meanwhile, heard about the racism inside the Canadian program his entire childhood. Growing up in Montreal to parents of Jamaican descent, Walton knew he wanted to be a professional athlete from the time he was seven years old, excelling in everything from baseball to hockey to basketball, the sport in which he eventually won MVP of the MacArthur Classic All-Star Game. He got a scholarship to Dawson College, one of the best Collège d'enseignement général et professionnel (CEGEP) schools in the province, where his coach and mentor was former Montreal star Varouj Gurunlian.

Walton knew he wanted to play on the national team since he was 19 years old, when he saw Tony Simms at the 1984 Olympics on CBC and told his mother that he would be on the team four years later at the Seoul Games. But on Walton's very first trip with the national team in 1986, after struggling to contain his excitement at the hotel during breakfast, one of the coaches said, "Dwight, relax, settle down. You're acting your roots." Walton says, "And the whole table just went silent, like 'Did he just say what we heard?'"

"It's a crippling story to be pigeonholed in that regard — that just told me he had no respect for me," he says. "I finally get to the pinnacle of my sport in this country and to be treated like that on my first trip, on the first morning with the team, I'll never forget it."

Sometimes, these players would be sitting on the bench behind white players that had no chance of guarding them in practice, but who would play ahead of them in the most important games. And as a result, they would sit there with tears in their eyes. But what's most astonishing is that these players persevered, refusing to quit despite the systemic and overt racism they faced.

"I'm the token guy, so I was supposed to be quiet," Simms said. "Unfortunately, I didn't feel like that." He told the coaches to send him home if they were going to treat him poorly. Walton, meanwhile, went on to be an assistant coach at Concordia University, a basketball analyst, and a part-time referee in the Montreal community, while Clarke created Triple Threat Basketball Club to ensure kids of all socioeconomic backgrounds could get support and basketball training.

"I was not going to allow that to break me down and to not want to be a part of something that I honestly believed and still believe to this day is bigger than me or any player that steps foot in," Walton says. "That's why I wanted to remain with Canada Basketball."

Walton made it to the Seoul Olympics just like he promised his mother, who referred to him as "my son, the Olympian" until she passed away a few years later, he says. "And to hear my mother say that with such pride and happiness, that made it all worthwhile."

International basketball was entering a new era following the emergence of the Dream Team at the 1992 Olympics. It not only showcased the game on a truly global stage — inspiring a new generation of kids from all over the world to fall in love with basketball — it also turned international hoops into an attractive option for pros looking to gain exposure and better contracts with their next club team.

The Canadians failed to qualify for Barcelona after losing to Venezuela at the 1992 FIBA Americas, when a 39-year-old naturalized American named Sam Shepherd dropped 44 points in a 76–72 upset that sent Canada home. And Canada disappointed again two years later at the 1994 World Championship in Toronto — where talented players like Llewellyn and Yearwood were cut because they didn't fit the mould, while others simply didn't bother showing up to training camp because of prior issues with the federation.

"At that point, there was just too much talent within the city to be finishing second last [in the group] when all our best players are sitting at home," Llewellyn says.

While Canada is seen as a relatively progressive country, Black players had to work twice as hard to get half as far when it came to the men's basketball team. And things only began to change when some of those players exposed Canada Basketball for creating systemic barriers. They were no longer willing to sit by and watch from the sideline as the national team languished in obscurity and let some of its best players slip through the cracks.

As Team Canada establishes itself as a global powerhouse by 2025, we have those trail blazers to thank for its turnaround.

CHAPTER 4

THE SYDNEY OLYMPICS

JOHN NASH

Steve Nash executes a jump pass for Team Canada at the 2000 Olympic Games.

"I hope there are some kids back home — they're six, maybe seven years old — and they've never played hockey, and they see this, and they want to play basketball."

— ROWAN BARRETT

Sherman Hamilton was born in Toronto's Jane and Finch neighbourhood in 1972 before moving to nearby Malton, Ontario, when he was young — a small suburb sandwiched between Mississauga and Brampton.

There was only one basketball court nearby, which had one functioning rim that was usually occupied by older players. So, Hamilton and his friends would stand by and watch Morning Star Secondary standout Bobby Allen and his friends play until they could take the court themselves at night. In the meantime, they practised their shooting form by heaving tennis balls into the eavestroughs of neighbours' houses. "We used to take one step on the ground and one step on the wall, and we used to go up and dunk it on the eavestroughs," Hamilton says. "We used to bust the eavestroughs on everybody's houses."

Hamilton knew he had to get better in order to play with the older players in Malton, honing his skills on the "Black Circuit" — a series of inner-city tournaments held across Toronto, Montreal, and Nova Scotia in the summers where all the best players competed. But instead of forming super-teams, each neighbourhood friend group would create their own team and play for pride, with plenty of smack talk sprinkled in.

"There was no hiding," Hamilton says. "You had to play against everybody. And they were older, they were younger, but if they were a player, you were going to see them at some point."

Hamilton also played at Westwood Secondary School in Mississauga, where he competed against top-ranked players who went on to form the core of the 2000 Olympic team, like Michael Meeks at Cardinal Leger Secondary, Rowan Barrett at West Hill Collegiate, Keith Vassell at Mother

Teresa, and Greg Francis at Oakwood. "We were fiercely competitive," Meeks says. "In games we hated each other . . . it was like, whose school is better?"

Rather than striving for individual accolades or the best player dominating the ball in order to boost their stats and get recruited, Toronto-based players learned how to play together in hostile gyms with school and neighbourhood pride on the line. "It was a team thing," Meeks says. "And you repped your neighbourhood, you repped your school.

"You always kind of hung your hat on how your program did as a whole."

Hamilton was an athletic two guard who could jump out of the gym and shoot the stripes off the ball. But he had no understanding of how to get recruited by NCAA schools until a coach from Division II Florida Institute of Technology saw him play on the "Black Circuit" and offered him a scholarship. He played there for one season, won freshman of the year, and transferred to Virginia Commonwealth University (VCU) for his sophomore year.

In the summer of 1993, after playing for the junior national team, he was invited to a tryout for the senior team. However, he felt something shift in his back a few days into camp and told the program about feeling discomfort, asking for treatment and advice. "They were hemming and hawing with me," he says. "They were done with me at that point, because I wasn't going to make that team."

The national team didn't have enough money to hire a proper performance staff and didn't always treat the players well back then, expecting them to treat the experience of being there like a privilege rather than it being a two-way street. And after injuring a disc at training camp and having to get back surgery, Hamilton was frustrated with Canada Basketball. "After that experience, I was just kind of like, 'This is nonsense,'" he says. "I was done."

Hamilton was never the same above-the-rim player that dunked daily during his freshman year, playing with numb toes his entire sophomore season at VCU, when he could barely get off the ground. But his coach, Sonny Smith, let him play through mistakes and learn the point guard position, telling him that he had to learn how to keep his dribble alive and set up his teammates since he might never get his athleticism back.

He completely transformed his game at VCU, averaging 9 points and 5 assists in his first season there before going on to play point guard for almost 15 years overseas, and for nearly a decade in the red and white. But after his initial bad experience with Canada Basketball, it was going to take a significant change to pull him back into the program.

▪

Stephen J. Konchalski got cut from the freshman team at Archbishop Molloy High School in his hometown of Queens in 1958 — a basketball factory on a 48-game winning streak at the time. The 5'11" guard made a vow to get better, playing pickup on blacktops and at community centres across New York City every day until he was good enough to make the varsity team the following season.

As a senior, Konchalski was recruited to a little-known school in the small town of Wolfville, Nova Scotia, called Acadia University. He moved to Canada and guided the school to its first national championship in 1965, setting the all-time scoring record with 1,479 career points over his four years there. After graduating, he got a job coaching the Loyola College men's basketball team in Montreal, where he met Donohue at one of his training camps. "And I just said if there's any chance of me getting involved in a national team program, I'd love to do it," Konchalski says.

In the spring of 1973, Konchalski got a call that a manager's position was open. He later found out that he was the fifth person they offered it to, as there was no money in it and little glory: mostly packing bags and organizing travel schedules. He told Donohue, "I'll take the job. But I want to be a coach," Konchalski says. The following season, after one of the assistant coaches couldn't fly to the World Championship in Puerto Rico, he slipped into the position of assistant coach. "And I was there for 16 years," he says, going to three Olympics and four World Championships.

Meanwhile, Konchalski got the head coaching job at St. Francis Xavier University (StFX) and turned it into a basketball powerhouse with a modern style of play that he learned growing up in Queens, taking advantage of the immigration that was flowing to Canada's East Coast by the time he arrived in Antigonish, Nova Scotia, in 1975. "I like players to feel . . . comfortable on a court that I don't over-coach with the great details," he says, preferring a "more of a free-flowing style of play, pressure defenses, up-tempo game."

During his 46 season run at StFX, Konchalski won three national titles and became the all-time winningest coach in U Sports history, with a record of 919-576.

But it was always a dream of his to follow in Donohue's footsteps and coach the national team. And when Ken Shields stepped down in early 1995 after Canada Basketball cut his budget, despite making a signficant profit from the 1994 World Championship, the organization hired Konchalski (also known as Coach K) to be its next head coach.

Upon taking over the national team, Konchalski tried to mend relationships with Black players, calling Hamilton and offering him a spot on the team and promising him a better environment, while bringing in a diverse group of young players from Toronto like Phil Dixon, Rowan Barrett, William Njoku, Martin Keane, Hamilton, and Meeks — all of whom he'd seen playing against each other in high school while recruiting for StFX.

Meeks was born in Jamaica and moved to Brampton when he was young; attending Cardinal Leger Secondary. It was one of the best schools in the Greater Toronto Area (GTA) at the time, helping put Brampton basketball on the map.

As a 6'10" big man who could shoot the ball from deep, Meeks was at the forefront of the shooting revolution, but he was small for a traditional centre and struggled to bang in the paint. "Back then, my one defining characteristic was the ability to shoot the three," Meeks says. "There was a lot of physical development I had to undergo."

He started playing on the school's senior team when he was in grade 10 and between that, a few AAU games in Buffalo, and Team Ontario, he earned a scholarship to Eastern Kentucky before transferring to Canisius a year later.

One of his goals was always to make the national team. After being cut from the junior team in 1991 alongside Nash, the two shared a ride to the airport and Nash told him "we are never getting cut again," Meeks says. And they weren't. But Meeks came close.

After struggling in training camp due to his lack of size and strength compared to the other centres, Konchalski walked around the court cutting players before the team flew to the Los Angeles Summer League to play NBA teams and prepare for the 1995 FIBA Americas. When Meeks saw Konchalski approaching, he took his ball and moved to the next hoop, repeating the process over and over again to avoid Konchalski for as long as he could. "Finally, he gets me. He's like, 'Mike, I think you've had a great camp. You've really developed. I want to thank you for your time here, but it's come to an end,'" Meeks says.

However, one of the players that Konchalski offered an alternate position to turned it down, so he doubled back and offered Meeks an alternate position — the same one he'd had in 1991. Meeks was disappointed the next day as he watched the team's final practice from the sideline. But then former U Vic centre Spencer McKay stepped on somebody's foot and rolled his ankle toward the end of practice. And just like that, Meeks was on the team.

In their first game of NBA Summer League, the Canadians were getting blown out and Meeks hit a couple threes during garbage time. The Canadians struggled again the next game, when he got to start the second half and found a rhythm, hitting a bunch of threes to help the Canadians eke out a come-from-behind win. "And I started every game ever since," Meeks says, becoming the first player from Brampton to make the national team and one of the first stretch bigs in the history of the game. He now works with Canada Basketball as the manager of youth player development.

Aside from changing the personnel, the other thing Konchalski did given the racial climate at the time was hire Simeon Mars as an apprentice coach out of Eastern Commerce high school; he had a tremendous amount of influence over young players in the city like Jamaal Magloire. "I knew that that would reconnect the Black community with the national team program," Konchalski says.

The national team also went on a six-city tour of Canada to expand the open tryout system and create a more extensive national team database, changing the old protocol of leaning on U Sports coaches for recommendations. "I just said the whole country has to feel that they have a chance to play for the national team," Konchalski says.

Konchalski ended up cutting five players from the 1994 World Championship team ahead of the 1995 FIBA Americas, going from having five Black players to nine. "That had nothing to do with Ken's controversy," Konchalski says. "That was all just to do with my evaluation of players and the style of play that I wanted to play."

That didn't mean they were going away from Nash. In fact, the most important thing Konchalski did during his time as head coach was call Nash at Santa Clara and tell the up-and-coming point guard that he wanted to build the national team in his image. After watching him at the '94 World Championship, Konchalski knew that Nash was a great player who could run the free-flowing, up-tempo style that Konchalski wanted.

"I told Steve, 'This is your team. I'm giving you the basketball and this is your team,'" Konchalski says.

It was a perfect fit, as Nash ran the offense and made everyone's life easier by pushing the pace and taking advantage of the speed and athletisism of his teammates. When the players got together for training camp, "it was dunks everywhere and flying around — it was insane," Barrett says. "It was rough, it was physical, it was athletic. There was IQ, there was skill, it was just everything. I'd never really seen that before with the national team.

"I think that outside of just race, I think that the style of play, the way that the game was being played had to evolve. It had to evolve to include players like myself."

With Konchalski in charge and Nash running point, there was more available freelance play and creativity allowed, as players were trusted to express themselves more. Plus, Nash was creative and adaptive enough to accentuate their strengths as a masterful playmaker. "That's also a part of the growth and evolution of the game in our country," Nash says. "Exposure, inclusion, and maybe some of those moments in the past helped us evolve in this direction.

"The game was changing. It was becoming less rigid, and obviously, maybe some communities were the forefront of some of those trends."

After finishing fourth at the 1995 FIBA Americas, one spot out of Olympic qualification, Konchalski took a more veteran squad to Uruguay for the 1997 FIBA Americas. He pulled Pasquale out of retirement and leaned on older players like Yearwood, understanding that it would be too difficult for a young, inexperienced team to succeed in that trying environment.

Canada started the group stage 3-1 with wins over Puerto Rico, Venezuela, and the Dominican Republic before losing a tight game to

Team USA, setting themselves up for a win-or-go-home game against host Uruguay in the quarter-finals. It was in El Cylindro, the same building where they famously won nine years earlier when Hatch's forehead was split open before the game. And the crowd was just as wild this time, throwing coins and setting off fireworks to intimidate the Canadians.

Canada was under the canopy getting ready to take the court before the game as sports psychologist Cal Botterill thought about what to say. "And Steve just kind of looked at Cal and says, 'I got this,'" assistant coach Joe Raso says, recalling Nash running out from under the canopy and approaching centre court, where he started to do soccer keep-ups with the basketball on his feet. Nash did a semicircle around the court before going down the middle and knocking the ball into the basket with his head. "People were booing us, whistling, throwing stuff," Raso says. "At the end of it, the crowd yells 'Nash, Nash, Nash!'"

Canada won 63–56, beat the Cubans the next day, finished fifth at the tournament, and qualified for the World Championship the next summer.

However, Konchalski knew that the team he took to Uruguay would not be the same one going to the World Championship. "That team was put together for one reason: to qualify," Konchalski says, understanding that with the 2000 Olympics three years away, he needed to make the roster five years younger at each position so that they could start growing together to eventually have success in Sydney.

Konchalski cut veterans and brought a younger team to the 1998 World Championship — one he knew was too inexperienced to succeed. "We took some blows in that tournament," Hamilton says after going 1-7 and finishing 12th out of 16 teams. "But we also grew. Because losing is learning."

However, once the tournament concluded, the Canada Basketball board decided to let Konchalski go, feeling that the team didn't perform as well as they should have even though their only two NBA players, Nash and Todd MacCulloch, didn't participate due to injuries.

Despite his short tenure as head coach, Konchalski played a key role in forming the core of the team that eventually brought Canada back to international basketball's biggest stage in 2000. "That core, the starting unit, it was Coach K that said, 'These are the guys I need to be involved,'" Hamilton says.

When he took over from Konchalski in 1999, incoming head coach Jay Triano made a couple small roster changes in order to make sure everyone was as hardworking and selfless as he knew they needed to be to reach the Olympics. After representing Canada as a player at the 1984 and '88 Games, he knew that it would take a team rather than a group of individual players to succeed. And he wanted Canada to get more experience playing together ahead of the 1999 FIBA Americas qualifying tournament.

Fortunately, the Australian basketball federation was willing to pay for the Canadians to travel to Australia and New Zealand in the summer of 1999 to play seven exhibition games across five cities, testing out their Olympic venues in the process. But with Steve Nash being traded from Phoenix to Dallas ahead of the 1998–99 season, when nagging injuries limited him to 40 games, the Canadians would have to do it without their lead guard.

After flying across the world, an 18-hour time difference, and a bad meal, Canada looked completely out of sorts in its first game against New Zealand, losing to the Tall Blacks. Triano wasn't sure how to handle the situation given that it was his first time coaching the team, when manager Jon Lee asked if he could speak to them.

Lee immigrated to BC from the Philippines when he was six, getting a job as a ball boy with the Grizzlies before eventually meeting Triano. He looked each player in the eye and said: "First of all, I hate that we lost. But I don't give a shit." He picked up a sweaty jersey off the floor and said, "This jersey here, it says 'Canada,' it should never touch the floor. . . . This is who we represent."

After two games against New Zealand, Canada began to develop an identity as a pissed-off underdog and put up a fight against the talented Australian team, literally. As the two teams started a five-game series, traveling together from city to city — with the Australians always in the front of planes and buses and the Canadians in the back — they started to get on each other's nerves and the games became increasingly hostile, reaching a boiling point about halfway through the series when fist fights started to break out after nearly every whistle.

"We weren't gonna get punked," Hamilton says. "So, we were gonna fight. The wiring for our group was similar."

"It's what we needed," Meeks says. "We needed to develop a rivalry kind of like what Rowan, Sherman, Keith, Greg, and I had playing each other in high school; we needed something that we could all be on board with."

Towards the end of the series, Canada started to get some wins and some of its role players began to play better, gaining confidence that if they could do it against a medal favourite like Australia, they could do it against anyone.

•

With Nash back in the fold, Canada started the 1999 FIBA Americas tournament in San Juan, Puerto Rico, by upsetting the Argentina squad featuring NBA players Luis Scola and Manu Ginobili, winning 77–70. But after reeling off wins against Cuba, Uruguay, Brazil, and the Dominican Republic, Canada lost to Puerto Rico 80–75, setting up a win-or-go-home rematch against the host nation in the semifinals. In the locker room after the game, Nash told his team, "They can't beat us twice."

Despite its two oldest players being just 27, Canada was experienced and had developed a defensive identity around big men Peter Guarasci and Todd MacCulloch and wings Hamilton and Rowan Barrett, while Nash and Meeks did a lot of the damage offensively. Plus, they were battle-tested after fighting the Australians. But the environment they entered in the Roberto Clemente Coliseum on July 24, 1999, was unlike anything any of them had experienced before, with hundreds of fans in the streets delaying their bus and following them into the arena. "The whole country [is] watching, the whole country [is] shut down," Barrett said. "We got into the locker room and they were banging on the doors."

"Puerto Rico would probably be one of the most hostile environments that I've been in," Hamilton says. "I still hate those guys."

It didn't get any easier when the Canadians took the court, as the crowd of 10,000 started booing, setting off fireworks, and throwing stuff at them, with riot police protecting the players. Meanwhile, a band was playing, making it impossible for the players to hear one another on the court, which led to a mistake that may have changed the course of Canadian basketball history.

Up 36–32 with eight seconds to go in the first half, Puerto Rico called a timeout to draw up a play. And after seeing that Puerto Rico went small on offense, Triano called for Meeks to come off the bench. "And Shawn Swords, who doesn't friggin' play, ran down and jumped in the game," Triano says. "And I was like, 'No. No. Okay, okay, go.'"

Swords was one of the few additions Triano made to the roster upon taking over the team earlier that year. Despite being less talented than most of the players at camp, he worked his ass off and showed his scrappy and competitive nature that he learned playing ice hockey in Ottawa before a car accident caused him to change sports.

Swords knew his role well. And even though he wasn't supposed to be in the game, he picked up the opposing point guard full-court, poked out the ball from behind, and got an easy layup at the buzzer. "I look like a friggin' genius," Triano says. "And I thought I had the wrong guy." That play changed the momentum of the game, with the Canadians celebrating and going into the locker room with a six-point lead and a newfound confidence.

Canada opened the second half with an 11–0 run, including two quick three-pointers by Nash, helping take the rambunctious home crowd out of the game. Then when the Puerto Ricans changed their defensive strategy by trapping Nash and double-teaming him every time he crossed half court, Nash started to smile. "And he's like . . . 'They're dead. It's over,'" MacCulloch says, as Nash was so confident in his ball-handling that he knew the aggressive defensive strategy would work against his opponents.

If Nash did have a weakness at that time, it was that he was too selfless, preferring to set up his teammates instead of scoring. In fact, he averaged just 7.9 points that past season with the Mavericks, along with 5.5 assists. But during practice the morning of the game, Triano told Nash that he had to score at least 25 points to win. He finished with 26 points on 10-of-15 shooting, capping it off with a late play where he broke through a double team and dribbled into a smooth pull-up jumper to ice the game. "It was just a poignant moment that underlined what was happening," Barrett says. "It was like, 'No matter what you do, you're getting beat today.'"

Canada lost to Team USA in the gold medal game but qualified for the Sydney Olympics for the first time since 1988, while Nash won tournament MVP over Americans Tim Duncan, Kevin Garnett, and Jason Kidd.

"I think a lot of people don't realize how much that whole tournament was a part of Steve Nash's coming-out party," Hamilton says. "Everybody thinks it was the Olympics, but that tournament he came out and he showed the world that he was ready.

"And we followed suit."

•

Canada's opening match of the 2000 Olympics happened to come against the host nation, Australia, who had thoroughly outplayed the Canadians in the exhibition series a year before. But the over-confident Australians underestimated how big of an impact the addition of Nash would have.

The 26-year-old point guard from Victoria had his hair down to his shoulders and his tongue sticking out of his mouth. He surveyed the floor and sized up his opponents before making a move: driving into the paint and dumping it off to teammates as bodies converged on him, hitting jumpers when the defense sagged off him, and picking apart the Australian defense as he proved too skilled and selfless to keep under control.

Meanwhile, Barrett started sinking jump shot after jump shot, rising several feet off the ground before releasing the ball, finishing with 21 points. Meeks came to life in the second half and added a game-high 27 points. Nash put the finishing touches on the game, ending with 15 points and 15 assists as he led the underdog Canadians to a 101–90 win. "Vindication, redemption," Nash said about Canada's twelve-year journey back to the Olympics. "There's been ups and downs and lots of turmoil, but the key is that they kept all these guys together."

That confidence carried the Canadians forward, as they easily dismantled Angola and Spain in their next two games to start the tournament a perfect 3-0 in Group B. However, Canada took its foot off the gas in the penultimate group stage game against Russia, losing 77–59 after Russia's massive frontcourt held the high-scoring Canadians to just 33 percent shooting and a dismal 3-of-15 from behind the three-point line.

The 18-point loss complicated Canada's path to a medal, as they would now have to beat reigning world champions Yugoslavia in order to avoid ending up on America's side of the bracket. Canada hadn't beaten

Yugoslavia since the 1983 World University Games, and as the heavy underdogs, the Canadians knew they had to junk up the game. Despite having Nash, Canada slowed the game down and zoned up on defense to force its opponent to beat them from the outside.

Still, Canada got off to a slow start, falling into an early 20–8 hole. But the bench of MacCulloch and Swords kept Canada in the game until the third quarter, when the starters came alive. Barrett, Meeks, Hamilton, and Guarasci all picked up the scoring until Nash took over late, making back-to-back three-pointers to tie the game at 65–65, when the Australian crowd began to root for the underdogs.

Then, Nash got a steal and passed it to Hamilton for a dunk that gave Canada their first lead since the early going. Yugoslavia responded with a run of its own and went back up 73–72 with 1:57 left. But Canada reeled off an 11–2 run to put the game away, with Nash scoring or assisting on 18 of Canada's final 21 points as he looked to be having the time of his life picking apart the Yugoslavian defense.

With Canada up by one possession in the final minute of the game, Triano offered $100 to whoever got the next rebound during a timeout. And when Yugoslavia took its next shot, he could have sworn there were five Canadians all fighting for the ball. "I took it as a personal challenge," MacCulloch says. "Coach needs a rebound, I will get us a rebound. And sure enough, Yugoslavia missed the shot. And I went in there with a little extra incentive and came down with the board." After a slow start to the tournament, MacCulloch finished with 21 points and 4 rebounds.

In the end, Canada conquered, beating Yugoslavia 83–75 as Guarasci carried Nash on his shoulders at centre court with the team celebrating around them. "That was all grit," Barrett said. "That wasn't X's and O's at the end. That wasn't Yugoslavia against Canada. That was heart against heart. And our heart won."

As the Canadian Press wrote, "the historical win would compare to Canada's national soccer team upsetting England at the World Cup." It was the greatest win in the history of Canadian men's basketball and should have been remembered as such.

Instead, the Canadian team was better remembered for what followed.

Jay Triano was born in Tillsonburg, in southwestern Ontario, in 1958 and fell in love with hockey, but an early growth spurt meant he couldn't keep up with the other kids on skates. Meanwhile, his father started coaching a local high school basketball team just as the Niagara region was becoming a basketball hotbed, with Niagara University and the NBA's Buffalo Braves across the border.

Triano was a standout player at A.N. Myer Secondary School in Niagara Falls, living for Friday nights when the entire city would come out to watch their games. And his dreams quickly turned to making the national team once he watched a scrappy Team Canada rally to win an exhibition game against Russia in Niagara ahead of the 1976 Montreal Olympics, where they finished fourth.

Triano attended Simon Fraser University (SFU) in Burnaby, BC, because he knew three players from the Canadian national team went there: following them around, lifting when they lifted, shooting when they shot, and diligently working on his game in hopes of getting invited to a Team Canada tryout. He was further inspired by his friend Terry Fox, who managed the basketball team when Triano arrived at SFU until one day he showed up in a wheelchair after losing his leg to bone cancer. Triano developed a friendship with Fox and watched him train to run across Canada.

"If his whole story doesn't inspire you from the way it started and the way it finished, I don't know," Triano says. "It was a big part of my life."

When the invitation did come to attend a Team Canada tryout at 20 years old, Triano thought he was ready. But he couldn't make a shot, turned the ball over constantly, and was getting bullied by grown men. "So that's when I started diving on the floor and just over-hustling, overworking, being physical," Triano says.

He thought he blew his chance when Coach Donohue taught him a lesson that Triano would carry with him on his 37-year coaching journey: good coaches don't just select the best 12 players for a roster, but the 12 who best fit a role. Triano's work ethic earned him a spot at the end of the bench, where he became the best cheerleader and teammate possible. And by going up against older players in practice three times a day, he got better. "And then a couple of injuries and a couple things happened and all of a sudden I'm starting," he says. "And it's a position that I never gave up."

Triano was drafted by the Los Angeles Lakers in 1981 but was dedicated to the national team, where he won gold in '83 and went to two Olympics during the heyday of the team, when he was a captain. He played in 66 official games and scored 1,032 points — a national team record.

When he was done playing in 1988, Triano got the job as the head coach of the men's basketball team at his alma mater, SFU, where he tried recruiting a local talent named Steve Nash, whom he saw holding his own at national team scrimmages at U Vic. But instead of selling Nash on false hope in order to land him to SFU, Triano told the young point guard the truth. "You need to play at the NCAA level if your goal is to play in the NBA," he said. Nash appreciated the honesty and told Triano that he would play for him one day regardless because he knew that it was Triano's dream to coach Canada at the Olympics, while it was Nash's dream to play for Canada there.

A few years later, after Triano became head coach, he and Nash walked into opening ceremonies in Sydney with their arms around each other. "We said we were gonna do this. This is really cool," Triano remembers them saying.

■

The Olympic basketball quarter-final crossover is one of the toughest and highest stakes games in professional sports, because no matter how well you play in the group stages, one team goes on to the medal round while the loser goes home.

Canada got matched up with France, who had gone 2-3 in group play and looked to be weaker than Canada but made some major changes ahead of the matchup. Eight minutes into a tightly contested game, France subbed in Makan Dioumassi, a long, athletic guard who almost never played in the previous games. His entire job was to shadow Nash everywhere he went, pressuring him when he had the ball and face-guarding him when he didn't — causing two Nash turnovers as soon as he got in the game.

"Most teams, they put a guy on Steve, he breaks the guy down two or three times and the guy quits," Barrett said. "But Dioumassi didn't quit."

France went on an 8–1 run as Nash struggled to find his rhythm, being constantly hacked by Dioumassi but not getting any whistles as the referees allowed more physicality than in previous games. Canada began to show frustration towards the end of the first half, when Meeks leveled Dioumassi with an illegal screen to get him off Nash. Meanwhile, Canada didn't have enough supplemental scoring without Nash consistently breaking down the defense, as the bigs missed easy baskets, Hamilton looked tentative, and Barrett found the worst time to have a poor shooting night.

"If they don't blow the whistle, he's successful," Triano said of Dioumassi. "If they blow it, Steve shoots 15 foul shots. That's international basketball, you never know."

France took a commanding 38–23 lead into halftime after Canada opened the game shooting 11–32 from the field and 0–5 from three. However, Canada started the second half with two quick threes to cut the lead to nine, keeping it in that range for most of the second half despite making uncharacteristic turnovers, missing easy baskets at the rim, and shooting just 2–13 from three. With France leading 63–52 with three minutes remaining, Nash found Barrett for a fast break layup before laying the ball off to MacCulloch for another layup — two of his game-high 23 points. Then, Nash drove into Dioumassi's chest to get two free throws, but despite complaining that the ball was wet, the referee handed it to him anyways and he missed the first shot.

Canada kept fighting, with a chance to cut it to a one-possession game in the final minute when Nash drove into the lane and gathered the ball to lay it up before discovering that he dribbled it off his foot and out of bounds. He looked to the sky as if to say, "What's going on?" "It felt like a weird day, like something was off," Nash says. "It just felt like I was experiencing something . . . almost was like an out-of-body experience."

After scoring 26 points and 8 assists versus Yugoslavia the previous game, Nash managed just 10 points, 8 assists, and 9 turnovers against the French, and Canada lost 68–63.

Shortly after they shook hands with the opposing team, Nash's body began to shake and tears started streaming down his face. Hamilton and Triano carried him off the court, with the image of Nash crying being posted to newspapers across Canada the next morning. "I've never seen a guy as gutted as Nash as that day," Doug Smith, who has covered basketball for over 30 years, says. "I've never seen a guy take a loss harder, because that was a really, really good team. And France wasn't."

The locker room was a mess, with grown men unable to control their emotions after losing to a team that they thought was inferior. Hamilton was selected for a random drug test, but he collapsed on his way to the bathroom, sobbing on his knees after his legs gave out. "That one broke me in that moment," he says. "It definitely broke me."

Triano told the team how proud he was of them, and they rallied to beat Russia in the consolation bracket and finish seventh in the tournament. With the entire country watching, Canada proved that it could compete with anyone in the world, as its 5-2 record matched that of France, who won silver, while only gold-medalists Team USA had a better record. "I hope there are some kids back home — they're six, maybe seven years old — and they've never played hockey, and they see this, and they want to play basketball," Barrett said.

"I think that, combined with Vince [Carter]'s impact in Toronto, helped galvanize a group of young kids to play basketball," Smith said. "Because they saw what they could do for the country."

In a few short years, Nash went from an unknown Victorian kid to the face of Canadian basketball, gaining the nickname "Captain Canada" during his incredible run at the 2000 Olympics. He nearly doubled his statistical averages the next NBA season before becoming an All-Star in 2003 and winning back-to-back NBA MVP awards in 2005 and 2006, fundamentally revolutionizing the game with the seven-seconds-or-less Phoenix Suns.

"I went to the Olympics in 2000 and it springboarded my career," Nash said. "It was the best experience of my career."

The Sydney Games were supposed to be start of a golden generation of Canadian men's basketball, with everyone expecting the national team to begin a period of sustained success. Instead, Nash would never play for Team Canada again in an international competition, the core group would break up, and Triano would be unceremoniously fired three years later. Team Canada would fail to qualify for the next five Olympics as controversies, funding issues, and a lack of commitment came to define the program.

CHAPTER 5

REVEREND RO RUSSELL

RO RUSSELL

Coach Ro Russell (third from the right, holding up a black shirt) and his Grassroots Elite basketball team celebrate winning the Adidas Super 64 AAU tournament in 2008.

"That was my initial ministry. I was determined to help those kids not fall by the wayside. . . . Using basketball as a tool for them to stay in school and become something of themselves."

— RO RUSSELL

In 1971, Canadian Prime Minister Pierre Trudeau introduced the multiculturalism policy in the House of Commons, reshaping the country's population. The policy eliminated Canada's previous ban on non-European immigrants, thereby opening up the borders to people from Asia, Africa, and the Caribbean for the first time ever.

Meanwhile, West Indian countries including Jamaica and Trinidad and Tobago had recently gained independence, and their nationals began immigrating in large numbers to Canadian hubs like Toronto: a predominantly white city of just 2.6 million in the 1970s when about 80,000 Caribbean people lived there; by the 1990s, Toronto reached 4.2 million people with a Caribbean population of 240,000. By 2014, the metropolis's population reached over six million — almost 20 percent of Canada's population, nearly half of them visible minorities.

Immigrants were chosen on a point-based system that took things like age, education, language proficiency, and work experience into account, allowing only the hardest-working newcomers into Canada. While many of the athletes outlined in previous chapters took to basketball in high school, with some getting scholarships to play in university, most first-generation Canadians were more concerned with getting good grades, staying out of trouble, and working to support their families than they were dreaming of playing pro ball.

But when their children chose hoops over hockey sticks due to it being cheaper, more accessible, and more inclusive, parents were not going to let them get away with half-assing basketball or anything else they chose to do in their new country. Instead, it was straight As and zero excuses.

"My grandmother and my mother . . . showed me what work ethic looked like and what responsibility to your family looked like," Rowan Barrett, who's family came from Jamaica, said. "And no matter where you start, they always had an expectation of where we would end."

Canada now welcomes almost as many immigrants and refugees as any country in the world. Not coincidentally, basketball is among the fastest-growing sports in Canada and the most popular sport among "fast-growing visible minority groups," according to a 2006 study. Another study found that basketball has the second-highest participation for team sports among children, behind soccer and ahead of hockey.

For second-generation Canadians who grew up watching Nash at the Olympics and NBA teams in Toronto and Vancouver since 1995 — Canadian immigrant offspring like Jamaal Magloire (Trinidad), Cory and Devoe Joseph (Trinidad and Tobago), Tristan Thompson (Jamaica), Anthony Bennett (Jamaica), Tyler and Dylan Ennis (Jamaica), Dwight Powell (Jamaica), Andrew Wiggins (Barbados), Shai Gilgeous-Alexander (Antigua and Barbuda), and RJ Barrett (Jamaica) — a career in basketball was a semi-attainable dream. It helped that they finally had someone who looked like them to look up to.

•

Vince Carter grew up in Daytona Beach, Florida, before becoming a high-flying basketball star at the University of North Carolina. He was drafted fifth overall by the Raptors in 1998 and spent the first six seasons of his career in Toronto, helping put a relatively unknown city and franchise on the map with his awe-inspiring dunks and exciting style of play.

"Vince, he was Canada when he played for the Raptors," Wiggins said. "He made every young person, old person, it don't matter who you were, you just loved basketball."

Carter was must-watch TV, with a skill set built on a one-of-a-kind athleticism. From acrobatic layups to big blocks to posterizing dunks, Carter did something special every time he touched the court. But no performance was more influential than the 2000 NBA Slam Dunk Contest, where Carter wore the classic purple and black Raptors dinosaur jersey and put on an array of dunks that just kept getting better, throwing down a 360 degree, between the legs dunk before capping off the performance by sticking his elbow in the rim after dunking, hanging there for the world to see. "I'd be at home after school watching highlights of this guy named Vince Carter dunking, and the crowd was going crazy," Thompson said. "That is kind of where I fell in love with the game."

"The Vince Carter Effect" was a key turning point in the history of Canadian basketball, inspiring countless Canadians to dream of playing professional basketball — especially visible minorities who saw themselves in the African-American star. But by the turn of the century, there was already an uprising bubbling beneath the surface. "I'm sure you've talked to a lot of people that will say that everything changed after Vince," former Ontario Basketball Association (OBA) president Rob Wright says. "I think everything was changing. Ontario was building a machine."

Throughout the latter half of the 1990s, OBA saw a 10 percent annual growth rate each year, with kids joining local clubs that played each other throughout the year and met in the annual OBA championships. The school system was growing, too, with 18 different school boards competing at the Ontario Federation of School Athletic Associations (OFSAA) championships each year.

The OBA and school system were great for instilling passion and fundamentals into kids who wanted to play recreational basketball within the province, promoting a Canadian experience. In fact, the OBA was a feeder system for the provincial and junior national teams and for Canadian universities.

But Ontario's system was not set up to develop elite athletes or to expose players to NCAA Division I schools like Duke or Kentucky, where they could potentially earn a full scholarship and prepare for a career in professional basketball. "A PSO [provincial sport organization] should be promoting the sport and the love of the sport and the development of the sport for the masses, not for the five kids that are going to get a scholarship," Wright says. "To balance the two would have been impossible."

The problem was that playing in the OBA or for Team Ontario could cost over $1,000 a year, which was prohibitive for many inner-city kids. As a result, a lot of them slipped through the cracks.

•

Ro Russell is widely considered the godfather of Canadian basketball, creating the country's first successful AAU program and helping hundreds of Canadians get NCAA scholarships.

Russell was born in Jamaica in 1969 and moved to Toronto at four years old, falling in love with hockey and spending most of his childhood playing until he started to face racism as one of the few Black kids in the Metro Toronto Hockey League. Parents would call him the N-word and "monkey" from the stands, while his teammates and coaches refused to acknowledge him for scoring. "It was more overt than it is now," he says. He quit hockey in favour of basketball when he was 14.

Despite the late start, Russell was determined to become as good at basketball as his peers were, going to the library to gather training material and practising daily until he could hold his own. Soon, kids from his Jane and Finch neighbourhood took notice and started paying him $1 an hour to train them. "I was obsessed with training," he says.

Russell started coaching a team of kids in the community when he was 15. But after realizing that he could get a free education in America out of the sport, he got in a car with a friend during March break of his senior season at Runnymede Collegiate and crossed the border, trying out for as many NCAA teams as he could. "It was really pure," Russell says. "Because you had to be so determined and had to work to get somewhere."

Eventually, Keene State in Keene, New Hampshire, offered him a scholarship, and Russell played there before transferring to Gordon College in Wenham, Massachusetts, where he got a degree in physical education while learning the American basketball ecosystem and making connections across the country.

In the summers, Russell would return home and keep his basketball skills sharp at the legendary George Brown College men's league and pickup runs, where all of Toronto's best players met in the evenings. From legends like David Joseph, Simeon Mars, Jay Triano, Leo Rautins, and Paul and Mark Jones to American titans like Danny Ainge and Tracy McGrady stopping by, "It's still kind of this holy grail," says Paul Jones, the former Oakwood Collegiate star turned Raptors broadcaster. "People came from all over the city to play at George Brown" from the late 1970s to the early 2000s.

A lot of players there were good enough to play in the NCAA and maybe even the pros. But without the infrastructure to develop or expose players to American colleges, they were stuck playing for U Sports schools that couldn't even cover the full cost of tuition. And by the time Russell learned that there was a new way of making it in basketball, it was too late for his cohort of first-generation Canadians.

But for second-generation Canadians such as Cory and Devoe Joseph — who would sit in their strollers or shoot on the side hoop while their father, David, played at George Brown — the potential was staggering. Russell could see the basketball explosion that was waiting to happen, and because the Ontario programs weren't set up to help inner-city kids, he decided to take it into his own hands.

"That was my initial ministry," he says, gaining the nickname "Rev" after helping countless kids move out of their dangerous neighbourhoods and make a better life for themselves. "I was determined to help those kids not fall by the wayside . . . using basketball as a tool for them to stay in school and become something of themselves."

When Russell was 19, in 1989, he started Elite Toronto Development, an AAU program that put the best young Canadian players together and traveled to exposure tournaments in the United States. Russell registered the program as a non-profit at a time when the Ontario government was giving free gym time to help keep kids off the street. He usually booked gyms along the Bloor subway line at Central Technical School and Central Commerce Collegiate, spreading the word first by phone calls and eventually by MSN Messenger.

Building off the ethos of the George Brown runs, "Ro's Runs" became the best basketball in the city. People would come from all throughout the GTA to play, running five-on-five scrimmages into the late hours. "You had all the best guys in the city, every age group," Jermaine "Rock" Anderson says. "You had the best of the best, and it was a chance to play against older guys and see where you're at."

As Vidal Massiah puts it, "It was an environment where if you didn't bring it, if you weren't tough, if you couldn't play, you're gonna get exposed."

Elite Toronto Development's first tournament was the Eastern Invitational camp at Buffalo University. And after getting in two big vans and driving down, they dominated the American competition. "All the scouts and coaches are like, 'Oh my gosh, you're from Canada?'" Russell says. "'I didn't know they played basketball in Canada.'" They later started driving through the entire United States, playing against better competition in bigger tournaments, cementing themselves as a force to be reckoned with.

But things didn't fully take off until Russell partnered with Wayne Dawkins, who grew up in Toronto's west end playing basketball for York Memorial, a rival of Russell's Runnymede. The two struck up a friendship and started working out together until going their separate ways for college. Dawkins went to Eastern Michigan.

Dawkins eventually became a teacher and a "community builder," first in the youth ministry in church and then by running basketball camps. He lived in Jane and Finch but set up weekly runs with all the players in the nearby neighbourhood of Jungle, including a local phenom named Denham Brown, who played at Bathurst Heights Secondary before Dawkins coached him at West Hill.

So, while Russell had a stranglehold on Jane and Finch, Dawkins created a program with Saeed Al Naji composed of mostly kids from Jungle, eventually becoming Toronto Elite Development while Russell had Elite Toronto Development. The two programs were rivals competing in all the best AAU tournaments in the States, where they often met in the finals. They eventually decided to put their egos aside and merge, and one of their athletes, Junior Reid, came up with the name Grassroots Canada.

Shortly after, in 2001, Grassroots went to Douai, France, for the Under-19 World Junior Basketball Championship — Canada Basketball didn't have the resources to send a team — and they advanced all the way to the final against Team USA. Brown dropped 44 points on a teenaged Carmelo Anthony before losing 102–99. "And then it was over," Dawkins says. College coaches like Jim Calhoun from the University of Connecticut (UConn) and Rick Majerus from Utah flew in private jets to Jungle to recruit Brown. All of a sudden, everyone wanted to play for Grassroots, and it became a priority over high school and the OBA.

•

Despite the common saying that if you are good enough at basketball, they will find you, "The Russell Doctrine" said that if you want to make it big in basketball, you go play AAU in America instead of waiting for them to come to you — you compete against the best in order to prove that you are the best. And that's exactly what Russell and Dawkins gave young Canadians an opportunity to do.

AAU is a series of amateur basketball circuits that are great for young players to get exposure to NCAA scouts and coaches. Funded in large part by apparel companies like Nike and Adidas — who sponsor teams with gear and host tournaments across the United States — AAU has become the most popular way for elite young North American players to test themselves and ultimately get recruited.

But back in the '90s, AAU carried a negative connotation, as it was considered by many in the Canadian sporting establishment to be "Black basketball." And that didn't help Russell make any friends when he decided to eschew the local OBA and school system in favour of regular trips down south. "Nobody talked to Ro Russell ever," Leo Rautins says. "He was alienated by the basketball people."

There were other early adopters of AAU in Canada including Tony Marcotullio in London; Dave Smart's Guardsmen in Ottawa; and Bob White in Montreal. But Russell was the first to get a Nike sponsorship, expand it beyond the summers to a year-round program, and make enough connections with American coaches that he helped hundreds of kids from Toronto get NCAA Division I scholarships. He is a big part of the reason why since the turn of the century, Toronto has produced as many NBA players as any city in North America. "He's the man behind everything," Tristan Thompson said about Russell.

"I think there should be a statue of him," adds Jermaine Anderson.

However, to get sponsored by the biggest apparel companies and invited to the best tournaments, an AAU team needs stars. And after Brown left for UConn and Russell and Dawkins went their separate ways in 2002, the newly named Grassroots Elite needed a new phenom.

■

Junior Cadougan fell in love with basketball playing with his older brother, Kerlon, on indoor hoops fashioned out of coat hangers and milk crates. He eventually graduated to the outdoor court by his Jane and Finch house — the same court Russell had grown up on a decade earlier.

Born in 1990, Cadougan loved basketball but felt like it was a pipe dream to go pro until he saw Brown get recruited out of the hood in 2002. "I'm seeing NCAA coaches come to the neighbourhood to watch him," Cadougan says. "That gave me motivation that that dream is there and it's possible."

Despite living in the same neighbourhood, Russell never thought anything of Cadougan because he was a pudgy 5'7" kid who didn't look like a great athlete. But when he finally saw him play in a real game, Russell learned that Cadougan was deceptively quick, with a nasty crossover and the ability to explode to the rim. "At first because you're thinking, 'He's only 5'7", I don't know how good a 5'7" kid is gonna be,'" Russell says. "But Junior could get up there."

During Cadougan's first trip to the United States with Grassroots in grade 7, Russell told him to change into his basketball uniform in the middle of a game they were losing. He got in the game and dropped 32 points. "From that day on, the recognition and all of these new scout websites and all this stuff started to go crazy," Cadougan says. "They hadn't seen a kid that young from Canada put in work like that."

Grassroots started practising at the legendary Falstaff Community Centre off Jane Street and Highway 401. Despite the tiny gym being hemmed in by concrete walls just a metre outside its bounds, all the best players in the GTA started coming to train there in the early 2000s. Cadougan was joined by the likes of Cory and Devoe Joseph, Olu Ashaolu, Myck Kabongo, Brady Heslip, Nik Stauskas, Tristan Thompson, Dwight Powell, and Rock Anderson at Falstaff. Those Grassroots teams were so dominant that they barely lost a game in Canada for a 20-year stretch, with Russell one day having the revelation from the sideline that: "I can make my own NBA team from this," he says.

Grassroots had its fair share of adversity as it climbed its way up the AAU hierarchy, fighting against American referees and competition organizers who didn't want to see them win. And because they were the first generation of Canadians competing in the States, it was a nerve-racking experience for a lot of the kids to hop on a bus, be without their family or friends, eat different food, sleep in hotel beds, and go into a hostile basketball environment where they might see John Calipari or Kobe Bryant sitting on the sideline.

But Russell had his ways of motivating kids. One thing he would do was cut out American newspaper articles that said Canadians were soft and didn't play defense, similar to how European players were viewed at the time. And he would read them to the boys on the way to tournaments.

Plus, by the early 2000s, American basketball websites and magazines started ranking high school players as early as grade 9, creating top 100 lists of the best players at each position in each graduating class. But Canadians were never on those lists. So, as a way of motivating his players, Russell came up with a saying that they were going to "take names" at these AAU tournaments, meaning that when they played against a highly ranked player in their class, they would use it as an opportunity to get noticed.

"Put a chip on their shoulder, let's go after them and be ranked better and get their [college] offers," Russell says. "That was the motivation, and really we rose from the bottom all the way to the top."

Point guards like Cadougan, Joseph, and Kabongo would pick up opposing guards the entire length of the court, talking smack from opening tipoff, not switching off them all game. "Full-court, mano a mano, not ducking no smoke," Kabongo says. "Rev kind of instilled in us that wherever we go, we're going to take names because we didn't have no names, no one knew us."

It all came to a head at the Adidas Super 64 tournament in Las Vegas in 2008, when Grassroots was at its peak and had a team composed of Cadougan, Ashaolu, Heslip, Thompson, and Powell. Despite entering the 64-team tournament with zero expectations, Grassroots made it all the way to the final, where they matched up with the top AAU team in America, the Compton Magic.

The two teams went back and forth, with a sea of Compton OGs with tattoos and bandanas stomping their feet and throwing up gang signs from the bleachers, trying to intimidate the Canadians. But it didn't work. "We got to prove ourselves, we got to make a name for ourselves. Not just for ourselves, but for our country," Ashaolu says of their mindset. "We're from Toronto. We're not any soft pushovers . . . We let them know we come from the same environment you do.

"I mean, we're tough as nails as well."

Grassroots won in double overtime after Thompson dominated the boards and sunk the final free throws to ice the game, combining with Cadougan to score 41 points. It concluded an all-time performance from one of the best teams in the history of AAU basketball, let alone from Canada.

"What [are] they [gonna] say now?" Thompson shouted at the end of the game. "We just showed the US that we've got basketball players in Canada." Thompson won tournament MVP and was ranked as the number-one player at his position, while *USA Today* and *Sports Illustrated* published stories about Grassroots.

"We made a major statement," Russell said. "It's the biggest win in our program's history and Canadian amateur basketball history. . . . Now people will take us seriously."

That was the moment that everybody knew Canada had pros — not just NCAA players but future pros coming up the pipeline. In fact, every single player on that team got an NCAA scholarship, most of them went pro, and three of them went to the NBA — something that is practically unheard of for a single AAU team.

▪

A few years earlier, in the summer of 2005, Junior Cadougan was watching The Score TV network when he saw a documentary on a young basketball player named Olu Ashaolu. Ashaolu was a year older than Cadougan and grew up in Rexdale and Brampton, where he and his older brothers played for Grassroots. In grade 9, he became one of the first Canadians to leave home and play for a prep school in the United States.

"And that's when the motivation to go was happening because I'm like, 'Who's this kid from Canada on TV?'" Cadougan says.

Cadougan was coming off a dominant grade 9 season at Eastern Commerce when he asked his mother, Suzette, a native of Trinidad, if he could leave their dangerous Jane and Finch neighbourhood in favour of a prep school in America to get year-round exposure to NCAA schools. But she wouldn't even consider it. "I thought he was too young," she said.

However, a couple months later, Junior, Kerlon, and their four-year-old brother, Shaquan, were on the porch of the family's townhouse with several friends when a gunman inside a passing car fired shots at the group. Five people were hit by bullets, including Junior, who was nicked in the shoulder. Shaquan, however, was hit four times in his legs and midsection.

After the shooting, Suzette gave Junior her blessing to go south. "It wasn't easy for me, but he'd be safer there," she said. "God kept Shaquan alive, so that gave me confidence to know He'd be with Junior." Two weeks after being shot, a 15-year-old Cadougan was on a plane to Community Christian School in Stockbridge, Georgia, to team up with Ashaolu and chase his dream of playing NCAA basketball.

"There has been a lot of crime in some of those neighbourhoods," said CIA Bounce co-founder Mike George. "For some parents, they see it like sending their kids to boarding school; it gives them a sense of security."

As for the players, prep school was a way to literally prepare for the NCAA so that they could make a smoother adjustment to the culture shock of being independent and playing against bigger, stronger, more athletic players. That need was made clear for Canadians after Brown struggled to make the transition from being the best high school player in Canada — dropping 111 points in his final game at West Hill — to barely playing at UConn, where he became a role player that failed to crack an NBA roster after being selected 40th overall in the 2006 NBA Draft.

Prep schools originally started in the New Hamptons as a way for kids to do a postgraduate year to boost their grades or SAT scores. But when Tracy McGrady leapt from the church-sponsored Mount Zion Christian Academy in North Carolina directly to the NBA back in 1997 — immediately signing a $12-million sneaker deal with Adidas, which gave significant money to both Mount Zion and its coach — prep schools started to multiply and take on a different use. They now act as sport-centric institutions that prepare elite athletes for the NCAA, with private donors pouring millions of dollars into the schools knowing that if they hit on just one player, it could mean a big payday.

There were many problematic prep schools in the beginning: fly-by-night "diploma mills" that had no intention of taking academics seriously and, in some cases, even screwed tuition-paying students out of graduating by not getting accredited by the NCAA. In fact, a *New York Times* investigation found more than a dozen institutions failing to meet the NCAA's standards in 2006, including one in South Charleston that scammed 16 foreign basketball prospects out of cash with a fake prep school before leaving them all in a two-bedroom apartment without food or money.

Even Russell fell prey to those scams when he was hired to coach Christian Faith Center Academy in North Carolina in 2011. A CBC News *Fifth Estate* investigation found that the nine Canadian high school players he brought with him were ineligible to attend the school because their visas were delayed, forcing them to miss out on a year of school despite having paid Russell tuition. "If you look at the failure list, it's mind-boggling," Rautins said about highly touted Canadians fizzling out in the States. "Kids academically put in bad situations. You see all these kids with potential, and it just went out the window."

■

Being two of the first Canadians in history to go off to the United States for high school basketball wasn't easy for Cadougan and Ashaolu.

After having to reclassify and repeat the ninth grade, as all Canadians do when they make the move south, they had to overcome the culture shock of living alone in Georgia. Not only were they playing basketball twice a day, working their way up in a cutthroat world with old-school coaches and intense practices, but they were living with other teenagers in questionable housing environments, eating different food, speaking different lingo, and shaking their heads at some of the things going on around them.

"It was a culture shock when I first got there," Cadougan says. "I was missing my family. I didn't want to really leave when I had to."

On Ashaolu's first day in Georgia, he moved into a big pink house with a bunch of international students and a host family, where all the athletes had to rotate doing chores. One day a forward from Mali had to take out the garbage, but he claimed that he was a prince back home, and taking out the garbage wasn't befitting for a Malian prince. "This guy was not having it," Ashaolu says. "He was just like, 'There's no way I'm taking out trash.'" Shortly after, the prince left the school.

"Obviously, desire has to be there, but you've got to be resilient, man. You got to have a certain sort of the toughness about you," Ashaolu says.

"It's a dog-eat-dog world and you get chewed out real quick if you're not able to stand on your own two."

Ashaolu and Cadougan were tough. And the bond they formed off the court translated onto it, playing every game together over a three-year stretch between AAU, the junior national team, and prep school, where they developed a natural two-man game with Cadougan running point and Ashaolu finishing his passes.

After Cadougan's first season, in which he averaged 19 points and was named to the all-underclassmen list by *USA Today*, both he and Ashaolu transferred to Christian Life Center Academy in Humble, Texas, to play against better competition. They both climbed the rankings as they continued to win on the prep circuit, with NCAA coaches witnessing their development every step of the way.

After four years of prep school, Cadougan was featured in *SLAM* magazine, was a five-star prospect, and got a scholarship to Marquette University, where he won two Big East championships. Ashaolu, meanwhile, went to Louisiana Tech for three years before transferring to Oregon. Despite neither one of them making it to the NBA, both had long careers playing professionally and continue to work in basketball.

But their legacy will always be associated with how they blazed a trail for the next generation of Canadians to leave home early in favour of prep schools in the States. In fact, the prep route that Ashaolu and Cadougan helped establish became a pipeline of elite Canadian players like Joseph, Thompson, Kabongo, Powell, Wiggins, and many more traveling south for their final few years of high school before going to the NCAA and the NBA.

"To this day, there's hoopers that are a little bit younger than me that are thanking me like, 'Yo, man, if it wasn't for you guys, we wouldn't even have thought of going the prep route,'" Cadougan says.

"We bust that door open a little, and it was an opportunity for Canadians to kick it down."

CHAPTER 6

ONE-AND-DONE

CONNIE JOSEPH

A young Cory Joseph practises his jump shot with an imaginary basketball.

"We've always had talented people, but I think Tristan and I being the first guys to get drafted in the first round together, that opened some eyes."

— CORY JOSEPH

To say that Cory Joseph was born into a basketball family would be an understatement. His father, David, arrived in Canada from Trinidad when he was 12, dropped soccer, picked up basketball, and became a star player at Jarvis Collegiate Institute before moving on to play at Mount Royal College in Alberta. He met Connie there, also a basketball player, and before long the couple moved to the Pickering, Ontario, area and had two sons and two daughters — one of whom was driven straight from the hospital to a gym.

"The amount of time that we spent in gyms when they were younger, it was just crazy," Connie says. "But it was because we all loved it . . . It was a family thing."

Cory was born in 1991 and honed his skills against his older brother Devoe, playing all day on the hoop outside of their house. Even in the winter, the boys would put on a bunch of layers and shovel the driveway so they could play together. "Your hands would get cold, so you couldn't play too long," Joseph said. "My mom liked it because we shovelled the driveway for her."

When they weren't getting in fights over games that went too far, Cory and Devoe took the TTC and GO buses around the GTA to find open gyms or good runs. "We didn't have as many programs," Cory says about Pickering in the early 2000s. "I was looking for basketball. I was looking for stuff to do."

They started playing organized basketball for the Scarborough Blues, reeling off a string of provincial championships when the boys were in middle school, only losing one title game on a buzzer-beater at the hands of Toronto 5-0 star Stephen Curry, who was living in the city while his father, Dell, was a Raptor. The boys also played for Team Ontario and the junior national team almost every summer.

Devoe was a natural scorer and knockdown shooter from the moment he stepped into Pickering High School. Cory, meanwhile, was more mild-mannered, a jack-of-all-trades point guard who could guard anyone and set his teammates up, rarely making splashy plays but also never turning the ball over or missing an open man. "Their parents . . . basically taught them everything that they needed to know," high school coach Ron Parfitt says. "They came in miles ahead of other kids."

The Joseph boys became a well-known duo in high school, winning back-to-back OFSAA championships together, with Devoe hitting a buzzer-beating jumper in his final high school game to beat Eastern Commerce for their second OFSAA win.

After five years at Pickering, Devoe went to the University of Minnesota on a basketball scholarship. But it was a complicated process as NCAA Clearinghouse changed the eligibility requirements the year he graduated, making Canadian grade 13s ineligible to jump to the NCAA. Devoe almost had to go to a junior college like many of his peers before his parents wrote letters to Clearinghouse and got him an exemption.

"Coming after my brother who was two years older than me really helped," Cory says. "I could sit back and see kind of firsthand the stuff that he went through."

By grade 10, there was no doubt that Cory was going to be good enough to play in the NCAA. But the Josephs didn't want to go through the same academic headaches that they went through with Devoe. Fortunately, after playing for Grassroots AAU since he was young, Cory was recruited by several prep schools including Findlay Prep in Henderson, Nevada.

The family was initially hesitant to send their 16-year-old boy so close to Sin City after his grade 11 season at Pickering, but Cory had a form of dyslexia and was struggling in the public school system. Findlay Prep, meanwhile, offered resources such as smaller class sizes, a semestered academic system, tutors, and accommodations for the ACT tests. "It wasn't a basketball-driven decision," Connie says.

"I didn't know what the States would do for me. But I was just following a dream," Cory says. "It's one of those things that you follow your dream and you work super hard at it. And it kind of just comes together."

And he wasn't alone. By the time Cory left Canada in 2008, about 80 Canadian boys were chasing their hoop dreams in American prep schools, often as early as the ninth grade. Many of them struggled at first, adjusting to poor living conditions or going to schools that didn't take academics or basketball seriously.

But as more Canadians experienced life in America and handed down knowledge of the system, the good schools started to stick out from the rest. And Findlay was on top of that list.

Findlay Prep is not named after the school it was attached to — Henderson International, where the 10-man basketball team attended classes — but after Cliff Findlay, a wealthy Las Vegas businessman who built an empire selling cars.

In 2006, Findlay started the prep school in Henderson, a small city of 300,000 just 26 kilometres outside of Vegas, and established an endowment of $500,000 to fund the school. He also paid for a 3,000-square-foot house for the team to live in, each player's $17,000 tuition at Henderson International, and a travel budget that was more generous than most universities'. "Always treated it like college," said Mike Peck, Findlay's head coach. "That was our objective, that when they left us, we didn't want them to be surprised by anything at college." The school won three national high school titles and produced 18 NBA players and over 70 Division I NCAA athletes, with an all-time record of 381-43.

Because there are more practices than games in any given season, the best prep schools bring together a team full of high-level prospects and have them compete against each other several times each day in between weight training and games, with iron sharpening iron as the kids push each other to get better. Plus, the talent at Findlay was so overwhelming that a line of coaches from top college programs would fill the gym to watch their practices, while their games would air on major cable networks.

"A lot of [Canadian] guys play basketball, but it's kind of like a hobby; they never see themselves on CBS," said Tristan Thompson, who also attended the school.

"Here it's a lifestyle."

But there were also drawbacks to the wild world of American basketball — ones Thompson became intimately familiar with.

After leaving home in grade 9 for St. Benedict's Prep, in Newark, New Jersey — an all-boys Catholic private school run by monks with barbed wire surrounding the campus — Thompson raised up the basketball ranks, becoming the number-one power forward in the country following his performance at the Adidas Super 64 in the summer of 2008. But he butted heads with head coach Dan Hurley the following season, getting yanked from a game that St. Benedict's was dominating after Thompson took a rare three-pointer and jogged back on defense, as Hurley felt that his star player was disrespecting the sport. It was the boiling point in their relationship and eventually led to Thompson's dismissal that same season.

Thompson found himself at a bit of a crossroads as an elite rebounder, rim protector, and finisher who was developing a reputation as a troublemaker after moving between AAU clubs and prep schools.

So, midway through the 2008-09 season, Peck and the other Findlay coaches gathered Joseph in their office and asked if he could vouch for a fellow Canadian that he had played with at Grassroots. "I just kept reassuring them like, 'Look, he's a great guy,'" Joseph says about Thompson. "'You don't have to worry about him coming in and being a disruption to the chemistry or any type of flow going on over here because I personally know him.'"

Joseph reached out to tell Thompson that they would love to have him at Findlay and that it would be a perfect fit. Thompson joined midway through the season and was brought off the bench in an effort to test him and see how he would handle the demotion. But Thompson and his parents never complained. "I don't understand," Peck says about his reputation. "He just accepted it. Just didn't care. Wanted to win, compete and win."

Thompson fit into the team seamlessly because that's what he had done his entire life. Not only did he have Joseph to make the transition easier, but as a self-proclaimed "people person," Thompson knew how to communicate with everyone from the coaches to the players, bringing his high energy and bubbly personality to every practice and game.

"I think I get that from my mom," he says. "She's always been the bright spot of the room and brought the energy. So, for me, I think to be a great leader, you got to be able to understand every person's personality and how to get the best out of somebody.

"I've just always been that type of person that knows how to read a room."

•

Tristan Thompson fell in love with basketball watching Vince Carter's Raptors with his three younger brothers in the Brampton suburb of Toronto. His Jamaican mother, Andrea, had met his father, Trevor, and immigrated to Canada before settling in the Flower City.

Andrea worked at two different supermarkets and as a bus driver when the boys were growing up, giving Tristan a lot of responsibility over his three younger brothers, including taking care of Amari, who was born with epilepsy. "Just the way I was brought up, my mom, she was a woman that worked three jobs," Thompson says. "She's always been a hard worker. That's what she instilled in me."

Andrea would leave him in the mornings with a list of instructions, including getting his brothers fed and off to school, doing household chores, and finishing his paper route and homework on time.

"I've never had to ask him to do his homework," Andrea said. "Not once."

Thompson originally played soccer, but his coach told him he was going to be too tall for the sport, so him and his brothers began to play basketball religiously on the driveway hoop outside their house. They would pull it down to seven feet and practise all of Carter's dunks before going to the local YMCA and trying to hold their own against older players.

Tristan had started posting notes on his mirror every morning as early as 12 years old with goals of becoming the number-one player in the country and getting a college scholarship — only crossing off a goal once it was accomplished.

One day, the family saw a billboard promoting a local OBA team called the Brampton Blue Devils, which was coached by Tony McIntyre and built around his sons Tyler, Brandon, and Dylan Ennis. Thompson joined the program and immediately shined, showcasing a natural ability to rebound and overpower kids at the basket, eventually going on to play at the powerhouse Brampton high school St. Marguerite d'Youville Catholic Secondary.

During high school, he grew about six inches, from 6'0" to 6'6". But he never had trouble growing into his body like many big men do, eventually flourishing to 6'9" and becoming one of the best rebounders to ever come out of Canada. "His instinct for rebounding is the best I've ever seen," his high school coach Carlo Zoffranieri says. "He would get his hand on every single ball on both ends of the floor."

Thompson played briefly for McIntyre and Mike George's AAU team, CIA Bounce. But the NBA goal didn't become fully realizable until "Coach Ro got there," his younger brother, Dishawn, says. "We just never knew how to get there — it wasn't realistic until Coach Ro got there."

Russell saw Thompson playing for CIA Bounce and was taken aback by his hustle, saying "this kid has a motor unlike anything." So, he recruited him to join Grassroots for some tournaments before CIA Bounce gave him an ultimatum, making him choose between one or the other. Thompson chose Grassroots and leveraged his experience on the AAU circuit into an opportunity at St. Benedict's Prep before transferring to Findlay, where his game took off. Coach Peck had him transition from being more of a finesse player who took a lot of mid-range jumpers to a pure rim-running big man who embraced contact on both ends.

Together, Joseph and Thompson led Findlay to its first national ESPN Rise NHSI championship in 2009. They went undefeated and won their second straight championship the next season, with Joseph leading the team in assists and winning tournament MVP, while Thompson led the team in rebounds and blocks.

That year, they became the first Canadian boys since Toronto's Olu Famutimi in 2003 to be named to the prestigious McDonald's All-American Game.

"People back home don't get how big this is," Russell said. "For two Canadians to get these two spots on the All-American team, the stars gotta line up." And for Joseph and Thompson, they did.

Texas University assistant coach Rodney Terry had been trying to recruit Canadians since Devoe Joseph spurned him for Minnesota in 2008. However, in scouting Devoe, Terry discovered the younger Cory, recruiting him and Thompson since they were high school sophomores before landing the two Canadians in the fall of 2010. "I almost fell off my chair when he chose Texas," Terry said about Cory.

Both Joseph and Thompson transitioned seamlessly to the Big 12 — a member of the Power 5 NCAA conferences, which also include the Big Ten, Big East, ACC, and SEC. They started nearly every game their freshman season, helping Texas to a 28–8 record and a four seed in the 2011 March Madness tournament.

Joseph averaged 10 points and a team-high 3 assists to just 1.5 turnovers while shooting 41 percent from three, proving to be well beyond his years as a freshman point guard. He decided to enter the 2011 NBA Draft at the last minute despite head coach Rick Barnes being adamant that he wasn't ready. And because he wasn't invited to attend the draft in person, he opted for a small gathering at the family's Pickering house where the San Antonio Spurs selected him 29th overall. "It was like oh my god!" his father David says. "The place went crazy."

Fifteen minutes later, the street was full of friends and family members who showed up to celebrate Cory's selection. Later in the evening, the family got a knock on the door and saw four police cars responding to a noise complaint from one of the neighbours. But when they explained that Cory had been drafted, the police started taking pictures with him. "It was dope," Joseph says. "Just to see the community was behind me. And the love I was receiving was amazing."

Joseph went on to win an NBA championship with the Spurs in 2014 before signing a four-year, $30-million deal with his hometown Toronto Raptors in 2015, where he had two of the best seasons of his career.

Thompson, meanwhile, was more physically developed and ready for the NCAA, averaging 13 points and 8 rebounds for the Longhorns. He won the Big 12 Freshman of the Year and was a finalist for the National Freshman of the Year award. At the same draft, Thompson was selected fourth overall by the Cleveland Cavaliers, making him the highest Canadian selection ever. "I need some more time for it to sink in, but it's definitely an honour and it shows how much the Canadian basketball culture has grown," he said.

It was the first time that two Canadians were selected in the first round of the same draft since Rautins and Stewart Granger in 1983, giving a kid from Brampton and one from Pickering guaranteed contracts worth several million dollars while providing hope to countless Canadian kids that it was possible to make it to the NBA.

"Before people thought that they could probably go to college in the States," Russell says. "But when Tristan [and Cory] went to the NBA, it was like now you could go the NBA."

After Cadougan and Ashaolu became guinea pigs for the prep school system, Joseph and Thompson were able to take advantage of the knowledge that was handed down to them by preceding generations, going to Findlay Prep and becoming the first Canadians to go one-and-done in college before moving on to the NBA. It created a new pathway for other Canadians to follow.

"Kids realize they have different options now and they realize that it can actually happen," Joseph said. "We've always had talented people, but I think Tristan and I being the first guys to get drafted in the first round together, that opened some eyes."

CHAPTER 7

THE KID FROM KEELE STREET

LEO RAUTINS

A young Leo Rautins attempts to finish over two members of the American national team.

"He gave guys an opportunity that the national team probably wouldn't have looked at, maybe because of their past or maybe they had that reputation of being a troublemaker. He opened up the door."
— JERMAINE "ROCK" ANDERSON

When Leo Rautins was 16 years old, he and some friends drove to an AAU tournament in Buffalo, New York, where he played so well that Canisius University offered him a scholarship on the spot. Upon returning home to Toronto at 2 a.m., Rautins fell asleep. But a couple hours later, his dad woke him up, telling him to get ready for an open tryout for the Canadian men's national team.

Rautins had recently been cut by Team Ontario, so he didn't see the point in going. But he relented because it was unusual for his dad to be so convincing. "He would never tell me to go play," Rautins says. "But for some reason that morning, he wakes me up, says there's an open tryout, go!"

Rautins's natural feel for the game stood out playing against grown men, making quick use of the tryout as he sunk a couple jumpers, had a block, and threw down a big dunk in about five minutes of scrimmage play. Afterwards, Rautins was untying his shoes when head coach Jack Donohue walked over to him and invited him to training camp. A 16-year-old Rautins would soon become the youngest player ever to represent Canada. "From that point on," Rautins says, "my life started to change in crazy ways."

After coming off the bench for his first few exhibition games in 1976, Canada's top player, Ross Quackenbush, sprained his ankle and Rautins started against the powerhouse Yugoslavians, where he scored 25 points. "And from that point on, that was my team going forward," Rautins says. "I became the best player." He exploded onto the scene as an 18-year-old sensation at the 1978 FIBA World Championship, where Canada finished sixth. He also helped Canada finish second at the 1980 FIBA Americas before picking up its first ever win against Team USA at the World's Fair tournament in Knoxville, Tennessee, in 1982, scoring 24 points in the championship game.

Rautins went on to become the team captain, scoring 554 career points, the eighth most of all time, despite being held out of international competitions once he went pro.

Rautins was born in Toronto's "Little Lithuania" neighbourhood around Keele and Bloor in 1960. His parents met in a prison camp after having to flee their native countries of Latvia and Lithuania following the Soviet Union's invasion of the Baltic States. They came to Canada and had two sons, George and Leo.

As it was the national sport of Lithuania, it was natural for Rautins and his older brother to take to basketball, and Leo would follow George to every pickup run he went to, from the nearby Oakmount Park to gyms in Hamilton, Windsor, Niagara, and Buffalo.

After attending a few basketball camps down south, George got a scholarship at Niagara University and became a star, joining the Canadian men's national team before being drafted 158th overall in the 1975 NBA Draft. After watching his brother play for Canada at the 1974 World Championship, Rautins knew that he wanted to do the same.

"All I wanted to do is play for Canada," Rautins says. It was especially important given that Canada had been the only country to let his refugee parents in. "To represent your country, especially a country that allowed my parents to have a life, to have freedom, to have everything, it's always been a major factor in the way I look at it," he said.

"The Kid from Keele Street" became obsessed with basketball, searching for any books, magazines, or videotapes that he could get his hands on. Meanwhile, he started playing organized basketball through the Lithuanian Church of Resurrection and for Aušra, a local sports club for children of Lithuanian descent. He also played in a men's league from the eighth grade onwards, learning the game by playing against grown men, who would take him to the local establishment afterwards. "You take a bad shot and they slap you upside the head. If you don't pass the ball, they tell you, 'What the hell you doing?'" Rautins says. "So, you learn to play the right way."

Rautins attended St. Michael's College in 1973, a private Catholic high school at Bathurst and St. Clair with a top-tier basketball program coached by Dan Pendergrast. He would sneak into the gym through the priests' residence whenever he wanted, tiptoeing through the cafeteria and making the three-foot drop from the balcony to the gym floor, once calling up 40 of his friends to play a game on Christmas Day. And after growing into a 6'8" athletic marvel who could dribble, pass, and shoot, Rautins led St. Mike's on a 71-1 run, cementing it as one of the best teams in the city.

"He could handle the ball like a point guard and play like a big too," St. Mike's teammate Greg Hook says. "The greatest passer I've ever seen to this day . . . It was mind-blowing — it was like playing with grade 2 kids and he was just totally dominating."

By the end of Rautin's time in high school, all the best NCAA schools were coming north of the border to scout him at St. Mike's. With over 150 scholarship offers to choose from, he was one of the most recruited kids in NCAA history and the first basketball phenom to come out of Canada.

"Leo was a spectacular player and could do everything," says Jim Boeheim, the head coach of Syracuse, where Rautins transferred after his freshman year at Minnesota. He played for the Orange from 1980 to 1983, averaging 12 points, 6 rebounds, and 5 assists there while scoring a total 961 points in 85 games.

He was named a captain of the team because no matter how good Rautins got, he never had an ego. It stemmed from the fact that he came up alongside his brother, George, who was better than him and made him wait his turn on the side hoops before playing on the main court. He also learned the game from grown men who would have snuffed out any grandiose behaviour at the outset. "He was so far ahead of us and never once would he roll his eyes," Hook says. "He was always encouraging guys and would go out of his way when guys at the end of the bench got in to make sure that they got to lay up or they got something going."

By the end of his college career, despite being hampered by injuries,

Rautins became the first Canadian to get selected in the first round of an NBA Draft, going 17th overall to the Philadelphia 76ers in 1983. Unfortunately, his lone full season in the NBA was marred by a knee injury and a stress fracture of his left ankle; he played just 28 games. "He probably didn't get to be the player I think he could have been," Boeheim says. "He was a really ready-made NBA player." Instead, injuries derailed his career.

After having back surgery in grade 5, when doctors told him he might not ever be able to walk again, Rautins broke his nose five times, fractured almost every finger, smashed an elbow, and has undergone spinal surgery and 17 knee surgeries. Still, Rautins had a ten-year pro career overseas where he was an all-star in leagues in Italy, France, and Spain before returning to his hometown to work for the start-up Raptors in 1995. He got a job as a studio analyst and a colour commentator for the TV broadcast alongside the original play-by-play man, John Saunders. And while it was a dream job, getting an up-close seat to the Raptors' ascension, Rautins simultaneously watched his beloved national team go downhill.

Team Canada's great success at the 2000 Olympics was sandwiched between disappointing eras of racial tension in the 1990s and a lack of commitment in the early 2000s, with Canada finishing 13th at the 2002 World Championship after Nash was held out by the Dallas Mavericks.

The Nash-Triano era came to an official end following the FIBA Americas tournament in 2003. Despite Nash returning to play for the first time since 2000 and winning tournament MVP, Canada lost in a rematch to host team Puerto Rico and failed to qualify for the 2004 Games. Triano was subsequently fired by CEO Fred Nykamp, which caught everyone off guard, including the team's best player, who didn't feel like coaching was the issue. "It's certainly not going to help me playing for the national team again," Nash said. He later said, "In my mind right now, I'm not going to play for Canada anymore."

Nykamp tried to convince Nash that the organization had a new vision — one driven by the program's new long-term development model that was meant to create so many good Canadian players that Nash wouldn't have to put the team on his shoulders at every tournament. But Nash was done, in part because of Triano and in part because he wanted to maximize his NBA career.

"Of course, it hurt when Jay left," Nash says. "But honestly, my recollection is that as a 6'2" in shoes, 178-pound guard who handled the ball and had a lot of responsibility to create for his team, the NBA wore me out in a lot of ways.

"Getting to the Olympics was really important. And having done that, I now wanted to see if I could push on and have a great NBA career."

So, after 10 years of playing for the national team — playing the most official games (74) and scoring the second most points (923) of all time — Nash left. And with its lone superstar out of the picture, incoming head coach Leo Rautins had his work cut out for him if he was going to bring Canada back to respectability.

■

While Rautins was a great player, a smart basketball mind, a natural leader, and an enthusiastic public figure, it was very controversial decision when Canada Basketball hired him to lead the national team in 2005. After all, Rautins had no coaching experience whatsoever, and as a result, he faced a lot of criticism from the fans and media early in his tenure. "I know it really stressed him out," his son Andy, who played for him on the national team, says. "There was extra pressure on him, because people felt a type of way about Jay and Steve heading out."

Shortly after taking over the job, Rautins realized that it wasn't going to be easy to turn the program around and win in an international environment where the whole world was pouring more resources into basketball, while Canada couldn't even get its best players to show up. After all, the core of Nash, Barrett, Hamilton, and Meeks was past its prime, moving on to focus on their pro careers and families. And Canada's best young players were primarily inner-city kids from Toronto who had been jaded by Canada Basketball's previous treatment of Black players and coaches. Plus, with the explosion of AAU, they no longer needed the provincial and national teams to get exposure.

"The relationship back then was very strained with the national team and the guys coming out of Toronto," Ashaolu says. "The whispers I always heard were 'forget the national team, you don't need them, it's not important.'"

"For the people that were shunned, or their kids, or people that saw that, they were like . . . we've got AAU. We've got Division I scholarships," Paul Jones says. "And the national team became an option. It wasn't the goal anymore."

The most famous example of a player the national team could never secure was Jamaal Magloire, the 6'11" big man who grew up in Scarborough to parents of Trinidadian descent before falling in love with the competitive nature of basketball.

Magloire attended the storied Eastern Commerce, which was essentially a prep school in a public school's body, starting practice at 6 a.m. with kids from all over the province who had tutors and academic advisors to help them. The coaching staff, led by Simeon Mars, pushed Magloire to develop from an uncoordinated big man who got by on his size and strength into a skilled and smart player who could leverage his athleticism and improved touch to dominate the paint. He quickly became a fan-favourite in the small and crowded Eastern Commerce gym, where fans would hang from the rafters to cheer on the team.

"It was electric," Magloire says. "Everywhere we went, we were like a rock band. Our gym would hold 30 people, but we would fit in 100 because the gym was so small and people wanted to see us play."

After leading the team to back-to-back OFSAA championships in 1995 and 1996, Magloire got a scholarship from the University of Kentucky where he played for four years before being drafted 19th overall to the Charlotte Hornets in 2000. He became Toronto's first NBA All-Star in 2004 amidst a 12-year NBA career that ended in his hometown as a Raptor.

Magloire insists that he never had any issues with the national team, saying, "I know some people have had challenges, but I can't directly say I have." However, after a brief stint with the junior national team when Magloire was 18, Rautins could never recruit him to play for the senior team no matter how hard he tried. Of course, NBA teams were reluctant to let their athletes play internationally back then, but Magloire might also have been jaded by the program after his mentor and head coach at Eastern Commerce, Mars, was passed over first as a player and then — after being hired by Coach K as an apprentice coach in 1995 — was let go three years later when Canada Basketball chose not to renew his contract.

"I saw it myself that they weren't participating," Canada Basketball chairman Brian Cooper says about Black players in the 1990s and 2000s. "I remember having a conversation with Jamaal Magloire . . . I said, 'Why isn't this happening?' And he said, 'Well, it's a long, long history. Guys have been overlooked.'"

That was the environment Rautins walked into in 2005. And as a former player himself, he knew that he had to change the perception that there was racial bias in the selection process while getting enough money and resources to improve the standards so that the athletes who did choose to play would feel confident that the national team cared about them. In other words, he needed to show the athletes and their coaches that Canada Basketball would invest in their development and help them improve and get exposure. "The first thing I did, I went to all the AAU guys, I went to Ro Russell," Rautins says. "I said work with us. I'll help you. I'll help your guys."

However, each party was hung up in its own world. The AAU coaches didn't understand all the developmental benefits that came with representing the country on the biggest stages in games that mattered, while the national team's mandate was to win medals rather than to help kids get NCAA scholarships. And, as a result, there was an underlying divide, with the different entities pulling kids in different directions.

"One of the challenges in Canadian basketball, particularly at that time, was a fairly splintered development system or pathway for kids," former Canada Basketball manager Andrew Cook says. "You had different competing entities for the kids that weren't necessarily working together."

Instead of helping support the kids by scheduling competitions at different times or allowing coaches to work in both organizations, each entity chose to work alone and tried to take sole credit for each kid's success story. At one point, kids were even given ultimatums to either play AAU or play with Canada, and vice versa.

It created an environment where the best players were simply not showing up for the national team. And, eventually, something had to give.

When he took over as head coach in 2005, Rautins wanted to reset the culture. So, he opened up the doors and hosted open tryouts with a new group of players without any expectations as to who would be on the team and what their roles would be, giving everybody the opportunity to prove themselves.

Jermaine "Rock" Anderson was one of those young guys. The future captain of the senior men's team grew up in Toronto around Queens Quay before moving to Keele and Wilson as a teenager, where he was introduced to basketball through his older cousin.

In grade 8, Rock went to a high school tournament and saw Eastern Commerce play. "And just seeing from like a cultural standpoint, how they would enter the gym and the music playing and then watching them play. For me, I'm just like, 'This is a school that I'm going to,'" he says.

Rock went to Eastern and had a lot of success under coaches Desmond Rowley and Roy Rana, winning OFSAA in his senior season. At the same time, he joined Grassroots and improved his game, realizing how much harder he needed to train in order to succeed south of the border.

Like a lot of Torontonians in those days, Rock had no relationship to the provincial or national programs. After just one year playing in the OBA, he started focusing on AAU, where the national team wasn't even discussed. "We felt like it was pointless without even actually saying it," he says.

But Rautins reached out to Rock in 2005 — by then a starter for Fordham University in the Bronx — and invited him to camp. "He gave guys an opportunity that the national team probably wouldn't have looked at, maybe because of their past or maybe they had that reputation of being a troublemaker," Rock says. "He opened up the door."

While he didn't have the tactical expertise some international coaches did, Rautins was a former player who understood the pro game and could communicate effectively with players. He saw what they needed to do to improve and move up in their careers and wasn't afraid to tell them. "I see Leo as in many ways a father figure because he genuinely cared," Rock says. "He was open and honest."

Rock remembers when the camera caught him being upset on the broadcast because he wasn't playing much. Rautins later approached him in the airport and told him straight up that he was young and needed time to improve. "Somebody else might have said, 'Oh, this guy is an asshole,'" Rock says. "But I was actually extremely appreciative that he was putting it to us in that way."

"It was almost like he was your teammate," former captain Carl English says. "He was great at keeping communication with you all year and building the team. We knew that he cared about us."

In fact, Rautins was brutally honest with his new core of young players including Carl English, Joel Anthony, Aaron Doornekamp, Brady Heslip, Myck Kabongo, Jesse Young, Levon Kendall, Juan Mendez, and Rock Anderson, showing them a lot of confidence and loyalty even if they originally struggled to make the transition to the senior team. Their first tournament together was the 2005 FIBA Americas championship, a qualifier for the upcoming World Championship. Rautins completely turned over the roster, allowing a group of young guys to make their Team Canada debuts, with just one holdover from their previous competition in 2003 under Triano: Denham Brown.

And while the other 11 players were young and inexperienced, placing ninth in the 10-team tournament and failing to qualify for the 2006 World Championship for the first time since 1967, a new core was being formed — one with a renewed sense of energy that would end up growing very close bonds and coming back year after year, keeping Canada Basketball afloat during its most challenging era.

"We enjoyed our time together so much," Andy Rautins says. "We just wish we had more time to grow as a team together."

Despite the national team being desperate for NBA players in the 2000s, it was primarily composed of European pros who got used to the lack of resources, the bad travel and sleeping conditions, the lack of a reasonable daily stipend or carding money, and the underwhelming performance staffs because they were desperate to represent the country during a time when the program was in need of support.

"It was a transition time," assistant coach Dave Smart says. "Everything was new so that international basketball was not the thing — the [AAU] circuit was the thing, the NBA was the thing, the circuit led to Division I, Division I led to the NBA.

"Leo did a great job of getting guys to play in a time when that was not anybody's priority."

CHAPTER 8

CAPTAIN KELLY

CHIP BANTOCK

Kelly Olynyk boxes out an opposing big man during his time at Gonzaga.

"This kid's a big part of what I think our future is going to be. He's a talented kid. He plays with balls."

— LEO RAUTINS

Two years after Rautins took the job, Canada had the 2007 FIBA Americas Championship in Las Vegas, Nevada — a qualifier for the 2008 Olympic Games. And while Rautins was busy mending relationships in the grassroots community and improving the resources of the program, he felt the team needed an immediate injection of talent if they were going to qualify for the Olympics.

Unfortunately, Canada's two NBA players, Nash and Magloire, were both off the table. So, Rautins felt that Samuel Dalembert was their next best shot, fighting hard to recruit the 6'11" Port-au-Prince, Haiti, native ahead of the 2007 FIBA Americas. Despite being born outside Canada, Dalembert lived in Montreal for high school, arriving from Haiti as the tallest soccer player in the city before transitioning to basketball. His skills developed quickly, and he ended up moving to a prep school in New Jersey before earning a scholarship to Seton Hall University.

Dalembert averaged 8 points and 6 rebounds during his sophomore season in the Big East and was drafted 26th overall by the 76ers in 2001. He improved each season and posted career-best averages of 11 points, 9 rebounds, and 2 blocks in 2006–07. "Sam can have a huge impact on this team," Rautins said. "We have a chance to see what we can do with a top quality centre."

With help from the national team, Dalembert received his Canadian citizenship in the summer of 2007, just in time for the tournament. And despite there being concerning moments when Dalembert isolated himself away from the team and was late to practices, he performed well and helped Canada beat Brazil, Venezuela, the US Virgin Islands, Uruguay, and Mexico while leading the team in points, rebounds, and blocks.

Team Canada finished fifth at the 2007 FIBA Americas, its best result since 2003 and good enough to qualify for the last chance Olympic Qualifying Tournament in Athens, Greece, the following summer. Canada joined a 12-country competition with teams like Germany, Greece, Croatia, Slovenia, Puerto Rico, and Brazil expected to compete for one of the three available Olympic spots. Meanwhile, Rowan Barrett came out of a five-year retirement to rejoin the national team and provide veteran leadership, while Joel Anthony — the Montreal-born big man who had just finished his rookie year with the Miami Heat after going undrafted out of the University of Nevada, Las Vegas (UNLV) — made his national team debut.

But from the moment camp got underway in Toronto, things fell apart. First, Denham Brown, who was a big part of the team the prior summer, didn't show up to camp. Then after Canada was badly outhustled and out-rebounded during an exhibition loss to New Zealand in Toronto's Ricoh Coliseum, Rautins called out his team. "I think every player should be absolutely embarrassed about what they did today," he said. "I mean, if that was a park and you were playing there and people walked in and pushed you around and did whatever they wanted to do . . . it's absolutely embarrassing."

Once they got to Athens, Canada played the 19th-ranked Slovenians in the opening match. Slovenia made quick work of the Canadians, winning 86–70 behind a dominant 14 point, 9 rebound performance from big man Rasho Nesterovic. "The effort was unacceptable," Rautins said. "The way we came out to play was just extremely disappointing." Dalembert was dealing with a back problem and struggled in his matchup, going 1-for-8 from the field with just two rebounds while allowing Nesterovic to go off.

The next morning, the team got up early to watch film in the hotel to prepare for South Korea — the program's most important game in four years and a must-win if they were going to qualify for the Olympics. But Dalembert was "falling over, sleeping during the video," says Rautins, who felt disrespected after fighting hard to have Dalembert join the team.

"The concern was that Sam hadn't been playing that well," assistant coach Wayne Yearwood says. "You could see that his interest was waning."

"Sam being there was just more of a distraction than anything else," Andy Rautins says. "His heart wasn't in it at any point."

But Rautins made exceptions for the one NBA rotation player on the team, overlooking the fact that he was late to practices and partying at night with a group of friends he brought to Athens, creating a double standard for the rest of the team. And it all blew up hours before the South Korea game, when, following the sleepy film session, Dalembert was late for the bus to the arena and then started mumbling under his breath about how he was done with the team.

Rautins heard Dalembert and asked him to get off the bus, where the two of them got to talking. "Sam goes, 'I'm your best player,'" Rautins says. "I said, 'You're my best player? Let me make something clear: We haven't won one game with you that we couldn't win without you.'"

The two were chewing each other out, with the rest of the team now watching from the bus, peering through the windows as their coach and star player appeared ready to come to blows. "He goes, 'Fuck you,' And he got back on the bus," Rautins says. But he got Dalembert to return outside. "I go, 'What did you say? Fuck me? No. Fuck you and get off my bus! Get out of my fucking hotel and fuck off. Get lost.'"

Canada still had a game to play without Dalembert. And despite having every excuse to lose, they rallied from a 77–66 deficit to score 13 straight points in the game's final three minutes to secure the 79–77 victory and keep their Olympic hopes alive. "My job once that happened was to kind of rally the whole team together and play a game," English says. "We need to come together. We got a job to do. We're representing our country — all that other stuff can take care of itself later."

However, Canada's Olympic dreams came to an end a couple days later in the quarter-final, when it was outclassed by a more talented Croatian team 83–62. It was a massive disappointment for the program, which had hired Rautins in 2005 in hopes of qualifying for the 2008 Games. But despite the media criticism and the Dalembert situation creating an even worse reputation for the national team when it came to recruiting NBA players, Canada Basketball extended its contract with Rautins until the 2010 World Championship in Turkey.

English and Rock led Canada to a 4th-place at the 2009 FIBA Americas Championship — Canada's best finish under Rautins. But Canada faltered a year later in Turkey. The team finished as the 22nd best team in the 24-team tournament after going winless against Lebanon, Lithuania, France, New

Zealand, and Spain due to a mix of poorly timed injuries and a lack of star talent. "It was a different level," Andy says. "So we took our licks, but we never gave up. We always played really hard to make up for what we lacked, but just it just wasn't enough."

A year later, after failing to qualify for the 2012 Olympics, Rautins announced his resignation from the national team after six years of having to clash with the board over money, the players over commitment, and the media over respect.

"The players have given me everything that I've asked [but] I think for the benefit of this program going forward, a new voice in the locker room will be the best thing," Rautins said.

"This hasn't been a job. This has been a passion . . . something that I've loved doing."

While Canada would have to wait four more years for a chance to go to the Olympics, there was one silver lining from the 2010 World Championship: a 19-year-old big man with long blond hair and a funky game named Kelly Olynyk.

Kelly Olynyk was such a big Raptors fan growing up that he would take a portable radio into his bed to listen to Chuck Swirsky call the games on The Fan 590 or watch them with his sisters Jesse and Maya at their home in Scarborough. At half time, Olynyk would use the 15-minute commercial break to run to the driveway hoop and practise the moves he saw the Raptors make.

Once, however, his sister locked him outside during halftime as a joke. He was so desperate to get back inside before the second half started that he punched a hole through the glass window to unlock the door.

"He was fanatical about it," his mother, Arlene, says. "I watched people, friends, tell me that, 'oh you know my grandson's fanatical.'" She would respond, "I don't think you know what fanatical means."

Olynyk was born in Toronto in 1991 after his father, Ken, left his post at the University of Lethbridge to take a job coaching the men's team at the University of Toronto while working as an "visiting" coach with Lenny Wilkens and the Raptors. Arlene played high school basketball in

Kamloops, BC, before going to play at Lethbridge, where she met Ken and later became a referee. "While Ken was coaching and I was reffing, both at the university level, we were watching game film until two in the morning," Arlene says.

Olynyk grew up around the game, traveling from his father's U of T practices to the Raptors games, where his mother had a side job as the first female scorekeeper in the NBA. She got two tickets for every game, enabling Olynyk to meet his heroes like point guard Alvin Williams. "I was in a gym 24/7, 365, whether my mom was reffing or my dad was coaching," Olynyk says. "I was always around the game."

When he wasn't shooting on the driveway hoop, Olynyk was playing organized basketball for the Scarborough Blues alongside his friend Cory Joseph. Ken had started a team for their age group so Kelly would have somewhere to play. "We were really, really good," Olynyk says. "Obviously, we had a few guys on that team who went to the NBA, which is pretty unheard of."

The family moved back to BC around 2003 when Ken got a job at Thompson Rivers University in Kamloops, a small town of less than 100,000 people three hours inland from Vancouver. But the basketball scene in Kamloops lagged far behind that of Toronto, lacking any club infrastructure. "There was zero opportunity to play," Arlene says. Instead, the teenaged Olynyk stayed engaged in multiple sports throughout the school year while playing pickup basketball in town.

Fortunately, his parents knew what it was going to take for their son to make it in basketball. After playing for four years at SFU and then one year at Laurentian under Ken Shields, Ken Olynyk became a U Sports coach while working with Canada Basketball's junior program on and off between 1983 and 1996. He learned from international programs like Russia and Yugoslavia that had big men who could dribble, pass, and shoot. "I just thought wow, you got to learn to be a basketball player, not a position," Ken says. So, as a coach, he would have every player rotate through the positions, going from point guard to post to the wing.

By the time Olynyk got to South Kamloops Secondary for grade 9, he was a 6'3" point guard with a perimeter-oriented skill set who could do a bit of everything. However, while quarterbacking the Titans during his grade 11 football season, Olynyk took a hit that broke the humerus bone below his left shoulder, forcing him to get three screws in his shoulder and miss his entire grade 11 basketball season. "I didn't cry when I got hit," Olynyk said. "But I started to cry when they told me I wasn't going to play basketball that season."

The silver lining was that Olynyk could still practise with his right hand, dribbling and putting up 500 shots a day while his left hand was in a sling. "I asked Kelly, 'Can you work without a guarantee?'" Ken said. "He worked his butt off, but there was no guarantee."

Olynyk joined the Under-19 boys' national team in 2009, when he went to the FIBA World Championship and averaged 11 points and 8 rebounds, gaining interest from NCAA schools like San Diego and Gonzaga. Then, after participating in Canada Basketball's inaugural National Elite Development Academy (NEDA) at McMaster University in Hamilton, Ontario, for a couple months — training with former national team player Greg Francis and some of Canada's best teenagers while attending school online — he returned to Kamloops in December of his senior year for the basketball season and dominated. In fact, he was named the Basketball BC outstanding high school player of the year after leading the tournament in scoring, rebounding, and assists for the Titans, who finished third in the province.

Olynyk's parents wanted him to stay on the West Coast and be close to home for college, so he committed to Gonzaga University in Spokane, Washington. Unfortunately, the start of his tenure as a Bulldog didn't go as planned.

■

Olynyk was a reserve who could barely get off the bench in his first two seasons in Spokane, playing behind fellow Canadian Robert Sacre while struggling to fit into the role head coach Mark Few envisioned for him. After Olynyk grew to 7'0" during his freshman year, Few wanted Olynyk to play in the post like a prototypical big man. "I had never done it," Olynyk said. "It was like telling a quarterback to go kick a field goal."

"We were fine with the skill package on the perimeter, but not if that was exclusively all we got," Few said. "It was a problem for the first couple of years."

After a disappointing freshman season, Olynyk was selected to represent Canada at the 2010 World Championship, where Rautins was so impressed with the tall, gangly teenager that he gave him the final roster spot despite facing criticism from inside and outside the organization. Olynyk sat on the bench for the first two games of the tournament before dropping 13 points in 19 minutes against France in his senior team debut. "I was kicking myself in the rear end," Rautins said about not playing him sooner. "This kid's a big part of what I think our future is going to be. He's a talented kid. He plays with balls."

"That team really helped me realize that I could play at that level," Olynyk says.

Renato Pasquali was an assistant coach on the team in 2010 and an influential figure in European basketball. He could tell that Olynyk was going to be a special player and that Few was limiting his game by playing him in the post at Gonzaga, so he offered Olynyk a professional contract at BC Kyiv in Ukraine for about $200,000 a year.

"Listen, Kelly was making nothing," Pasquali says. "I was offering him a chance to show himself to Europe where he could make millions of dollars."

However, Maurizio Gherardini, who brought Pasquali into the program, begged him to rescind his offer because he didn't want to ruin Canada Basketball's relationship with Gonzaga and other NCAA schools, understanding that they would not be happy if a player joined the Canadian team for a summer and didn't return to school.

That's when the decision to redshirt began to crystalize for Olynyk, realizing that he was a good player who could succeed in the NCAA as long as he tweaked a few things. "If things aren't going the way you want them to, you have to change something or else you're going to stick with the same result," said Olynyk. "[Redshirting] made sense in a way, and it gave me time to build my body, work on my skills, and develop into the player I wanted to be."

Olynyk took control of his own destiny with the long view in mind, returning to Gonzaga and sitting out his junior season, using the time to get in the weight room with trainer Travis Knight. The issue wasn't just that Olynyk needed to get stronger but that it was taking too long for his brain to communicate with the rest of his body. After going through a seven-inch growth spurt and sprouting up to 7'0", Olynyk "had skills that in his mind he knew what he wanted to do, could do," Knight says. "But he had trouble just from a coordination standpoint, from a balance standpoint, doing those things consistently at a high level."

The goal was to make things more automatic so Olynyk did things as a matter of reflex rather than having to process decisions before acting on them. "And one of the ways to do that is to occupy the working memory with another task," Knight says.

Knight had Olynyk shuffle in and out of an agility ladder while catching tennis balls, progressively increasing the difficulty by labelling the balls with words that would correspond to actions such as move backwards or to the left, eventually requiring him to do math on the fly to determine which way to move or which hand to catch the ball with. "There was no real time to think," Knight says. "I think it helped him learn how to make decisions faster. And I think he learned how to be a little bit more instinctive with his movements rather than sometimes you get paralysis by analysis."

As Olynyk's brain-body connection improved, so, too, did his ability to execute highly coordinated movements that many athletes take for granted, such as running and jumping to dunk. In fact, Olynyk's vertical increased from 32 inches to 39 after a year of working with Knight. "Once we improved that rate [of communication]," Knight says, "everything opened up."

Having nearly 18 months to work out five times a day helped Olynyk make a huge transformation in his body and processing speed, using the team's practices as his games. He would destroy Gonzaga's starting lineup with the scout team and walk-ons. "My goal was to make it so that coaches went back into their little meeting every single day and say, 'Why the F are we redshirting Olynyk?'" he says. "So, every time we practised, that was like my game."

Olynyk returned to the starting lineup in 2012–13 and averaged 18 points, 7 rebounds, and 2 assists with a field goal percentage of 63, the best in the West Coast Conference (WCC). He won the WCC Player of the Year and was a Wooden Award finalist, seeing his name for the first time on NBA Draft boards. "Nine months ago, this wasn't what I envisioned for today," Olynyk said. "It came quicker than I expected."

Gonzaga, meanwhile, had one of its best seasons in the history of the program, going 32-3 and 16-0 in the WCC, with Olynyk and fellow Canadian point guard Kevin Pangos at the helm. Shortly after losing to Fred VanVleet's Wichita State Shockers in March Madness, Olynyk left for the 2013 NBA Draft. He was selected 13th overall before going on to play in the NBA for more than 12 years, making more than $110 million in his career.

Meanwhile, inspired by watching Nash at the 2000 Olympics and seeing his dad coach the junior national teams growing up, Olynyk represented Canada at every healthy opportunity between 2010 and 2024 — when he was named captain of the best Canadian team in history. "[My dad] just instilled that pride and that respect and that give back to your country for everything that your country has done [for you]," he says. "Watching him coach and compete, and then watching obviously the [Canadian] teams before me, I think that was a huge thing.

"Like, if I ever have that opportunity, that's what I'm doing."

CHAPTER 9

A CHANGING OF THE GUARD

ON POINT, SANJAY KHURANA

Former player and current general manager of the senior men's program, Rowan Barrett, talks with his son RJ during a Team Canada training camp.

"It kind of opened the door for the professionals to come in and say, 'Okay, I'm being treated first class, I'm being treated like my NBA team.' It makes for a better opportunity to get our best to show up."

— WAYNE YEARWOOD

Canada has been behind the international eight ball when it comes to funding the national basketball program ever since the sport's international debut in 1936.

Canada's economy was recovering from the Great Depression, so the government forced athletes to pay their own way to the Berlin Games. The only reason the Windsor-based basketball team was able to go was because head coach Gordon Fuller had a connection with Ford Motor Company, which paid for the team's 10-day boat trip there.

A few years later, at the 1952 Games, player-coach Paul Thomas learned that even the most destitute nations were outspending Canada when it came to basketball. "We were given a daily stipend of $2 a day," he said. "India got $12 a day."

Even when Donohue took the job in 1972, Canada Basketball couldn't afford to put a competitive offer together until Carling O'Keefe breweries agreed to hire him as a motivational speaker who gave pep talks to O'Keefe staff, lending him to the national team on the side. "We didn't have shoes," Doc Ryan, who played for Donahue, says. "I mean, that's how bad it was back in the day." He noted that players had to practise three times a day without time for a summer job, but never got enough carding money from the government to survive.

Travel was also huge issue, as the organization would book the cheapest route to every destination, taking upwards of five trains or connecting flights to each tournament, which they still do in the winter windows. Their accommodations weren't much better, as the team would stay in dorm rooms at Humber College in Toronto for training camp, with players rooming two to a dorm in small beds that didn't fit the big men, whose legs would dangle off as they slept. At competitions, they would continue sleeping two to a room all the way up until the late 2010s.

The dire state of the organization became public at the 2000 Olympics, when Nash gave up his first-class seat to the team's seven-footers while he sat in economy. He also secretly funnelled $30,000 to Triano to divide between his 10 non-NBA teammates to go on a shopping spree. "Before it was kind of like, Let's squeeze these guys into any hotel we can. Let's save on budgeting, not worried about the food as much," Andy Rautins says. "That frustrated a lot of guys, especially considering that we sacrificed our summers."

After all, having lackluster amenities, travel, food, and support staff is not synonymous with elite performance or health. And many believe that the national team suffered as a result of a lack of funds.

•

While Canada was struggling for basic necessities, basketball countries like Spain, Italy, Germany, France, Australia, and America were pumping millions of dollars into their national programs by the mid-2000s. The top programs were outspending Canada's men's program by more than five times while rewarding players monetarily for each medal.

That injection of cash enabled European federations to have training camps every summer, sometimes lasting up to 45 days before international tournaments, where a group of 30 players and ten support staff would participate until the day before a competition. Canada, meanwhile, would practise for half the time and with half the personnel, hurting its ability to grow the talent pool and install a Canadian style of play.

European federations never had to worry much about developing young talent, either, as there are established domestic leagues with privately owned professional clubs that identify and develop players from the age of 10, enabling the federations to focus simply on regulatory matters and building the national teams. But Canada Basketball has always had the dual mandate of investing in programs to identify and develop athletes as well as building the national teams.

Things started to improve when Wayne Parrish became the CEO of Canada Basketball in 2007. The Toronto native worked as a sports journalist before transitioning to the business side of the newspaper industry, where he started to hear rumblings of an opening at Canada Basketball after former CEO Fred Nykamp left for a cushier job at Canada Soccer. The organization earned $8 million in sponsorship and licensing revenues compared to about $1 million for Canada Basketball at the time, also receiving significantly more money from FIFA than Canada Basketball ever got from FIBA.

Parrish knew that the program was in financial straits when he got the job. But it wasn't until he was able to look over the books that he realized they were in significant debt and the banks wouldn't loan them any more money. "It was dire," he says. "I didn't know if we would be able to survive."

National sports organizations (NSOs) are notoriously challenging to fund in Canada because the majority of the money has historically come from the government, which has never prioritized basketball. In fact, Canada's government has funded over 7,000 ice arenas and zero basketball-specific facilities.

Plus, the government's funding model was based primarily on high-performance results including the ability to qualify and win medals at international events, which put team sports like basketball at a unique disadvantage compared to individual sports that could win multiple medals in any given year. Parrish worked to establish a coalition of 19 team sport NSOs that demanded Sport Canada change the funding structure to see the potential benefits of investing more into team sports, eventually getting $6 million annually to split between them in 2010. "And if you look back . . . at the growing success of Canadian team sports within the Olympic framework, it really can be traced to that moment in time and the success of that lobbying effort," Parrish says.

That along with a five-fold increase in support from MLSE in the form of a three-year agreement valued at $1.5 million improved the organizational standards for the men's and women's programs, helping flip Canada Basketball from a top-down organization with a "you're lucky to be here" culture to a bottom-up organization where players were put at the forefront. "Just the lifestyle, which was important," Rock says about what changed. "You have to create a standard for guys to just want to play and give up their summers."

And while Parrish was creative enough to find the money, Rautins began the process of funneling it to all the right places, moving the players from dorms to hotels, traveling directly, allowing family members to join them on trips, hiring more support staff, and paying players better per diems and a more livable carding salary in order to make the experience as attractive as possible.

"It kind of opened the door for the professionals to come in and say, 'Okay, I'm being treated first class, I'm being treated like my NBA team,'" former assistant coach Wayne Yearwood says.

"It makes for a better opportunity to get our best to show up."

•

Following Rautins's departure in 2012, a new regime came in to lead the Canadian men's program. Led by general manager Steve Nash and assistant general manager Rowan Barrett, the childhood friends and former teammates made good on a decade-long promise to improve the program from the inside once they were done playing.

After meeting at tryouts for the Under-19 junior national team in 1991, the two immediately bonded over their shared love for the sport and desire to reach the highest levels. "From day one, we had a friendship that was important to me," Nash said. "He took care of me when I was young, and he didn't need to."

They stayed close friends throughout their entire national team careers, running the stairs to get in extra work during training camps and hanging out with each other's families in the offseasons. But as two of Canada's most committed players, Nash and Barrett were always frustrated by the lack of resources in the program, including how they would have to take multiple connecting flights to every competition and sleep two to a dorm room right up to and including Nash's final tournament at the 2003 FIBA Americas in Puerto Rico. "We were upset," Barrett says, noting that a key conversation took place following the competition. "What do we have to do? And it was like, Well, whenever we're done, we're going to come back and we're going to try to help change this."

Barrett grew up in Scarborough to Jamaican parents, discovering the game during a camp at the local YMCA. But he was more into soccer and track and field as a kid, racing his friends in the 100-metre sprint taped to the school's track during recess and dreaming of becoming an Olympic sprinter like Ben Johnson, who lived down the street.

It wasn't until grade 9 at West Hill Collegiate that Barrett started to fall in love with basketball, making the freshman team and playing in pickup runs with his friends all over town. And while it started as a social thing, his passion evolved after seeing Michael Jordan, his tongue sticking out, his red and white sneakers, and the swagger and confidence he played with. "I was like, 'Who's that guy?'" Barrett says.

Jordan was more relatable than any of the sprinters or hockey players that Barrett had previously looked up to, as Barrett was a 6'6", long, lean, fast, and strong athlete who could jump out of the gym, picking up the nickname "Ducky" because of his size 13 feet.

After Barrett helped the bantam team win the city championships during his first year at West Hill Collegiate, a couple older players told him about an upcoming Five-Star Basketball Camp in America, noting that he might be good enough to do something with basketball. "I was armed with a mission," Barrett says. "I took the invite, gave it to my mom, and I told her, 'Mama, I don't want any Christmas presents or any birthday presents. I just want to go to this camp.'"

Barrett came back from the Five-Star camp a more skilled and confident player, and it propelled him to an exemplary high school basketball career, highlighted by 59- and 56-point games in his senior year, when he won the slam dunk contest and was MVP of the *Toronto Star* all-star game. He was the number one player in Canada and landed a scholarship to St. John's University in New York in 1992. "He has the explosiveness, the talent and the jumping ability to do extremely well," West Hill head coach Richard Dean said. "I'd put him in the same category as Leo [Rautins] and Phil [Dixon]."

Still, Barrett had relatively little experience playing against American competition and was like a fish out of water when he started playing in the Big East. Not only did he have to get used to playing on the perimeter after being able to dominate in the paint due to his size and athleticism advantage in Canada, but the insane crowd sizes along with the speed, skill, and physicality of the NCAA game were overwhelming at times.

He barely got off the bench during his freshman season but ended up developing a nice jump shot in the summer and had a decent college career, averaging 10 points off the bench in his senior year. After going undrafted in 1996, Barrett turned pro and played everywhere from Venezuela to Cyprus to France while representing Canada nearly every summer. He played 58 games (8th all-time) and scored 754 points (3rd most) between 1993 and 2008, co-captaining the team alongside Nash to a seventh-place finish in Sydney.

•

Following a nearly 20-year playing career, Barrett retired to work at a bank in 2008. But he would occasionally volunteer for Canada Basketball and other youth basketball programs around Toronto, catching up with old friends and former teammates who had created club programs while Barrett was busy playing overseas.

When Rautins stepped down as head coach in 2011, Barrett saw the opportunity he had been waiting for to improve the organization from the inside. He started sending Nash video clips and articles about young Canadian players like Andrew Wiggins and Anthony Bennett who were projected to go to the NBA. "He was kind of shocked, right? Having been one of the few Canadians in the NBA for so many years," Barrett says. "His interest was piqued."

Nash was still in the final chapter of his NBA career as a member of the Los Angeles Lakers. But despite having reservations about joining Canada Basketball as an executive while he was playing on the other side of the continent, he understood that his presence could fundamentally shift the organization from a resource standpoint — that he could help bring in an influx of cash that was desperately needed.

Plus, Nash wanted to help change the image and build a culture where guys would choose the national team over the increasing opportunities that were popping up in the summers, such as working out at their NCAA or NBA facilities, joining professional leagues, or working with skills coaches. "[We were] trying to create a culture where it means something to play on the national team," Nash says. "But also where the national team provides players with kind of a player-centric program."

Nash accepted the job of general manager on two conditions. The first was that his pal and former coach Triano return as the head coach. And the second was that the board had to raise enough money to run a professional outfit as the team attempted to qualify for the 2016 Olympic Games, no longer having to scramble for money like the previous summer when a last-minute private donor coughed up $50,000 for the players' insurance.

The goal was to double the yearly budget for the men's program from $500,000 to $1 million, even if some federations were spending as much as $5 million a year by 2012. "The funding that [top countries] have available to them is exceptional. We felt we needed to address that," Parrish said. "What we really needed to get all of those guys to come to the table was a single event, something to galvanize them and that in my mind was always the prospect of Steve taking on this role."

Former Raptors owner John Bitove and businessman David Kassie helped put together a committee of 32 Canadian businessmen called the "6th Man" group including then Bell Canada CEO George Cope and CN chairman David McLean. Nash got on the phone with whoever was hesitant to ask for a donation of $100,000 each over a four-year period for a total of about $3.2 million. "It's amazing how powerful Steve getting on a conference call [is]," Parrish said. "How galvanizing that is for these individuals."

It all came together at a massive training camp in the summer of 2012, where Nash's presence along with an influx of cash helped the national team bring 27 of Canada's best young players to Toronto's Air Canada Centre for five days of training with NBA coaches, while staying at an upscale hotel nearby. From NBA players like Joseph, Thompson, and Olynyk to young guys like Kevin Pangos, Tyler Ennis, Andrew Nicholson, and Anthony Bennett to program veterans like Jermaine Anderson and Robert Sacre, there was a different energy with all the best players in the building.

"A couple of years ago, we'd be lucky to have at least five of the top players in the country at training camp," Thompson said. "Now, we're building something real special.

"You go back in the day before I was born, they said the best players from the GTA could beat the national team. Now we've got the best players from the GTA."

Even Magloire was there, wearing a practice piny and helping coach the youngsters. His presence was symbolic of the changing of the guard taking place. "With Steve Nash and Rowan Barrett leading the helm," Magloire said, "it definitely is a new phase in Canada Basketball."

Nash, assistant general manager Barrett, and head coach Triano understood that continuity, chemistry, and a long-term commitment to the national team mattered when it came to international success, crediting their run at the 2000 Olympics to just that. And the camp was the beginning of a years-long process meant to instill a sense of national pride into the athletes. "Playing for Canada at the Olympics was the greatest experience of my career, bar none," Nash said at training camp. "It's no secret what this country means to me and to be a part of Canada Basketball again is a huge honour and pleasure."

"If that message doesn't resonate with our young kids," Triano said, "then we have to re-evaluate who we want representing our country."

That camp represented the beginning of a new era for Canada Basketball — one where the players would be put at the forefront of the organization, which would do everything possible to recruit its best players so they could start winning medals.

But one player was missing from the Air Canada Centre during that all-important training camp in 2012 — someone that Canada Basketball had been pursuing since he was a little kid dunking on his peers in nearby Vaughan, Ontario. His name was Andrew Wiggins.

CHAPTER 10

THE CHOSEN ONE

GUS GYMNOPOULOS

Andrew Wiggins dribbles at Vaughan Road Academy, where he was the best prospect to ever come out of Canada.

"I didn't know how to feel back then, because it was so new. And some people would start to notice me and show me some love and appreciation. And being a 13-year-old kid, you're kind of just trying to soak it all in."

— ANDREW WIGGINS

On October 12, 2009 — five years after the invention of Facebook and YouTube and two years after the first smartphone — a 39-second highlight clip was uploaded to the YouTube channel Hoopmixtape with the title "Best 13 Year Old in the Nation 6'6 Andrew Wiggins!"

A few days earlier, at the Elite 80 Fall AAU Showcase in Wilson, North Carolina, Wiggins was dominating his competition, rising several feet off the ground to sink jumpers without a contest and crossing over his opponents before dunking on them, looking like a man amongst boys. A few months later, the video had been viewed over a million times, marking the beginning of Wiggins's ascension.

Wiggins was born in Thornhill, Ontario, a suburb north of Toronto, in 1995. His parents, Mitchell and Marita, met when they lived in the same dorm at Florida State University in Tallahassee in 1980, chasing their dreams of becoming professional athletes.

Mitchell was a 6'4" shooting guard from Kinston, North Carolina, who went in the first round of the 1983 NBA Draft, making a name for himself as a hard-nosed defender across four seasons in Chicago and Houston, where he went to the NBA Finals. However, after testing positive for cocaine use the following season, he incurred a two-and-a-half-year suspension from the league and moved on to play professionally for 15 more years.

Marita, meanwhile, was born in Barbados and raised by her extended family after her parents moved to New York City for college in order to seek a better life for their children. They eventually settled down in

Concord, Ontario, where Marita rejoined them when she was nine, attending nearby Vaughan Road Collegiate Institute for high school. She blossomed into a world class sprinter and won silver for Canada in the 4x100 metre relay at the 1984 Olympic Games before being inducted into the Canadian Olympic Hall of Fame.

Mitchell and Marita had six children: three boys and three girls, settling in Vaughan, a suburb of Thornhill, in 2002. It was a quiet existence outside of the spotlight, attending church on Sundays and playing sports at the nearby park when they had free time, which would come to be named Marita Payne Park. "They never stressed anything," Wiggins said. "They wanted us to be kids, have fun. When we were younger, we didn't take basketball seriously like that."

All the children ran track and played several sports until they got to high school, when Mitchell put his arm around each of his boys and told them that if they were serious about basketball — the sport that he played and that they all gravitated towards — now was the time to specialize. "Just following my dad's footsteps. Being on his hip everywhere he went," Andrew's older brother Nick says. "Sports was the avenue that made my family successful, so we just followed my parents."

"They all had a dream to follow what I did," Mitchell said.

Luckily, the Wiggins household was also walking distance to the Dufferin Clark Community Centre, where the Wiggins boys would hoop all day on weekends and all night during the week, honing their skills alongside a group of neighbourhood boys who all fell in love with the sport. Mitchell became a regular fixture in the community centre, running kids through basketball camps and shooting games to teach them fundamentals, while pulling kids aside during games to give them pointers.

"Mitchell Wiggins played in the NBA, but you go to that community centre, he would greet you as if you've known him for years," Vaughan native Troy Reid-Knight says. "I think that gave a lot of people confidence because you're thinking, 'Oh, he played in the NBA. What he's telling me must work.'"

As the boys got older, Vaughan became a basketball hotbed due to the presence of Vaughan Road Secondary, the Bathurst Jewish Community Centre, and Dufferin Clarke — home to some of the best runs in the city. All the top players from the surrounding area would hoop there after school, developing a familial atmosphere. "We had some real heated basketball games there," says Cy Samuels, who will never forget the day Wiggins cracked the glass backboard with a ferocious dunk while the rest of the players stood by in shock. "It was just a real close-knit community. And a lot of us really loved each other and really were close to each other, so it was easy for us to kind of gel there."

Mitchell Jr. was an athletic marvel and Nick was a knockdown shooter. And after going to prep schools in America, they would return to Dufferin Clarke in the summers to school the youngsters. "It definitely became home," Nick says. "It became a comfortable space for us to go . . . it became our sanctuary. It became our safe home."

Andrew Wiggins embodied the best of each of his brothers, eventually growing to 6'8" with a 6'11" wingspan and a 44-inch vertical — a dynamic player who could shoot the laces off the ball, sprint down the court in a flash, and jump as high and as quickly as anyone. He grew up playing elementary school basketball at Glen Shields and rep basketball with the OBA's St. David's team. He also had a brief spurt with Grassroots AAU, playing up an age group after getting used to going against his older brothers, who showed him tough love on the court.

After Wiggins spent the first few months of his freshman season at an American prep school run by Ro Russell, Mitchell and Marita saw that the school wasn't taking academics seriously and pulled him out, transferring him to Vaughan Secondary — where Marita had gone and all of Andrew's siblings went to school.

■

Gus Gymnopoulos grew up in Toronto's east end and played basketball at Victoria Park Secondary before moving on to Concordia University in Montreal. He got his teaching degree and started coaching the basketball team at Vaughan, which had never been very good but started to have some success behind Nick and Mitchell Jr.

Gymnopoulos had no idea how big of an impact the younger Wiggins would have on the program until Andrew's first day of school in grade 10, when he was finally eligible to play after sitting out the second half of his freshman season due to OFSAA eligibility rules for transfers. "I was sitting in the phys ed office and I got a call and it was Purdue University," Gymnopoulos says. "Two days later, Syracuse University calls." Both schools told him they were coming down to watch Vaughan practice. "It was nuts."

Wiggins immediately joined a group of experienced players on the senior team, and despite being 15 years old, he took them over the top, leading the Voyageurs to a 45-1 record, with the one loss coming in a game he left early due to cramps. "I remember one time in practice . . . Andrew basically took off from the foul line and dunked on our teammate," Reid-Knight says. "Everyone started screaming.

"But the dunk was so bad, it was one of those things where you didn't want to laugh because it could be any one of us on any given day."

Wiggins was clearly the best player on the floor in every matchup, able to do a little bit of everything from the wing position, scoring 50 points one game and only passing the next, as long as Vaughan got the win. The only guy who gave the team problems was Kevin Pangos, the Newmarket, Ontario, native who was a threat to pull up from anywhere inside half court, going toe-to-toe with Wiggins and regularly dropping 50 balls against Vaughan during his time at regional rival Denison Secondary.

But Wiggins's biggest moment came at the historic Sun Youth tournament in Montreal, where the entire city had seemingly shown up to watch Vaughan play the Dawson College CEGEP team coached by Wayne Yearwood. Vaughan was ahead by four when Gymnopoulos called a timeout and ran a play to have Wiggins set a screen for Reid-Knight and then roll to the rim. "Andrew flew to the basket," Gymnopoulos says, as Reid-Knight threw him a lob that was a few feet wide of the basket. Still, Wiggins caught it and managed to throw it down while getting fouled. The Montreal crowd went wild. "It was the craziest thing I've ever seen probably to this day," Gymnopoulos says.

His game was full of contradictions because despite regularly leaving the crowd in awe, Wiggins was never a showboater. In fact, he refused to embarrass his opponents. Yet he drew unprecedented crowds to that small Vaughan gym and everywhere the team traveled that season, drawing the attention of new Canadian blogs and social media brands that began covering Canadian hoops in the early 2000s like HooptownGTA, HoopStars Canada, On Point, and North Pole Hoops. "People are just drawn to him," Gymnopoulos said. "There's just something magnetic about him."

"Honestly, I didn't know how to feel back then, because it was so new," Wiggins says. "And some people would start to notice me and show me some love and appreciation. And being a 13-year-old kid, you're kind of just trying to soak it all in."

It all cumulated at the OFSAA championship in 2011, when the Voyageurs overcame a tough Oakville Loyola team in the finals on the back of a 25 point and 13 rebound performance from Wiggins, who took over when the crowd began to chant "Over-*rated*. Over-*rated*." "That did it," Reid-Knight said. "[Wiggins] always responds well to negativity."

It was the school's first ever provincial championship, culminating what was one of the greatest individual seasons in Canadian high school hoops history, up there with guys like Phil Dixon, Denham Brown, and Bobby Allen. Years later, after Wiggins and his two brothers had their jerseys retired together at Vaughan, he said his season with the Voyageurs was still the favourite of his career. "Nothing compares to playing at home," Wiggins said. "Playing in front of my family and friends."

Vaughan went on to win OFSAA again the next year following Wiggins's departure, with the school going on to produce future pros like Kassius Robertson, Nickeil Alexander-Walker, and Andrew Nembhard. "It was an experience that I would never expect to happen at Vaughan," Reid-Knight says. "Andrew brought all of that. Within one year, he changed the whole dynamic and the culture of what was going on there."

"[Andrew] made our school such a desirable place and one of the powerhouses" in the city, Gymnopoulos says.

But Wiggins was still a Canadian secret during his time at Vaughan. And it wasn't until he played for the famous CIA Bounce AAU program that he became an internationally recognized name and the top prospect in the class of 2014.

•

The AAU basketball scene had grown by leaps and bounds by the time Wiggins was at Vaughan in 2011, with programs like Grassroots, Northern Kings, Canada Elite, Triple Threat, and many more popping up in order to meet the newfound demand from young Canadians who were taking basketball seriously.

None was bigger than CIA Bounce, which had surpassed Grassroots as the top program in Canada by the early 2010s after Tony McIntyre merged his Brampton-based Bounce program with Mike George's Malton-based CIA program to create CIA Bounce in 2006.

McIntyre grew up in Mississauga playing hockey and lacrosse before suffering a career-ending hockey injury. He moved to Brampton at 19, a densely populated suburb northwest of Toronto that was becoming a basketball hotbed due to the influx of Caribbean immigrants moving there in the '80s and '90s. He fell in love with basketball, and after marrying Suzette Ennis, he started coaching his kids Brandon, Dylan, and Tyler Ennis with the Brampton Blue Devils storied OBA program.

McIntyre had a group of middle-school-aged neighbourhood kids that were starting to show real potential, including Tristan Thompson, and wondered how to get them exposure so they could get D1 scholarships. Eventually, he went to the executives at Brampton Blue Devils hoping to convince them to let him start a traveling AAU team. But they refused.

McIntyre started his own program, Brampton Bounce, and began taking teams to small tournaments within a five-hour radius of Toronto. They had immediate success, winning tournaments in America and seeing more players from all over the GTA show up to their tryouts. "The big thing of coaching when I started was I just wanted to see if I could get one kid a scholarship," McIntyre says. "I had a group of kids that knew how to play and they were dedicated and they were in the gym and a great group of parents and it was like, 'I got to do something.'"

Bounce was one of the first clubs to provide kids with year-round training, so that the kids wouldn't have to restart when they returned to basketball in the winter after playing other sports all summer. They also incorporated a dryland component to the training, taking kids outside to run hills and do sand workouts to develop a different set of muscle groups.

Meanwhile, in nearby Malton, Mike George started a team out of his local church, Humberlea Church of God. George grew up in the area before pursuing his education degree at York University, where he played basketball. He returned home and became a high school teacher and community builder, creating the basketball program Christians in Action which later became Characteristics Inspiring Achievement (CIA).

George recruited local kids like Melvin Ejim, Taévaunn Prince, Kofi Mensa, and Maurice Walker and started winning on the AAU circuit, regularly matching up against Brampton Bounce in the finals of tournaments. The two programs eventually developed a Peel-based rivalry, with kids having to decide to play for one program or the other. "We decided we had the same goals for these kids, to put our differences aside, come together and build a program that would be able to house more players," McIntyre said. "We're able to put a bit more power behind it, combining our resources and knowledge."

They merged around 2006, creating CIA Bounce, winning every game in Canada for a two-year span and regularly dominating American AAU tournaments as well. "We've had a lot of talented guys in Canada for a long time," George said. "But we never had them under one roof before."

Still, as CIA Bounce worked its way up the AAU hierarchy, they weren't flush with cash. Kids would share jerseys, with the grade 7 team running off the court and handing their sweaty jerseys to the grade 8s, who would flip them inside out. Plus, McIntyre and George were putting meals, hotels, and gym time on their personal credit cards to help the kids.

But things really took off when one of George's students at Cardinal Newman Catholic High School suggested he go on the game show *Deal or No Deal* to raise money for his basketball team. "She was just like, 'Mr. George, you should do it. You'd be really good,'" he says. George went home and decided to apply, assuming one of his friends was pranking him when he received a call a few weeks later telling him he had been selected.

George appeared on the show in January of 2007 and won $144,000, donating half of it to the program. It gave CIA Bounce the resources to travel and compete in bigger tournaments throughout the United States. The money also allowed them to buy more uniforms, form more teams, and buy more gym time where they could focus on smaller groups. "It just came right at the exact time that we needed it," McIntyre says.

The program was ahead of its time, taking advantage of video and social media to create highlight tapes for players and their own YouTube channel, Bounce TV. "They just made it really cool," says Canada Elite co-founder Shane James. "And I think everyone wanted to play Bounce at that time."

Bounce recruited all the best talent, eventually creating one of the best teams in AAU history in 2012, with Andrew Wiggins joining the program alongside top-ranked players like Tyler Ennis, Xavier Rathan-Mayes, Duane Notice, and Tanveer Bhullar. They attracted the attention of Nike, which sponsored the team and invited them to play on the prestigious EYBL Circuit, where they went undefeated until the finals of Peach Jam, when the Oakland Soldiers beat them 51–50 to win the title. Wiggins averaged 22 points and 9 rebounds in the tournament, playing so well that he became the number one player in the entire 2014 graduating class.

"We did some really, really special things," Rathan-Mayes says. "That was a time that we all look back on, and something that we're really proud of, something that we were able to do and accomplish, and for not only ourselves, but for our country.

"That CIA Bounce program really changed how people viewed us as a country."

•

After just one full season at Vaughan, Wiggins needed better competition than Canada could provide and moved on to Huntington Prep in Huntington, West Virginia — a relatively new prep school set in a small, blue-collar, sports-oriented college town near Kansas.

The head coach, Rob Fulford, had been recruiting Wiggins since he was 13, at one point watching 24 consecutive CIA Bounce games in person. "We developed a relationship with him," Fulford said. "We recruited him harder than anyone else."

What stood out to Fulford was the same quality that would later get the young Wiggins in trouble, which was that everything he did looked so effortless. "He could just dominate a game from a talent perspective," Fulford says. "It just was a clear difference between Andrew and everyone else."

But there was nothing quiet about the show Wiggins was putting on the basketball court, as Huntington quickly became the most popular high school team in the country, going from having 50 fans at a regular home game prior to his arrival to packed gyms with over 1,000 fans there to see the Canadian high school phenom with their own eyes. "A lot of people just wanted to see him play," Rathan-Mayes says. "We tried to go and put on a show the best that we could every single night."

But being at the centre of the basketball universe didn't come naturally to the quiet kid from Vaughan. After all, shyness, like athleticism, runs in the Wiggins family: Mitchell Sr. said the reason it didn't work at his first college, Clemson, was that "I was so quiet, you couldn't get a whisper out of me." While a track teammate of Marita's said, "She was very quiet, still is very quiet and very unassuming."

Unlike LeBron James, who was happy to engage with the media and put on a show for the crowd since being crowned "The Chosen One" as a teenager, Wiggins was soft-spoken and shy, preferring to pass the attention on to his teammates instead of beating his chest after a big dunk. Many people wanted Wiggins to be the version of an alpha athlete that they were used to seeing on TV, like James and Kobe Bryant. And that dissonance created a tension with the basketball media and certain segments of the fan base, who wanted more from Wiggins.

"I think we all have a certain kind of perception of what we want a great athlete to look like," his junior national team coach, Roy Rana, says. "We want them to be fiery. We want them to be emotional. We want them to be extroverted. We want them to be demonstrative.

"That's not Andrew."

The criticism picked up during Wiggins's second and final season at Huntington Prep when, in February of 2013, a *Sports Illustrated* article questioned his work ethic, suggesting that he only showed up in big games while lofting through less important ones. "Andrew Wiggins' work ethic and motor have yet to catch up to his athleticism and raw ability," it read, bringing up examples of previous Canadian prospects whose careers stagnated as a result of poor decision-making or a lack of skill development. And it questioned the role models in his life, including Russell and his father, Mitchell Sr., who was pushed out of the NBA for cocaine use decades earlier.

The day after the article came out, Wiggins dropped a career-high 57 points in a statement win. "I think it pissed him off," Fulford says. "He wanted to prove a point."

"Just responding in a positive way," Wiggins says. "Not saying anything, not . . . going on Twitter and saying anything . . . whenever you think you got something to say, just go on the court and do my thing."

Wiggins compiled one of the most memorable seasons in high school basketball history that season, averaging 23 points, 11 rebounds, 3 assists, and 3 blocks per game and winning the Naismith Prep Player of the Year and the Gatorade National Player of the Year awards, earning a trip to the McDonald's All-American Game. After that, he left to go to the University of Kansas.

But the spotlight didn't stop there. In fact, when Wiggins arrived at Kansas City International Airport in June of 2013, he emerged from the gate to find 15 fans waiting for his autograph after his itinerary had been posted on an online message board. When classes started, students began Twitter-stalking him, tweeting pictures of the back of his head in class and posting his whereabouts when he was spotted at local stores. Meanwhile, back home in Canada, Wiggins picked up the nicknames "Maple Jordan" and "Air Canada," and all of his Kansas games were broadcasted on the national TV network TSN.

While all this might seem normal now, 2013 was the beginning of the social media era. And between the fans stalking him, the student sections taunting him at away games, and the rapidly expanding media landscape criticizing his every move, it was hard for Wiggins to feel comfortable. "We talk about it sometimes, but he doesn't like talking about it. That's how bad it stresses him out," his wife, Mychal Johnson, said at the time. "Sometimes he doesn't know what to do."

"It was a lot," Wiggins says now. "It was a lot."

Wiggins just wanted to be a normal kid. He happened to love basketball and be really good at it, but he wanted an average life away from the spotlight, playing *Call of Duty* after games and announcing his college decision without any media present. In fact, his Twitter bio used to read "Just a average kid trying to make it."

But when he was asked about it during his freshman year at Kansas, Wiggins said, "I used to be an average kid, when I put that up. But that . . . was a while ago."

■

Some of the criticism directed towards Wiggins was warranted. Even Fulford acknowledged that he was no gym rat — that things came so naturally to Wiggins that he needed to fall in love with the process of improving if he was going to reach his ceiling. "I don't think at any point ever that anyone had to go tell Michael Jordan or Kobe Bryant to pick it up," Fulford said.

Wiggins quietly improved under head coach Bill Self at Kansas, averaging 17 points, 6 rebounds, 2 assists, 1 steal, and 1 block as a freshman for the number-two-ranked Jayhawks, who went 24-9 before losing in the second round of the NCAA tournament. He even set the Kansas freshman single-season scoring record with 597 points.

Still, there were times that Self had to get on Wiggins to play harder or be more aggressive offensively, instituting a special rule at some practices that only Wiggins was allowed to shoot. "Andrew is the type of guy who could score 28, and you'd say, 'Why didn't he score more?'" Self said. "Critics want him to do more. I understand that because the game comes so easy to him, it's so natural."

Some of that on-court reticence came from the way Wiggins was raised, learning the game from his brothers and dad, who carved out a 20-year pro career as a defensive role player. "His dad taught him how to play basketball the right way," Reid-Knight says, noting that Mitchell Sr. always harped on the importance of being selfless and making the right reads. "Playing within your game and not forcing an action."

After one season at Kansas, Wiggins declared for the 2014 NBA Draft and was selected first overall by the Cleveland Cavaliers — a foregone conclusion since Wiggins was in the tenth grade. What made the selection even more amazing was that his CIA Bounce teammate, Brampton native Anthony Bennett, went first overall to Cleveland the year prior, giving Canada back-to-back first overall picks for the first time ever.

The 2014 NBA Draft also featured Canadians Tyler Ennis, Nik Stauskas, and Dwight Powell getting selected, giving Canada a record 12 NBA players. That year Canada overtook France as the second-most represented country in the league behind the United States — a record Canada has held ever since.

However, the best player in the world, LeBron James, returned to his hometown Cleveland in free agency that same summer. And before playing a single game in the NBA, Wiggins and Bennett were both traded to the rebuilding Minnesota Timberwolves in exchange for Kevin Love, making Wiggins the cornerstone of a franchise that had not been to the playoffs in 10 years. "I just gave in to it and figured I'd be good wherever I go," Wiggins said. "The whole thing has worked out. [Minnesota has] put me in a situation where I can grow a lot more than on the team that drafted me."

Wiggins got off to a slow start in his NBA career before breaking out against the team that snubbed him, dropping 27 points in his first game against James's Cavaliers. He followed it up with a stretch of six straight 20-point games, eventually becoming the first Canadian to win the NBA Rookie of the Year award after averaging 17 points, 5 rebounds, and 2 assists a game in 2014–15.

While he never turned into the NBA superstar that many people had him pegged to become when he was a teenager, Wiggins went on to have an incredible career, spending five and a half seasons in Minnesota before getting traded to the Golden State Warriors in 2020. In the Bay, Wiggins became the third Canadian NBA All-Star and won an NBA championship as the team's second-leading scorer in the 2022 NBA Finals, when he averaged 18 points and 9 rebounds.

But, for better or worse, the huge spotlight and unbalanced criticism that started to shine on Wiggins when he was a teenage phenom never left him, especially in Canada — a basketball-crazed nation that was growing hungry for a superstar.

As Wiggins once said, "I know I can never live up to expectations."

CHAPTER 11

HEARTBREAK IN MEXICO CITY

ASSOCIATED PRESS

Nik Stauskas, Andrew Nicholson, Brady Heslip, Anthony Bennett, and Dwight Powell walk off the court in disbelief during their matchup against Venezuela at the 2015 FIBA Americas Championship.

"It was just the basketball Gods went against us. And it cost us a chance to go to the Olympics."

— JAY TRIANO

When Nash, Barrett, and Triano took over the Canadian men's program in 2012, the entire goal was to qualify for the 2016 Olympics. It was seen as a near-guarantee after producing 12 NBA players by 2014, including the first overall draft picks in 2013 and 2014.

"I said to Steve, 'Man, this is not an easy job,'" Triano said. "It used to be we had hard time convincing NBA players to play for our country. [Now] we're going to have to cut an NBA player off of our Canadian national team."

Triano used the 2013 FIBA Americas Championship in Venezuela to get some of his younger NBA players acclimated to the FIBA style of play, as it was the first tournament with the senior team for guys like Tristan Thompson, Brady Heslip, and Andrew Nicholson and just the second for Cory Joseph.

Canada was expected to be among the top four teams in the tournament, which would have been enough to qualify for the 2014 World Cup in Spain. And things looked good after they got a string of early wins against Jamaica, Brazil, Uruguay, and Mexico to start the tournament. But Canada struggled with foul trouble, outside shooting, and late game execution, losing its final three games by a combined total of just 18 points — finishing sixth in the tournament and outside of World Cup qualification. "We knew it was gonna be a growing period and we were gonna have to learn how to play together," Triano says. "We just didn't gel.

"We had NBA players, but we didn't have a star."

After all, most of Canada's athletes were four-year college players who ended up being role players on their pro clubs, especially early in their careers. Asking them to be the go-to scorers for the national team was unrealistic. Wiggins, of course, eclipsed those boundaries.

"I think what his presence did, it was: here's a guy that could be the superstar," Parrish says. "And I think it perked people's consciousness to believe that there was someone who could be this good and be part of the upper echelon."

Canada Basketball had invested in his development since they discovered him in 2009, enrolling Wiggins in the inaugural Centre for Performance (CP) and Targeted Athlete Strategy (TAS) development programs and getting him to play for the Under-17 team at the 2010 World Championship in Hamburg, Germany. Wiggins helped Canada win its first and only medal at the tournament, and two years later, he joined the Under-18 team and won a second consecutive bronze.

"He was always a little bit uncomfortable in environments that he wasn't used to," coach Rana says. "To be able to get him to that World Cup in Hamburg was a big win for us, and it was a great moment because I thought we developed a little bit of trust."

Wiggins took a three-year gap from the national team as he went through his final year of prep school and college, focusing on becoming the number-one pick in the NBA Draft and the $25-million contract that came with it. But after winning the NBA Rookie of the Year in 2014, Canada Basketball was desperate to have him participate in the 2015 FIBA Americas Championship, as they believed it was their best chance to qualify for an Olympics since 2000. And when it was announced that Wiggins would make his senior team debut at the competition, everybody was expecting them to finally break through.

"We're at the most important stage there is; we've got to qualify and it's not going to be easy," Wiggins said. "There is a little pressure, but it's always positive pressure. It makes us hungry, makes us work harder.

"We don't want to disappoint anybody."

■

The improved professional standards and presence of Nash had helped change the perception around the national team, with more top players wanting to be a part of it — partly because it was becoming realistic that they might finally make history and qualify for the 2016 Games.

And the hype kept building at the Pan Am Games in Toronto in the spring of 2015. Canada put on a show behind a jaw-dropping performance by a teenaged Jamal Murray, who came off the bench to score 22 points in the fourth quarter and overtime as he helped Canada come from behind to defeat Team USA in the semifinals, eventually winning a silver medal. The women, meanwhile, won gold at the Pan Am Games before qualifying for the 2016 Olympics later that summer, putting the pressure on the men to do the same.

Triano had some tough decisions to make ahead of the 2015 FIBA Americas tournament in Mexico City. There was a core group of overseas pros such as Jermaine Anderson, Carl English, Jevohn Shepherd, and Andy Rautins that helped steady the program during its most challenging years. They were growing frustrated with the unequal treatment between themselves and the new NBA players who were getting single rooms and first class flights, which created a divide because the federation couldn't financially service everybody the same way.

"Guys just didn't understand the grind that we went through," Andy says. "And the amount of years that we put into Canada Basketball before they even got there or decided that they would bless us with their presence.

"I think the NBA guys kind of came in and expected preferential treatment and to get most of, if not the majority of the credit for any success that we would or could have had. And that rubbed a lot of guys the wrong way."

But, like it or not, a new generation was coming to take their spots, and Triano overturned the roster to a new group with nine NBA players and an average age of just 23.8. Wiggins, Bennett, Melvin Ejim, Dwight Powell, Philip Scrubb, and Nik Stauskas all made their senior team debuts at the tournament, making half of Canada's 12-man roster FIBA rookies. "I think there were too many NBA guys knocking on the door," Triano says. "We're gonna have to make this shift now to make sure that our best players are playing."

The obvious downside was that they lacked experience and continuity compared to their South American counterparts, who had been consistently playing together instead of taking summers off to prepare for the

NCAA or NBA. But the upside was that it was clearly the most talented group of Canadians ever assembled, with more speed and athleticism than most teams in the world. "God spent a little more time on some of these guys," advanced scout Joe Raso said.

"I think we had the best team in the tournament," Phil Scrubb says. "And one of the better teams we've ever had."

With a few weeks of practice before the competition, the game plan was to install a system that took advantage of the team's youth, creating pressure with a swarming defense that would help them get out on the break, where they could use their speed to beat teams down the court. And things looked to be on the upswing when Canada finished with a 4-0 record at the Tutu Marchand Cup exhibition tournament in Puerto Rico, including a win over Argentina, where Wiggins dropped 18 points in his senior team debut.

Canada entered the FIBA Americas as heavy favourites to not only finish in the top-two and qualify for the Olympics, but to win the entire thing for the first time ever since the United States was not participating after having already qualified for the Olympics through the World Cup. Still, in its first game, Canada lost a rematch against Argentina by a score of 94–87, as Raptors forward Luis Scola dropped 35 points and 13 rebounds in the win. "I believe experience is a big part of this tournament because there are a lot of different things the younger players aren't used to," Scola said. "There's a mix of styles and rules so there's a lot of confusion at times."

"People forget were a fairly young team," Triano said. "We're fairly new at this, so this is a good growing experience."

But instead of succumbing to the pressure, Canada responded with arguably the greatest stretch in program history, reeling off seven straight wins by an average margin of victory of 26 points. Everything was clicking, as Wiggins led the team in scoring with 15 points per game; Joseph set everybody up with 6 assists per game; Olynyk took on secondary-creation duties with 12 points and 5 rebounds a game; and Heslip and Stauskas knocked down over 45 percent of their threes. "Analytically we were just dominant,"Triano says. "Best offense that FIBA had anywhere."

Canada finished first in the group with a 7-1 record, setting them up with a semifinal clash against a relatively weak Venezuelan team, who was

4-4 at that point after losing to Canada by 20 in the group stage. However, before the game, Nash issued a warning. "I think the only thing that we're playing against is experience," he said. "You go out and play one game for the Olympics and anything can happen."

•

Venezuela was coached by Nestor Garcia, an Argentinian who knew Canada well from his days coaching various South American club and national teams since 1990. But Venezuela was the clear underdog because of the absence of three starters, slowing the game to a crawl and using a physical defense to force 17 turnovers.

"We didn't respond well to their pressure," Scrubb said. "They were a good defensive team and their coach had them ready to play, and we came into the game expecting to win and didn't expect it to be as tough of a game as it got."

Joseph and Wiggins combined to score just 14 points on 5-of-19 shooting. Olynyk, however, kept his team in it, proving to be too big, fast, and skilled for the Venezuelans to keep up with. He finished with a game-high 34 points on 11-of-13 shooting, including 3-of-4 from three. "I felt really good that game," Olynyk said. "I was in the zone."

However, after Venezuela installed a zone defense to force Canada to beat them from the outside, the Canadians tightened up. Canada shot just 5-of-17 from three, getting outscored 30 to 15 from the three-point line. "It was good coaching because they put all their marbles in one basket and they had us playing not to lose," Raso says. "When you can do that for a long part of the game, then it's a successful tactical approach."

It didn't help that Canada was missing one of its best shooters, Stauskas, who ate a piece of raw salmon at the team hotel two nights earlier and sustained a bad case of food poisoning, forcing him to go to the hospital and sit out the game.

Venezuela kept things close in the fourth quarter, going back and forth with Canada for a combined 29 lead changes and 15 ties. As the game wound down, the Mexican crowd started to cheer for the South American underdogs to beat the stacked Canadian team. "Everybody's rooting for the underdog," Doornekamp says. "Nobody thought it was gonna happen. And then when it was close, everyone was praying for it to happen."

But the Canadians looked to be in charge after an Olynyk jump shot put them up 75–68 with three minutes remaining. However, that's when Venezuelan point guard Heissler Guillent swished in a deep three pointer at the end of the shot clock to get his team within four. Then, after another Guillent three, Olynyk dribbled the ball up the court and slipped on the advertisement decal taped to the floor at centre court, doing the splits and throwing the ball away to Guillent, who picked it up as Olynyk grabbed his leg in what was deemed an unsportsmanlike foul for not making a play on the ball. Guillent went to the free throw line for two shots and the ball.

Canada called a timeout to draw up a play for Wiggins, as his moment had come with the game nearing its end. Wiggins drove to the basket and dropped a nice pass into the hands of a cutting Olynyk for an easy layup that restored Canada's lead to 77–76 with 50 seconds remaining. But after Wiggins was controversially subbed out for Doornekamp for one defensive possession that dominated the headlines the next day, Guillent responded with a layup of his own to move Venezuela back up by one.

Canada took its last timeout with 35.5 seconds on the clock and ran a play that ended up with Andrew Nicholson getting a foul and going to the free-throw line for a chance to take back the lead with 24 seconds remaining. But as Nicholson stepped up to the line, the pro-Venezuela crowd started to cheer like crazy, and he missed the first free throw before sinking the second to tie the game.

Venezuela took its final timeout and got the ball to Guillent, who waited out the clock, dribbling around half court with Joseph draped all over him, even poking the ball away at one point. Guillent regathered it near half court and heaved a long three towards the rim with seconds left in the game. It missed as the buzzer sounded, sending the game to overtime. Or so everybody thought.

Beneath the sound of the rising Mexican crowd and the buzzer, there was a whistle.

The referees gathered together at half court and determined that the baseline referee called a loose-ball foul on Canada's Doornekamp with

0.3 seconds remaining, who was alleged to have held down Venezuelan wing Jose Vargas going for the rebound in the mix of bodies all battling for positioning under the basket.

"Honestly, I thought it was a foul on the guy that jumped into me," Doornekamp says. "I thought, 'Wow, I can't believe they called that foul for me.'" But upon learning that the call went against him, "It was devastating."

Vargas stepped to the line and made the first free throw, giving Venezuela the 79–78 lead. Then he intentionally missed the second, throwing it off the front of the rim so that by the time Joseph picked the ball up off the ground for a last second heave, the full-time buzzer had already sounded.

Coach Garcia led the Venezuelans on to the court in celebration, running in circles as they could hardly believe their good fortune. "This is an historic day for Venezuela," Garcia said. Venezuela qualified for its first Olympics since 1992, when they also shocked a more talented Canadian team to advance.

Meanwhile, the Canadians slowly walked back to the locker room with their heads held in disbelief. "It was just the basketball Gods went against us," Triano says. "And it cost us a chance to go to the Olympics."

It felt like everything that could go wrong did go wrong in order to pull off the worst upset in Canadian basketball history. If it hadn't been for Joseph and Wiggins struggling to score or Stauskas getting food poisoning or Olynyk slipping on the decal or Guillent banking in a deep three late or one of the worst calls in FIBA officiating history, Canada would have followed what appeared to be a clear path to the Olympics — they would have changed the narrative around the program and set themselves up for future success by boosting their world ranking and getting crucial Olympic experience.

Instead, Canada had to come to terms with the fact that a team with seven NBA players coming off a historically dominant seven-game winning streak just lost to an undermanned Venezuela. Powell called it "crushing." Olynyk said, "It really haunts you every single day."

Meanwhile, Doornekamp still hasn't gotten over the foul call that changed the game all these years later, saying, "I remember that night just sitting in my room and . . . you just keep reliving it." He rejoined the national team for a brief spell in 2021 but had a hard time playing for them because he would be reminded of the foul each time. "That doesn't leave you," he says. "You can't help but feel blame."

The always stoic Wiggins, meanwhile, was disconsolate after the game, crying in the locker room and on the way to the bus after scoring just nine points on 4-of-11 shooting. "I remember standing there with my wife and Leo Rautins and saying, 'Oh my God, you know, there's something very, very positive in this,'" Parrish says.

"You realize how much it meant to him," Raso says. "And if anybody questioned his commitment or how important it was, his body language after the game showed it."

Canada responded the next day by taking down Mexico in the bronze medal game. Wiggins scored 18 points while Joseph finished with 8 points, 6 rebounds, 8 assists, and a buzzer-beating fadeaway jumper that fell through the net at the buzzer, clinching a meaningless 87–86 win.

When the game was over, Joseph went over to Canada Basketball CEO Michele O'Keefe and hugged her. "I'm really sorry," she recalls him saying. "I was a day late."

■

A year later, Canada found itself in a group with France, Turkey, Senegal, and New Zealand in the 2016 last chance Olympic Qualifying Tournament (OQT) in Manila, Philippines, where only the winner would advance to the Olympics.

With the pain of the previous summer lingering and a number of personal obligations and contract stalemates getting in the way, Canada had trouble recruiting its best talent. Wiggins decided to focus on the upcoming Timberwolves season, Stauskas on the Kings, Powell on the Mavericks, and Nicholson on Orlando. Olynyk, meanwhile, suffered a shoulder injury that would require surgery that same year.

Canada brought in a bunch of new faces and had little chemistry or continuity from the previous years. Plus, several players showed up late to camp or skipped parts of the exhibition tournament in Italy, only meeting in Manila before the tournament.

After beginning the OQT with tight wins against Turkey, Senegal, and New Zealand, Canada matched up with France in the final for a chance to go to the Olympics. France was considered favourites after winning bronze at EuroBasket the previous summer, with a core of Tony Parker, Nicolas Batum, Nando De Colo, and Boris Diaw, who had been playing together for years.

Meanwhile, Canada had a strong frontcourt with Thompson, Khem Birch, and Anthony Bennett, but Joseph was asked to carry too much of the scoring load without Olynyk or Wiggins in the fold. He averaged a team-high 19 points per game, while Melvin Ejim was the second leading scorer, averaging 13 points after barely playing a year before. "Cory at that time was probably our best scorer," assistant coach Nathaniel Mitchell says. "And even he would say it was tough to expect him to go out there and get 20, 25 every game. That's not what he does."

Joseph poured in 20 points on 9-of-16 shooting while Ejim added 19 of his own against France. But nobody else on the Canadian team had more than nine. Meanwhile, Canada turned the ball over 21 times, leading to 21 points for France, who executed on the fast break with a veteran poise.

Canada kept it to a one possession game until four minutes remaining when French point guard Tony Parker hit a couple of back-breaking threes with Joseph draped over him, scoring nine straight points to finish with 26 points and 4 assists. "He got pretty hot in the fourth quarter," Joseph says. "That just kind of helped them get over the hump."

France won 83–74 and sent Canada home. But despite being undermanned that summer, it wasn't an issue of talent. Instead, what stood out between the two crucial losses to Venezuela and France that held Canada out of its fourth-straight Olympics was the different levels of commitment those two programs had over Canada. After all, a 34-year-old Parker played for France despite having a kid weeks before the tournament, representing his nation in all but three summers between 1997 and 2015. Canada, meanwhile, couldn't even get its best players to give them two consecutive summers.

The media and fans were quick to turn on the organization and some of its best players, questioning why there wasn't more commitment or national pride from Canada's top NBA players. What the public struggled to understand is how physically and mentally taxing it is for NBA players to finish a grueling season and immediately commit several weeks to the national team.

Wiggins, of course, became the lightning rod of discontent, taking the majority of the heat for choosing to spend that summer focusing on the Timberwolves instead of playing for Canada. The *Toronto Sun* even reported that the program had to pay him to play in 2015, when in reality they offered his father, Mitchell, a player development job instead. "There's never been an issue with Canada Basketball or FIBA or anything like that where I didn't want to go back," Wiggins says. "It's always been a personal choice because I needed to lock in in the summer and just work on me."

Still, Wiggins admits that "there was a lot" of criticism from fans and the media. "At some point, I just knew whenever I wasn't playing, I knew I was gonna get some people saying certain stuff and stuff online," he says.

But it was a systemic issue that held Canada back. After all, several members of Canada's frontcourt showed up late to training camp, while Joseph and Thompson missed some of the exhibition games in Italy. The national team was desperate to add NBA talent at any cost, making certain exceptions for them to be comfortable while creating a double-standard that set a dangerous precedent which would end up hurting the program in the long run.

The basketball world was changing by the mid-2010s, with more and more money to be made in the NBA, more opportunities to develop in the summers and, as a result, international basketball becoming a less appealing option for Canadian players who grew up dreaming of the NBA, not the Olympics. Meanwhile, pro teams and agents started to exert more control over their players, not wanting their multi-million-dollar investments to risk injury playing internationally in the summers.

"You have to really, really want to be an Olympian," Triano says. "It's not an easy thing for these guys to do when the money is what it is in the NBA right now and they're trying to maximize their growth.

"I dreamed of playing on the national team and representing it — never got paid for it. And it was just something that I did and I loved. These guys now, that's not the case."

While top programs in Europe and South America built basketball cultures that made it impossible for NBA guys to say no to their country, Canada didn't have a culture of winning or history of commitment to fall back on. And as much as the program was trying to reinvent itself as an attractive environment for high-level pros, it came to a point when the NBA and international basketball were moving in two different directions.

"It doesn't seem to mean as much anymore in this generation — because you have so many options — to represent your country," Nash said as Canada's commitment issues lingered into the 21st century, when the money and business of basketball had begun to supersede the pure love for the game that players had during his heyday with the national team. "I don't know how we can shift the mentality so that these guys recognize the opportunity," he added about the exciting group of young Canadians coming up the pipeline.

"I mean, it's the golden generation."

PART 2

THE GOLDEN GENERATION

CHAPTER 12

BATTY AND BENCH

NICOLE ALEXANDER

Shai Gilgeous-Alexander is joined by his brother, Thomasi, and his cousin, Nickeil Alexander-Walker, playing for the JCC Warriors OBA basketball club.

"Shai was very, very, very competitive. And I think he kind of taught me earlier that when it comes to competition, there is no friends, there is no family."

— NICKEIL ALEXANDER-WALKER

While the lack of commitment from Canada's best players was the leading story in the summer of 2016, something else happened that would change the trajectory of Canadian basketball — and Team Canada — forever.

Shai Gilgeous-Alexander was born in Toronto, Ontario, in 1998 to Charmaine Gilgeous and Vaughn Alexander, who met when they were in high school.

Vaughn grew up in the Spare Ways neighbourhood around Finch and Leslie, where he witnessed poverty and gang violence and learned early that sports could be an escape. After discovering basketball at 13, his friends formed a community housing team with kids from Spare Ways, going to different neighbourhoods around the GTA to play against other community housing teams such as Jamaal Magloire at Flemingdon Park Community Centre.

Eventually, all his friends transferred to the nearby Georges Vanier Secondary, where Vaughn led them to a city title in the early 1990s. But they didn't take basketball seriously and got in fights with opposing teams, creating a hostile environment where student fans were banned from attending home games.

Even though Vaughn and some of his friends were talented enough to get Division I scholarships, they never saw kids coming out of Toronto making it to the NBA, so it wasn't a realistic dream for them. "Phil Dixon is probably the best player I've ever seen come out of Canada, hands down, and he didn't make it [to the NBA]," Vaughn says, referring to the Bathurst Heights legend who many believe was the greatest Canadian high school player of all time, going to the University of Utah in 1989 before playing overseas. "So, we were like, 'Yo, stop this, man. This is just not something that you do out of Canada.'"

Charmaine, meanwhile, went to Earl Haig Secondary School in North York, where she was a star sprinter who became a five-time All-American at the University of Alabama. She later represented her parents' native country of Antigua and Barbuda at the 1992 Summer Olympics, where she finished fifth in her heat in the women's 400 metres. "I never ran anything over 400 meters," she said. "That means I know what the goal is, and I don't do anything until I get the goal.

"That's how I'm orientated. And I knew I needed my kids to be like this. I had to raise them that way."

Vaughn and Charmaine ran a strict household. When Shai and his younger brother, Thomasi, came home from school, it was straight to homework and sports instead of video games or TV. They also had to leave the house looking proper, representing the family every time they stepped out in public. And they were held accountable if they ever showboated or acted like they were better than somebody else. "I don't like overhyped kids. I can't stand cocky people," Charmaine said. "I raise confident people."

Gilgeous-Alexander also got his confidence from his father, who always wore flashy clothes and seemed to know everyone in town. Vaughn was their basketball coach, teaching his boys how to shoot, showing them videos of Allen Iverson and Kobe Bryant, and taking them to watch Raptors games to inspire them. Before falling asleep, the boys would lie on their backs and flick a small basketball over their heads, working on the motion Vaughn taught them and dreaming of going to the NBA since they were five. "Back then, I wasn't just thinking that I hoped [the NBA] would happen," Gilgeous-Alexander said. "I actually believed I could do it."

"I was the only one that's thinking, 'Bro, you just need a scholarship,'" Vaughn says. "And those guys are like, 'Fuck scholarships, we're going to league.'"

Vaughn overdosed the boys with sports knowledge, trying to give them all the advice that he wished somebody had given him when he was younger about the importance of academics and how to get an NCAA scholarship. Sometimes, when he was shouting from the sideline at practices and games, people looked at him like he was crazy and told him to relax, that it's just a game, that it's supposed to be fun. "And I'm like, bro, I hear what you're saying, but not really," Vaughn says. "I don't got Kentucky scholarship money. So, to me, it's not a game, it's not for fun."

For Vaughn, it was a way of life — a way out of the situation the family found themselves in, which wasn't the worst but could certainly get better.

•

Vaughn and Charmaine separated in the late 2000s; Charmaine and her two sons moved to nearby Hamilton, a smaller city one hour west of Toronto. "I was skeptical," Vaughn said about the basketball training they would receive in Hamilton. "And you never want your kids away from you. But he was in good hands."

When Gilgeous-Alexander got to Hamilton halfway through grade 6, it was an adjustment for the shy, quiet kid who never wanted to leave his family and friends in Toronto. However, he met two of his best friends, Mark Castillanes and Maurice Montoya, in homeroom at Regina Mundi Catholic Elementary, who immediately bonded over their shared love of sport. "We're all just quiet individuals," Castillanes says. "Going through that whole year, we realized through sports that we had a deeper connection."

The boys started playing basketball for fun during recess and in the nearby parks after school. And when Gilgeous-Alexander joined the school team at the start of grade 7, they realized that "Shai's kind of different when it comes to basketball," Castillanes says, noting that the young point guard could make layups with both hands and had a quick crossover — simple skills most Hamilton-area kids hadn't mastered at that age.

They started playing together more, with Gilgeous-Alexander joining them in the Filipino Basketball Association, where he dropped 50 points in a game despite being known as more of a playmaker in those days. When they didn't have a court to play on, the boys would go to one of their houses and practise dribbling while they talked. And it all paid off as they won a city championship in grade 8.

"It was a big thanks to Shai, obviously, because he brought such a different type of game," Castillanes says. "You could visibly see this guy is gonna go somewhere."

The next year, the friend group all attended St. Thomas More Catholic School, which had one of the best basketball programs in Hamilton, having been to OFSAA a few years earlier. And after leading his elementary school team to the championship in grade 8, everybody expected Gilgeous-Alexander to make the junior team. But when the roster was posted following a round of tryouts, he wasn't on the list.

"I wasn't hurt by it," Gilgeous-Alexander said. "It was more a feeling of I'm not good enough, so I've got to get better."

Charmaine told her oldest boy that he could either cry about it or make them regret their decision.

As a social worker, she never made a lot of money and had to move the family around a decent amount before they got settled. But she always held a strong front. "No matter how horrible a situation looked, if I had to cry or scream, I would wait until they went to bed," she said. "They would never see me sweat. They would never see me frustrated."

She spent whatever free time she had doing stuff for the kids, taking the bus around Hamilton to organize different bingo fundraisers for school basketball teams, leaving everyone who crossed her path with the impression that she was a generous person who came from humble roots. "I probably got her determination and her work ethic," Gilgeous-Alexander said, noting that she rarely talked about the Olympics but often preached the work it took to get there. "She instilled that if you want something in life, you go get it. That approach to life in hitting adversity changed the course of my career on and off the court.

"Every person has trials and tribulations and adversity in their life at some point," he added. "But what makes you who you are is how you learn from them."

An extra motivated Gilgeous-Alexander destroyed the tryouts for the freshman team, where the coaches fell in love with his game and leadership capabilities, uplifting his teammates even when they botched an easy basket. They also realized that Gilgeous-Alexander was extremely motivated after not making the junior team, leading the freshmen team to a city championship.

It turned out that getting cut wasn't the only thing pushing a young Gilgeous-Alexander to maximize his basketball abilities.

•

Nickeil Alexander-Walker was born in Toronto 52 days after Gilgeous-Alexander and raised by his mother, Nicole Alexander, and her brother and Shai's dad, Vaughn.

The cousins became inseparable before they could even speak, sleeping in the same beds, playing on the same basketball teams, sharing meals, calling each other on the phone to talk about their dreams, and quickly becoming more like twins than first cousins.

"I feel like me and him are as close as you can get," Alexander-Walker says. "To have that bond and to go through the same things together, I think made us closer."

Both were naturally gifted athletes, but while Gilgeous-Alexander was a better soccer player growing up, Alexander-Walker excelled in basketball from the moment he touched a ball. "Just an instant connection, chemistry between me and basketball," Alexander-Walker says. "It's just a feeling I got by playing, everything went away and it allowed me to feel invincible and be everything I've ever wanted to be."

The cousins had immense success playing together on the OBA circuit in Toronto with the Scarborough Basketball Association and JCC. And while it was hard to leave each other behind when Gilgeous-Alexander moved to Hamilton at 12, they made a point to see each other on the weekends, when Gilgeous-Alexander would usually make the trip to Toronto and play with Alexander-Walker on the hoop outside their uncle's house in Scarborough or at Top Garage, a court that sits on top of the parking garages at Finch and Leslie where Vaughn and his friends learned the game.

"Every weekend I was either at his house or he was at my house," Alexander-Walker said. "Every day in summer we were together practising and doing things we love to do together."

Alexander-Walker was the superior basketball player in those days, with a bigger, more coordinated body, ambidextrous hands, and better jump shot. "Nickeil's basketball skills were like a fucking 13-year-old kid at six," Vaughn says. "He was crazy.

"So, for Shai to catch up to that was a task."

"Nickeil was better in every aspect," UPLAY Canada founder Dwayne Washington says. "Shai couldn't hold his fucking jockstrap."

But one thing Gilgeous-Alexander did have from a young age was a mental edge that set him apart. When the boys would play one-on-one they would go at each other's throats and do everything necessary to get the win, even if it ended in a few fights like when Alexander-Walker wanted to stop playing because something got stuck in his eye, but his cousin kept coming at him. "Shai was very, very, very competitive," Alexander-Walker says. "And I think he kind of taught me earlier that when it comes to competition, there is no friends, there is no family.

"Seeing that hunger in his eyes, him willing to take you to blows — me, I've never been one to want to fight my family, but we got into these heated competitions because he brought it there."

Vaughn and Washington used tough love on the two, telling Gilgeous-Alexander that he had to catch up to his cousin and telling Alexander-Walker that he would be a fool to let his cousin catch up to him. It was all in an effort to help them get the most out of each other through regular competition.

"Having a brother my age, who is damn near just as good at basketball, we used to go at it all the time," Gilgeous-Alexander said. "We've almost fought before, almost punched each other in the face, but we know it's all love and that's why we're both at the stage we're at today.

"Growing up with a guy like that will give you a competitive edge."

■

Canada Elite co-founder Shane James was at the HoopDome in Downsview Park when he saw a grade 8 Alexander-Walker playing pickup against grown men. He was surprised. "Usually when you see a young kid playing with men, they kind of take a back seat and they're quiet and they don't say much," James says. "But he was in mix, man. He was getting after it. He was talking shit. He was hitting guys. He was being physical."

James grew up in Scarborough and played for Grassroots before captaining the junior national team in high school. He got a scholarship to Loyola University Maryland in Baltimore in 2003 before playing professionally overseas. While he was in college, however, some kids from his former high school started asking him questions about how to get a Division I scholarship, so James created a program called Triple Balance Community Services to help the youth with homework, nutrition, basketball knowledge, and connections.

After his professional career came to an end, James returned to Toronto and merged with a nearby program called Youth Association for Academics, Athletics, and Character Education (YAAACE), run by Devon Jones, to form Canada Elite AAU in 2014, playing on the Under Armour circuit and helping more than 80 Canadian players pursue careers in the NCAA, U Sports, the Canadian Elite Basketball League (CEBL), and the NBA. James also created the Canadian Youth Basketball League (CYBL) to provide Canadian AAU teams with opportunities to compete against each other in the spring before heading to America for bigger competitions.

James was so impressed with Alexander-Walker at HoopDome that he invited him to try out for Canada Elite. But while he had a head start physically and skill wise, Alexander-Walker could get mentally overwhelmed as a youngster. He often asked too much of himself too quickly and was hard on himself when he made a mistake or had a bad game, allowing his emotions to get the best of him.

"He was very emotional when he was young. So, he'd get upset very easily," James says. "The key was being in control of his emotions. He would be at his best when he was able to forget about making shots."

There were times when James would sub him out of the game and Alexander-Walker would want to come right back in. If he was injured, he would simply tape it up and ask to play. During practices, it would be like the world had ended if he ever lost a ball-handling or shooting competition. "He would hate to lose," James says.

Alexander-Walker had dreamed of the NBA since he was five, but his lofty ambitions got him in trouble because he wanted everything to come quickly and struggled to remain patient when there were bumps in the road. But the turning point came during a game against CIA

Bounce: Alexander-Walker was excited to play in front of his friends and family in Toronto but ended up sitting on the bench all game. In the changing room afterwards, Alexander-Walker was crying when his mom came in and told him to get his stuff and go. But Alexander-Walker said he was going to stay and prove that he belonged.

"That really was the turning point for him," James says. "And after that, he was just a completely different kid. His work ethic just turned up 1,000 times. His attitude was much better, and then he just surpassed everyone." Within 12 months, Alexander-Walker was the best player on Canada Elite, with 20 Division I offers to boot.

Prince Oduro remembers seeing Alexander-Walker come to practice one day with an attitude, noting that he had clearly had a bad day and was taking it out on the basketball court. "He was hitting shot after shot. He was guarding guys 94 feet. He was getting mad as fuck, kicking the ball in the arena," Oduro says. After seeing Alexander-Walker drenched in sweat on the sideline after practice, he noted that there was no way Alexander-Walker didn't get better that day.

"He's one of the guys at that age group that really helped me realize 'Okay, this is what it takes to be good,'" Oduro says. "He gave me a different outlook on how to approach the game."

After following in Wiggins's footsteps and playing one season at Vaughan Secondary, Alexander-Walker left Toronto for St. Louis Christian Academy in Missouri. After just one season there, however, he heard about another prep school opportunity in Chattanooga, Tennessee — where he could chase his dreams alongside his favourite cousin.

■

In grade 10, Gilgeous-Alexander transferred to nearby Sir Allan MacNab Secondary School, where top talents from all over Ontario were flocking to play for head coach Dwayne Washington.

Washington grew up in the Bronx, New York City, honing his game on the outdoor blacktops before playing for the New York Gauchos, a youth basketball club that started in 1967 and produced countless pros like Stephon Marbury and Rod Strickland.

Washington attended a prep school in upstate New York before landing a basketball scholarship at Houghton College, a Christian Division II school in Houghton, New York, where he obtained a double major in psychology and education before pursuing his doctorate of education at the University of Toronto.

He started teaching at Ray Lewis Elementary School in Hamilton in 2005, which was on the road between New York and Toronto, quickly learning that the city was becoming a hotbed for basketball talent. While the list of alumni who went from Hamilton to the pros was limited, including StFX legend Tyrell Vernon and long-time pro Tyrone Watson, the area was home to tons of first- and second-generation immigrants who had a chip on their shoulders as the city sat in Toronto's big shadow.

There were a few OBA clubs in the area including Blessed Sacrament, Hamilton Wildcats, and the Ancaster Basketball Club; some good high school teams like Sir Allan MacNab and St. Thomas More; and Joe Raso's McMaster University Marauders men's teams were always competitive. However, there weren't any AAU teams in the area.

So, Washington started United Public Leadership Academy for You (UPLAY Canada) in 2007, with the goal of using sport to help develop better young men. "I'm known as a master skills developer," Washington said. "When players come to us, they'll get an explanation," he added. "We don't just show them how to use certain angles or arcs or how to use their energy; we tell them *why* and *when* to use those techniques."

UPLAY went on to become the top AAU program in Canada after RJ Barrett and Andrew Nembhard joined Gilgeous-Alexander there around 2016, taking the Nike sponsorship from CIA Bounce and competing on the EYBL Circuit. UPLAY has helped 113 Canadians get NCAA Division I scholarships, producing 13 NBA players while putting Hamilton on the basketball map.

When the superintendent at Sir Allan MacNab saw what Washington was doing with UPLAY, he brought him over to teach and coach the basketball team. Washington turned it into a "superpower magnet school that was attracting all the really, really good talent," Tim Francis, a fellow teacher and assistant coach there, says. "All of a sudden the program just sort of skyrocketed to another level."

Washington met Gilgeous-Alexander when he was in grade 8 and just 5'7" with spidery arms and size 12 feet that made him slow and uncoordinated, struggling to jump high or shoot far. Frederick Owens, a coach at UPLAY, joked to Charmaine that with feet that big her son could be one of three things: "a swimmer, basketball player, or a clown."

"I was kind of goofy [growing up]," Gilgeous-Alexander said. "Like a baby deer."

Gilgeous-Alexander learned how to survive as a relatively small, unathletic, pass-first point guard. Instead of getting by on size, speed, or jumping, he worked hard to better understand the game, relying on his feel, pace, creativity, and using different angles to score over bigger defenders. "His whole game is predicated around not being athletic," Washington said. "So when you see him take the layups he's extending his arm, he's using certain parts of the glass."

Washington would have Gilgeous-Alexander make layups using each part of his hand, from the inside to the outside to the fingertips, guiding the ball into the hoop. He would have him take 10 shots off a certain quadrant of the backboard, and if he missed the spot once, he would have to start over. Then he would have him stand in the same spot a few feet from the basket, sinking swishes all day to perfect his form.

"It was very tough," Washington said. "I couldn't work kids now the way I worked with him. But he could take a lot. He was a mental grinder."

Gilgeous-Alexander never complained; he never asked to shoot more threes, to practise his step-back, or to play more scrimmages. Instead, he was patient enough to stay in the same spot and repeat the same drill again and again. "He was like, 'coach, we got to work double hard — I'm not gonna be as big as Nickeil,'" Washington recalls him saying.

Gilgeous-Alexander had a steady mindset, avoiding the highs and lows that could often come with playing high level basketball as a kid. "It was like, 'Who is this guy?'" Washington says, growing so impressed with the youngster's mentality that he figured, "I gotta help this kid out . . . That was my whole life goal for that kid."

Washington taught Gilgeous-Alexander how to approach the ball-screen, taking tricks that he learned from his Gaucho coach, Strickland — the godfather of Kyrie Irving — and applying them to his new apprentice.

Gilgeous-Alexander would watch film of the best small point guards during lunch break, from Chris Paul to Allen Iverson to Nash. Then he would go to the court and practise a series of pick-and-roll drills designed to help him at the next level. "I worked on that for countless hours," Gilgeous-Alexander said. "That's where the base of my game is. That's where I started and I built up from there."

During his grade 10 season at MacNab, Gilgeous-Alexander came off the bench and averaged just eight points a game alongside a host of future Division I players, because Washington always took the long view with his athletes. "He actually didn't really care about winning at all," Francis says. "His priority was individual development of the kids." Washington focused on honing the skills that would be transferable to the next level like ball-handling and passing instead of just scoring, going so far as to tell Gilgeous-Alexander not to shoot until the fourth quarters.

"Growing up, I had the ball in my hands really young," Gilgeous-Alexander said. "I wasn't that good early, but I always had the ball in my hands."

By grade 10, Gilgeous-Alexander had devoted his life to basketball, hanging out with his friends less, going to sleep early, and spending five hours a day in the gym and watching film. During his two years at MacNab, Gilgeous-Alexander would go to the local YMCA every morning to train before school, watch film and play at lunch, and then go back to the YMCA for scrimmages in the evenings.

"We used to be always hanging out constantly in the summertime," Castillanes says. "Then we just didn't see him as much as we used to. . . . And we just kind of saw that whole seriousness grow into something that we couldn't comprehend at the time because we didn't think for us sports would take us somewhere. But for him, he had the chance to do something with it. And he did."

"I hope everybody understands the sacrifices he made," Washington says, explaining that he never drinks or goes clubbing, and that he had one girlfriend his entire life before marrying her in 2024. "That's fucking discipline. He watches video all day long. How people watch Netflix, he's watching video. He's Kobe. He's fucking Kobe."

Gilgeous-Alexander hit a growth spurt before grade 10, sprouting to 6'2" and then to 6'6" with a 6'11.5" wingspan by the time his senior year rolled around: a monster of a point guard who had the unique advantage of learning the game before he could rely on his physical traits to succeed.

"Most of my life, I was shorter," Gilgeous-Alexander said. "I think that forced me to be crafty and deceptive with my movements on the court, just to get to where I wanted to go.

"It was harder when I was smaller, and then I hit a growth spurt," he added, smiling. "And it turned out well."

•

Gilgeous-Alexander was still a relatively unheralded prospect when he transferred to a little-known prep school in Chattanooga, Tennessee, called Hamilton Heights Christian Academy after his grade 11 year in 2015.

He was reunited with Alexander-Walker, where the cousins lived with head coach Zach Ferrell and his family. For two years, they did everything together, bunking in the same room, sharing meals, attending church, babysitting Ferrell's kid, and playing basketball. In fact, they brought the same competitive spirit that they had playing one-on-one at Top Garage to practice, where they guarded each other every day. "They were constantly pushing each other to become better," Ferrell says.

But it wasn't until the summer of 2016, in between his sophomore and junior year of high school, that Gilgeous-Alexander's stock really took off. After both he and Alexander-Walker were cut from the Canadian Under-17 team the previous summer, they came back better and dominated at the Under-18 FIBA Americas in Chile, where Alexander-Walker led the entire tournament in scoring with 17 points per game while Gilgeous-Alexander led the tournament in assists with 5 per game along with 3 steals, helping Canada win a silver medal for just the second time in history.

"They just grew and got better and better," Rana, who let them go the year prior, says. "That's what both those kids have always been: just relentless workers, and you can see the growth and improvement every year."

While Alexander-Walker got injured towards the end of the FIBA Americas tournament, a 17-year-old Gilgeous-Alexander was so impressive that Rana suggested the senior team take a look at him as they prepared for the 2016 OQT in Manila. "For a big guard to have that type of feel, that type of vision, that type of playmaking ability, I think it made a lot of sense for us to give him as many opportunities to compete at the highest level," Rana says. "We were just trying to speed up his development curve."

Gilgeous-Alexander blew the staff away with his ability to cause havoc on the defensive end, using his size and length to give veteran point guards Tyler Ennis, Phil Scrubb, and Cory Joseph problems. Plus, he had the mentality to just keep going at the older guards no matter how many times they got the best of him.

"He made everybody's life difficult," assistant coach Raso says.

"I could tell he was going to be a great, great player," Scrubb says. "He looked pretty comfortable in a lot of situations around professionals."

General manager Rowan Barrett and head coach Jay Triano believed in him so much that Gilgeous-Alexander got the final spot on the team. And while he didn't play a single minute in Manila, it marked a turning point for the young point guard. "I think I learned professional basketball that year," he said. "I learned a lot of terminology, the physicality of it, the speed of it, and it for sure was a kick-start to my professional career.

"I got so much better. It was a faster pace of game, and I ultimately knew I wanted to go to the NBA."

Off the court, Gilgeous-Alexander learned about work ethic from being around pros for the first time in his life, seeing how they ate, rested, practised, weight-trained, and prepared for games. There was a dinner banquet where he was sitting at a table with Joseph, Thompson, Joel Anthony, Boris Diaw, and Tony Parker when Raso walked over and asked Gilgeous-Alexander: "How many NBA championships are at this table right now?" The answer was nine.

"That experience kind of helped me for this, being in the NBA today," Gilgeous-Alexander said. "I'm a little bit ahead of the game, being with those guys and seeing how they act on and off the court and how professional they are."

Gilgeous-Alexander returned to Chattanooga with a newfound confidence and a lot more interest from NCAA schools, breaking out in his junior campaign as he averaged 18 points, 5 assists, and 3 steals. As a result, the four-star prospect decommitted from Florida and went to his dream school, the University of Kentucky, where he played for one year before getting selected 11th overall in the 2018 NBA Draft. He went onto become the best Canadian basketball player of all time.

Alexander-Walker, meanwhile, averaged 16 points, 3 assists, and 3 steals in his final year, sorting through a host of Division I offers before committing to Virginia Tech, where he played for two years before getting drafted 17th overall in 2019. He bounced around the league before finding his footing on his third NBA team, the Minnesota Timberwolves, establishing himself as one of the best three-and-D players in the game and being rewarded for it with a four-year, $62-million contract in 2025.

Most importantly, they did it together — two cousins from Toronto who chased an NBA dream and leaned on each other every step of the way, staying up late to flick an imaginary basketball over their heads, talk about their goals, practise post-game interviews, laugh, cry, and push each other to get better.

"It's hard to really explain, to be honest, just the love that I have for him," Alexander-Walker says. "Being family. Us chasing a dream together and pushing each other to be better since we were born — it's hard to explain just how valuable it was to go through that experience with him."

"They're like batty and bench," Vaughn says. "They couldn't really do without each other."

CHAPTER 13

THE GOLD MEDAL BOYS

CHARLIE LINDSAY

RJ Barrett poses with a gold medal in his mouth after leading Team Canada to its first ever title at an international boys event.

"That's one of the most, probably is the most special basketball moment of my life."
— RJ BARRETT

By the time Gilgeous-Alexander was making a name for himself in the United States, Canada Basketball was using the influx of money Nash helped pull in to build a sustainable youth infrastructure back home.

The youth programing started with the Nike All-Canada Camp in 1997, run out of Nike's facility in Portland, Oregon. Canada Basketball would bring in about 60 to 80 of Canada's best high school juniors and seniors for a weekend-long camp, with seminars about college recruitment and scrimmages with up to 90 NCAA coaches watching.

"We really didn't have this opportunity," Nash said to campers in 1999. "I was seen by maybe two American Division I coaches. So, I think a lot of the obstacles for you guys have been alleviated."

Then, around 2001, Canada Basketball took an idea from federations in France and Australia and launched the Centre for Performance (CP) program that was run in conjunction with the provincial sports organizations across the country. A group of elite athletes would be identified by the provincial bodies and meet five times a year to work on player development drills that came from Canada Baksetball's long-term development model to create well-rounded international players.

Finally, a component was added to the Centre for Performance in 2009 called the Targeted Athlete Strategy (TAS), which identified players from as early as high school freshman and provided them with more individualized training and support, starting with 40 of the best 16- to 18-year-old players, like Wiggins, Pangos, and Bennett, enabling kids to get some affinity with the national team from an earlier age.

"One of the biggest challenges that we had in Canadian basketball . . . we were playing all these games, but are we really training and developing young players?" program manager Andrew Cook says, noting that kids could play over 100 games a year between high school, OBA, and AAU. "The idea behind CP was to train."

But these programs weren't just about developing global basketball players; they were also meant to improve Canada's results on the world stage, hoping to win gold for the first time since the 1983 World University Games.

■

Roy Rana grew up around Bloor and Lansdowne to Indian-Canadian parents and played high school basketball for Bloor Collegiate Institute before studying to become a teacher. He worked at C.W. Jefferys high school and then was recruited to Eastern Commerce in the early 2000s, succeeding former basketball coaches Simeon Mars and Desmond Rowley.

"Coaching became a real obsession, something I took very seriously," says Rana. "At the high school level, it was all about making an impact, changing young people's lives."

Under his reign, Eastern Commerce Collegiate won four OFSAA titles in an eight-year span, finishing first in the national rankings seven times and compiling an overall record of 256–39. Rana developed connections with so many of Toronto's best players through coaching at Eastern Commerce, Team Ontario, and his AAU team, Toronto Mission (which later became King Nation). Eventually, Canada Basketball hired him as the head coach of the first cadet team in history when FIBA announced a new Under-16 age group competition in 2009.

With no money to properly prepare for the inaugural FIBA U-16 Americas Championship, Rana had just three practices before heading off to Mendoza, Argentina, with a two-person support staff and a 12-man roster. "At the start, I was using my credit card for gyms. I was paying a lot of expenses myself," Rana says. "I was actually spending money to try and help the program."

While the directive was to simply have fun in Mendoza, a Canadian team led by Kevin Pangos and Anthony Bennett won bronze, qualifying for the next summer's Under-17 World Championship. There, a 15-year-old Wiggins joined the fold and helped Canada win bronze — still the program's only ever medal at a cadet world championship. "That was the beginning of really a transformational period for basketball in the country," Rana says. "[That] really started to kind of make people think twice about those perceptions, those judgments about Canadian players."

"It was huge for . . . that generation of people in basketball," Pangos says. "He just gave us the confidence, like, 'Hey, we can really do this.'"

Rana was succeeded by coach David DeAveiro at the cadet level and promoted to coach the under-19 junior team in 2012. The two coaches worked off each other to set the building blocks for Canada Basketball's age-group programs, which became an important developmental tool for Canada's best players. Together, they won nine medals between 2009 and 2017.

But it would be a long time before a player came along who was good enough to take one of Canada's teams over the mountain top.

▪

Rowan Alexander Barrett Jr. (RJ) was born in Scarborough, Ontario, in 2000 before moving to France, where his father, Rowan, was playing professionally. He would sit in the gym and watch Rowan's team practise, shooting the ball on the side hoops before playing against the other players' kids when practice was over. He wore No. 9, a twist of his dad's No. 6.

When the family moved back to Canada in 2008, settling in Mississauga, Ontario — a suburb on the opposite side of Toronto as Scarborough — RJ started playing for the local OBA team, the Brampton Minor Basketball Association, eventually competing alongside his friend Andrew Nembhard against all the best players of their generation.

"What [the OBA] did was it started to allow the best players from different schools to play together on one team," Rana says. "It also allowed more competition outside the GTA . . . [providing] competitive opportunities for the best players to play against the best players."

Unlike his father, who only saw Jordan on TV a couple times a week, RJ had role models in his own backyard. His mom, Kesha Duhaney, was a track star born to a family of Olympians, including parents who ran for the Jamaican national track team and a sister who was a world champion sprinter who competed for Jamaica at the 1992 Barcelona Olympics. "Believe me," Rowan said. "Her family spares no opportunity to let me know that RJ's athleticism came from their side."

RJ's godfather was Steve Nash, and his father took him to Raptors games to meet his favourite players, like DeMar DeRozan and Kyle Lowry. Plus, at nearby Vaughan Secondary, Andrew Wiggins was the best prospect in the country. "A guy that was closer to my age, and him being the number-one player in the country, that kind of inspired me," RJ says. "Because that's what I wanted to be. And I saw that that was achievable."

By the time RJ was 10, he had a dream board with his ideal NCAA schools on it. Then he told his dad he wanted to stop playing organized soccer and track and field and commit full-time to hoops, with dreams of becoming an NBA All-Star and Hall-of-Famer. "The loftiness of his goals really took me aback," Barrett said. "What do you tell your kid at 12 when he tells you something like that and you know the chances are so remote?"

He was taught to deal with obstacles before they arose, with his father talking trash to him at the free-throw line of otherwise empty gyms, and his parents grilling him in front of the TV in mock press conferences. And in an effort to accelerate his development, RJ tracked down the highest level of competition, playing against older players in hostile environments where he was forced to mature or succumb to the pressure.

Once, Rowan took a 12-year-old RJ to the cadet team training camp to get some work in alongside some older players before the team left for a tournament. RJ played one-on-one against the team's star player, Jamal Murray. "It was too much," RJ says. "He was making half court shots on me while I'm guarding him.

"He bust my ass. I wasn't ready back then."

RJ was quiet on the car ride home, but when he walked through the door, he hugged his mom and broke down in tears. When his parents asked RJ how he wanted to handle the situation, he said, "I want to work harder." And that was that. The rest of his career has been carefully calculated to achieve the lofty goals that he shared with his parents when he was 10.

"If you know RJ and what he's about, it's not by chance, right?" his Team Ontario head coach, Aaron Blakely, says. "Everything he did was very calculated and his family was very, very meticulous in terms of working with him about setting goals and kind of ticking boxes as he went through his youth.

"It's kind of playing chess while a lot of people have been playing checkers."

•

It helped that by the time RJ was a teenager, his father was running the youth programming for Canada Basketball. After witnessing the explosion of young talent in gyms across the GTA, Rowan Barrett went to AAU coaches like Russell's Grassroots, Vidal Massiah's Northern Kings, and McIntyre and George's CIA Bounce and explained that he wanted to bring the blue-collar world of grassroots basketball and white-collar world of Canada Basketball together for the first time in the country's history.

"What we needed to do was re-establish continuity that ran through all levels of basketball in this country," Parrish says. "He was able to reach out and connect in a collaborative way to all the other spheres of influence in the country."

Barrett was aware of the tension that existed between the grassroots community and the national federation from when he was a young player. And he was afraid that if they didn't mend relationships soon, the national team might never secure the best talent. "I thought we need to get on this right now or we could lose a whole generation of players if they're just disinterested, they don't want to play, and it just continues to go like this," Barrett says.

Barrett would go to local gyms like Falstaff and HoopDome and talk to parents and coaches, trying to get their kids to come out and play for the national team. And after working to identify the best Canadian athletes from RJ's 2000-born age cohort, Barrett started a program at Georgian College for the best 10- to 12-year-olds to train alongside some of the best grassroots coaches like Rana, Greg Francis, Raso, Gymnopoulos, Keith Vassell, O'Neil Kamaka, and Vidal Massiah in 2011.

In 2013, with hopes of creating something more sustainable, Barrett started the Junior Academy — a development program that brought together 40 of the best grade 7s and 8s over the course of six weekend-long training sessions and a week-long camp at the brand-new, privately funded Athlete Institute facility in Orangeville, Ontario. He hired Scarborough native Chris Cheng to run it after establishing himself as a connector in the grassroots community as the head coach of Team Ontario. And together with Cheng and Athlete Institute CEO Jesse Tipping, they put together a curriculum where kids were put through basketball drills, strength and conditioning sessions, and informational workshops about college recruitment, social media, leadership, diet, time management, and film study.

"I just remember being super excited to have the opportunity to go away on some weekends to go train and get better with the Team Canada coaches," inaugural Junior Academy member A.J. Lawson says.

They lived in the same dorms, practised three times a day, and learned the same terminology and systems that the senior national team was running at the time. It was all in an effort to teach them how to operate as professionals and to prepare them for upcoming junior national team training camps. Then, on Sundays, the players would scrimmage all day.

"So now you have a gym where you have 20 kids from grade 7, 20 kids in grade 8, but the makeup of those kids is lot of the best kids in the best AAU teams," Claude Nembhard, who's son Andrew was an inaugural Junior Academy member, says. "And that's not really happening before, because Canada Basketball probably didn't have someone that could get those guys in the gym."

"That was probably the biggest jumping points," Claude adds. "Rowan coming back and kind of having his hands on the ground, bringing in the community guys."

Claude was a former multi-sport athlete who grew up at Bayview and the 401 but had to stop playing organized sports when he attended York University, working to put himself through school. Upon graduation, he met his wife Mary, moved to Vaughan, and started coaching basketball at Dufferin Clarke in the late 1980s. "It was a drug," Claude says. "I just fell in love with the game."

Claude and Mary had two sons, Andrew and then Ryan, and moved to Aurora, Ontario, the day before Andrew was born on January 16, 2000. The boys grew up playing all sorts of sports, but they had a unique advantage when it came to basketball because of their father's obsession with coaching. "My pops brought me into the game," Andrew Nembhard says. "He's always been coaching me, and he always had a gym open for me every night of the week."

Claude started a training program called "True Basketball Fundamentals" when the boys were young before starting the Vaughan Avengers rep team, where Nembhard played two years up against '98s like Gilgeous-Alexander and Alexander-Walker. "When I started coaching Andrew, that was literally insane because I'd be up on the internet getting drills and scouring the internet for things to do in games," Claude says. "And I had two kids that were guinea pigs who just love the game. They couldn't sit still."

Claude also drove his boys to various gyms around the city so that they could watch Wiggins and Pangos compete at Vaughan and Cory and Devoe Joseph play together at Pickering. One day, while they were watching a young Cory dominate an OFSAA game by doing the little things like boxing out, guarding up, and making the right reads, Claude had an insight and "decided to model Andrew's game after him," he said.

Nembhard was a well-rounded athlete by the time he got to grade 7, dominating the OBA while also playing soccer for Toronto FC Academy. But the dual-sport lifestyle was becoming too difficult to balance, and he had a decision to make. Fortunately, the Junior Academy came along at exactly the same time. "My dad always told me when I was younger that if I want to take something serious, I'm gonna have to go full out towards it," Nembhard says about choosing basketball and the Junior Academy. "I think that's when my game grew the most, and I took advantage of those resources for sure."

"It was huge to learn from good coaches and be in situations where you're getting put on a team with other good players, and you have to adjust to playing with other good players. I think that's what the next level was. And I think that just gives you a little sneak peek."

Nembhard was a quiet competitor who hated losing to his younger brother Ryan, getting in fights over games on the Fisher Price net in their basement, when Claude and Ryan would team up against Andrew and play up to 11, with the rules dictating that Ryan had to score the final basket. "There's a lot of lights broken in the basement but, for the most part, Andrew's winning those games," Claude says. "But the odd time that

Ryan would get some kind of nice shot to win the game . . . it would be a problem in the house."

That competition prepared Nembhard to go against the best players of his generation, as the original Junior Academy included a number of future pros who are just now getting to the age where they can impact the senior national team such as Nembhard, RJ, Lawson, Marcus Carr, Ignas Brazdeikis, Simi Shittu, and Jaden Bediako.

"Growing up, we were all super competitive," Nembhard says. "We saw each other going through the ranks and were trying to be better than the next guy . . . And I think that's what makes it super fun."

The 2000-born age group bonded over their similarities after becoming the first group of Canadians to take the sport seriously before high school and to have a clearly defined pathway to the pros. They would sit in a dorm room each night and talk about their favourite players and dreams of making it to the league. Together.

"You're able to bond over the fact that you have to make the same sacrifices," Carr says. "It definitely felt like long-lost brothers."

■

By the time RJ got to high school in 2014, he had already been tabbed as the top Canadian prospect in his class. And after a year at St. Marcellinus Catholic Secondary School in Mississauga, it became clear that he needed better competition going forward, so he moved on to the illustrious Montverde Academy near Orlando, Florida.

Throughout the recruiting process, head coach Kevin Boyle was honest with him that he would begin the season as the 15th man on the best prep team in America. "Our biggest thing to him was he had to earn anything he got here," Boyle says. "This is the way we do things."

But that's exactly what RJ wanted: to go up against the top kids in practice every day, to be held accountable for making even the smallest mistakes, and to ultimately work his way up the pecking order based on merit — not the fact that he was a big shot in Canada. "He could have gone anywhere, and he went to a place where they're treating him like, 'You're nothing. You have to work,'" his AAU coach, Dwayne Washington, said. "It shows that he's been trying to really grow, trying to stretch himself."

Despite being the youngest player on a team full of future pros, RJ quickly earned a spot in the rotation after consistently showing up when the lights were the brightest. Even if he wasn't as dominant in drills or scrimmages, RJ found a way to contribute in the games, getting to the rim and finishing with his left hand no matter who the competition was.

In fact, RJ has never been a great practice player, according to Nathaniel Mitchell, who has trained him since he was a boy. He remembers putting RJ through a series of simple drills. "He struggled a lot in those skill areas," Mitchell says. "I remember [thinking], 'Oh man, it's gonna be tough.'"

But then Mitchell saw him play in an AAU game for Regional Elite Development Academy (REDA), who won a national championship when RJ was in grade 5 playing up an age. He realized that RJ had an "it" factor that separated him from other players and enabled him to play better when the lights were brightest. "I just remember him destroying kids," Mitchell says.

RJ followed it up by winning the Under-15 national championships with Team Ontario alongside Nembhard in 2014, winning tournament MVP after scoring 37 points in the finals against Lu Dort and Team Quebec. "It's been a trend that when things get difficult, RJ just gets better," Blakely says.

And at Montverde, after barely playing the first few games of his freshman season, RJ worked his way up the depth chart from the 15th man to the team's best player and leading scorer by the end of the season. "When I was growing up, I saw the work [my dad] put in and I've just been trying to work harder," RJ said. "There's always people coming behind me [wanting] my spot."

His breakout game came in a quarter-final loss to Lonzo Ball–led Chino Hills High School at the City of Ponds Classic in December, where RJ scored 31 points and realized that if he could do it against the best team in the country, he could make it to the NBA. But it wasn't until his junior season that he and Nembhard led Montverde to an undefeated season and its first national championship in three years, with RJ scoring 25 points and 15 rebounds in the final. "That's probably his biggest strength," Boyle says. "Anytime people start questioning RJ, he ends up quickly snapping out of it and really stepping up."

RJ was dubbed the number-one player in the 2018 recruiting class, a McDonald's All-American, the Naismith Prep Player of the Year, and the Gatorade National Player of the Year, becoming the first player since LeBron James to sweep all the major high-school awards and win the national championship. And while Wiggins was the first Canadian to dominate American competition from a young age, he was seen as an anomaly. RJ, on the other hand, had a more repeatable pathway to stardom as he took advantage of the best developmental opportunities in the country from the age of 10.

As a result of his father's connections and knowledge, RJ moved from program to program in order to fast-track his development, always having the ball in his hands and the freedom to make mistakes against older players and alongside the best coaches — opportunities ballers of his father's generation simply never had.

"I was nowhere near the kind of player [RJ] is at 15," said Barrett, who had the raw potential and athleticism to be an NBA player but never got there due to his late start and lack of resources. "Developmentally, he's had experiences I didn't have."

The inspiration behind the Junior Academy and other youth programming was to make sure that young Canadian players didn't have the same obstacles that Barrett and his generation went through, providing them with the resources necessary to succeed.

"It was definitely different from my dad's time. And he's honestly a big part of the reason why all of this is happening, and that we could do all of these things now," RJ says. "It's been easier for me growing up, especially just having a dad that kind of knows all the things that I need to do, all the positions that I was going to be in. He's been able to just kind of guide me, guide a lot of Canadian basketball players throughout their journeys.

"But I appreciate him going through that because it's easier for us now."

•

In each summer of high school, Barrett played for Canada's cadet and youth national teams, winning silver at the FIBA Americas Under-16 Championship in 2015 as the team's leading scorer and youngest player before finishing fifth at the Under-17 World Cup in 2016.

"It definitely helped me just being able to play basketball," Barrett says. "It's a different brand of basketball. It's a lot more just thinking and learning how to make plays, read, react."

In 2017, between his sophomore and junior season at Montverde, a 17-year-old RJ led the EYBL in scoring before joining Canada's Under-19 team for the World Cup in Cairo, Egypt. However, the team was short-handed after players like Nembhard, Shittu, Carr, and Bediako were all unavailable due to AAU commitments, NCAA visits, or injuries. "That was probably the weakest roster that I had in my whole career," head coach Roy Rana says. "Everybody chose not to play."

Led by RJ, Lindell Wigginton, Abu Kigab, Prince Oduro and a host of underrated role players, Team Canada went to Cairo with a big chip on their shoulders after the 12-man roster was posted on Twitter and criticized by fans. "People were basically talking bad about us in the comments, saying this team is terrible, why did they bring so and so, and how are we going to bring this product to a World Cup?" Oduro says, as the entire team gathered in one of the boys' hotel rooms to discuss the social media post.

"And that really fuelled us. I remember we were all sitting there reading the comments with each other, and we were like, 'Yeah, we have to show people.'"

Canada flew to Cairo and started the tournament with a 91–42 demolition of Mali. However, Canada lost its second game to Spain, 78–73, when they shot just 35 percent from the field and 20 percent from three as the starting backcourt of RJ and Wigginton struggled to break down the Spanish defense, combining to go 7-for-30 with six turnovers. The loss meant that Canada would end up on the same side of the bracket as Team USA.

But while the loss could have sunk a less tight-knit group, they rallied around it instead. "The most important piece was losing," Rana says. In the locker room after the game, Kigab started freaking out, smashing his phone on the floor and crying. Nobody said a word for a while, but once they all realized how badly he wanted to win, they understood.

"We spent a lot of time talking after that loss and refocusing and building confidence and bringing the group together," Rana says. "I think that was the trigger for that run."

"You see the vulnerable side of other people," Oduro says. "I feel like you just build a connection based off of that. I feel like that type of stuff is what drew the team closer and made guys want it more."

Canada won its next two games against Japan and Angola by a combined 47 points before matching up with France in the quarter-final — a program that had historically gotten the best of Canada, including at the 2000 Olympics and 2016 OQT. This time, however, would be different, as the Canadians reached a different gear on defense and led throughout, holding France to just 37 percent shooting and 21 percent from three. Canada won a defensive battle in which RJ's 27 points was just enough to win, 73–67.

"We always lose to France in the quarters — boys, girls, men, women, doesn't matter," Canada Basketball CEO Michele O'Keefe says. She remembers approaching Rana and team manager James DePoe in the hallway after the win. "And I said, 'What are you guys crying about?' They said, 'We finally beat France!'"

The win propelled Canada into the semifinal game against an American team chock-full of future NBA players like Immanuel Quickley, Cam Reddish, and P.J. Washington. Canada started off slow, getting outscored 23–17 in the first quarter. But they picked up their scoring and won the second quarter 28–19, heading into half up by three.

With Wigginton out with a concussion, Rana shifted RJ to the point guard position, running pick-and-rolls and making decisions with the ball in his hands all game. "He had an aggressiveness to him. He had an intensity to him. And he was a dog," Rana says. "He wasn't going to back down to anybody. He was going for it every single time. That confidence was really what stood out."

Before each game, RJ has a routine that helps him prepare for the moment. Once the starting lineups are announced, he brings his hands to each side of his head, flips an invisible switch, taps his leg three times, kisses both wrists now that his late brother, Nathan's name, is tattooed there, and locks in.

"There's Rowan Barrett Jr. and then there's RJ Barrett. And those are two different guys," RJ says. "Rowan Barrett Jr. is chillin', likes to hang out with his friends, play video games, hang out with family, play some cards, too."

However, once he flips that switch, RJ says he becomes a different person — he becomes RJ Barrett. "That's a dog," he says. "I'm ready to go after that."

Canada won both the third and fourth quarter behind a dominant performance from RJ, who aggressively attacked the rim and got to the free-throw line 15 times, proving that none of the Americans could guard him as he dropped 38 points, 13 rebounds, 5 assists, and just 1 turnover in the 99–87 win. It marked the first time in six years the Americans had lost in that age group.

"It's up there with one of the greatest Canadian performances at any level," Rana said.

Kigab, meanwhile, played a team-high 35 minutes, stuffing the stat sheet with 14 points, 6 rebounds, 4 assists, 4 fouls, and a block while giving everything he had to help the team avenge its loss to Spain. Literally. "He vomited twice in the last minute of the game because he played so goddamn hard," Rana says. "That's who Abu Kigab was."

Canada followed it up with a 79–60 demolition of Italy in the final, winning its first ever gold medal in an FIBA boy's basketball tournament. RJ led the field in scoring and was named tournament MVP. "That's one of the most, probably is the most special basketball moment of my life," he said.

"Being from Canada is something that I've always taken a huge, huge pride in. And there's some people that tried to make fun at the beginning," RJ says. "But then I really, really showed them when I was able to go over there when we went to Egypt and won the tournament.

"That put some respect on our name down there, for sure."

When Team Canada's plane touched down in Toronto the next day, they were greeted by a throng of media, family, friends, and supporters who were draped in Canadian flags celebrating their arrival. The team was honoured with the Canadian Press Team of the Year Award for 2017, becoming the first basketball team to be recognized since the award's inception in 1966.

"I underestimated how big winning that gold medal was until I got back to Canada," Oduro says. "All these news reporters and so many people there waiting . . . And once I got home, my mom was like, 'I saw you on the news.'"

"The country kind of galvanized behind it," Rana says.

In the airport, RJ was asked about his accomplishment. "I mean, I don't think my dad can say he beat the US," he said with a grin. "So I've got that on him."

As for next steps? "Pretty simple: go to college, go to the NBA, be a star," RJ said.

And that's exactly what happened. Three weeks after winning gold, RJ had the confidence to reclassify academically and move to college one year earlier. RJ landed at Duke University, where he led the Blue Devils to a 32-6 record and the ACC tournament championship while setting a freshman single-season conference scoring record with 724 points. After one season, RJ declared for the 2019 NBA Draft.

He refused to work out for the New Orleans Pelicans and Memphis Grizzlies, who held the first and second picks in the draft, instead focusing his attention on the spotlight that is Madison Square Garden and the New York Knicks. "This is the place I want to be," he said, and the Knicks obliged, drafting him third overall. He was the first of a record six Canadians to get drafted in 2019, setting a new benchmark for non-American selections in a single NBA Draft.

"Today is a momentous day for all our Canadian players drafted into the NBA," Rowan Barrett said. "This growth has not happened overnight and is the result of many years of planning, programming, and winning."

RJ had an up and down tenure across four and a half seasons with the Knicks before being traded to his hometown Toronto Raptors in 2023, where he has played some of the best basketball of his career. But similar to his father, RJ feels the most inspiring moments have come with the Canadian national team — a program he has remained committed to ever since he was a 17-year-old kid who lifted the team on his shoulders to bring home gold. "Competing for my country is one of the things that I always want to do," he says. "I feel like this is a way to give back. This is a way for us to show just how good Canada is, and also just to show how much we appreciate being [from] where we're from."

One day, RJ would like to follow in his father's footsteps and be "the captain of this team," he says. "Just like my dad was."

CHAPTER 14

HOMETOWN HEARTBREAK

JEREMY ZHENG

Dwight Powell, RJ Barrett, Trey Lyles, Andrew Wiggins, and Nickeil Alexander-Walker look towards the scoreboard during their matchup against the Czech Republic at the 2021 Olympic Qualifying Tournament.

"I wanted to see our best players compete. I wanted to see all of those NBA players come and play on a team so that we could actually fairly represent Canada as a basketball nation against the best in the world, instead of our second-string guys against everybody else's first-string guys."

— SCOTT LAKE

A couple years after Canada's boys won their first ever gold, the Toronto Raptors won its first NBA championship. A team constructed by a Nigerian named Masai Ujiri fielded the most international squad to ever win a championship, with players from seven different countries represented, including Montreal, Quebec's Chris Boucher.

When the final buzzer sounded inside Oakland's Oracle Arena on June 13, 2019, millions of people flooded the streets in downtown Toronto to celebrate the Raptors' win — something most long-suffering Raptors fans thought would never happen. It was a confidence booster for countless Canadian players like future NBA big man Zach Edey, who got in a car with friends and drove downtown to celebrate. "It made basketball seem like a lot less of a specifically American thing," he says. "It kind of [made me feel like] a thing that maybe Canadians can do too."

Hoping to build off the Raptors momentum and qualify for the 2020 Olympics, Rowan Barrett had a decision to make. Although he wasn't officially promoted to general manager of Canada's senior men's team until 2019, he had been doing the job that technically belonged to Nash since the mid-2010s. And after a long, drawn-out process, he made a coaching change, letting Triano go and hiring the rookie head coach of the championship Raptors to lead Canada into a new era.

"I think for us, if we are going to win medals, we owe it to our players to ensure that we have the best possible coaching staff available in the world," Barrett said. "I don't know of anyone today that believes Nick Nurse will not be a good coach for this job."

Born in Carroll, Iowa, in 1967, Nick Nurse was the youngest of nine kids, fighting for pancakes and orange juice each morning and growing competitive as a result. He developed into a standout athlete at Kuemper Catholic School, where he was the quarterback of the football team, a starting pitcher on the baseball team, and the starting point guard on the basketball team that won the state championship in his senior year.

Nurse walked onto the basketball team at the University of Northern Iowa, where he played for four years and set the school's all-time record for three-point percentage at 47. While he wasn't the biggest or most athletic player, Nurse was an effective communicator and knew how to make winning plays. "[He] couldn't run very fast, couldn't jump at all, but as soon as practice started, you could see he wasn't going to make a lot of mistakes," head coach Eldon Miller said. "He's a natural leader."

Nurse later went on to coach Grand View University, becoming the youngest college basketball head coach in the country at 23. He then coached nine seasons overseas in the British Basketball League (BBL), winning two BBL championship.

Ever since he used to watch VHS tapes of the 1990s Chicago Bulls, it was always Nurse's dream to coach in the NBA. And when no one was willing to give him a job despite his 276-103 coaching record overseas, he took it into his own hands to help Des Moines, Iowa, get an NBA G League expansion franchise, calling influential figures around the city before eventually landing the Iowa Energy in 2007. He became head coach and won the G League championships in 2011 with Iowa and again in 2013 with the Rio Grande Valley Vipers, becoming the first and only coach to lead two different teams to the G League titles.

Finally, in 2013, Nurse was hired as an assistant coach with the Toronto Raptors. The team's president, Ujiri, was a former professional player who knew Nurse from his time playing against him in the BBL, hiring the Iowa native to overhaul the Raptors offense by using innovative strategies to stay on top of new trends. "He thinks the game differently," Ujiri said.

But when Toronto failed to get past LeBron James's Cleveland Cavaliers — who eliminated the Raptors for the third straight time in the 2018 postseason — the Raptors let go of head coach Dwane Casey and hired Nurse to lead the team. After 29 years across 15 teams in five different countries, Nurse was finally an NBA head coach.

Nurse deployed a host of unorthodox tactics in his first season as an NBA head coach, making use of a versatile roster that had crucially swapped out DeMar DeRozan for superstar Kawhi Leonard in the off-season. He took it to another level in the postseason when he went with a double-big lineup against the Philadelphia 76ers and a box-and-one zone against Steph Curry and the Golden State Warriors, helping the Raptors win its first championship in 2019. "I thought if I ever got a chance to become a head coach, a lot of the things that I tried in some of those backwater places . . . I thought maybe would still work," Nurse said.

In the midst of his championship-winning season, Nurse heard of an opening at Canada Basketball and reached out to Barrett to tell him that he was interested in the job. Canada was having a hard time finding a coach who met its criteria of having NBA and FIBA experience after a deal with legendary Israeli coach David Blatt fell through once Blatt was diagnosed with multiple sclerosis. "I first called them to see if they were interested," Nurse says. When they were, he ran across the hall at the OVO Athletic Centre and told his bosses Ujiri and assistant general manager Bobby Webster about the opportunity. "And they green-lighted it without hesitation."

Shortly after the Raptors won the championship, Nurse was hired as the 17th head coach in program history — and the first American since 1998. Money, of course, was an issue until a generous donation from Canada Goose CEO Dani Reiss got the deal over the finish line.

Canada Basketball hadn't thought to reach out to Nurse because it felt unrealistic. But Nurse met all of its criteria given that he had FIBA experience working in the BBL and as an assistant coach of the Great Britain national team in 2012, when he went to the Olympics. Plus, his time working in the G League and BBL taught him how to put together teams on the fly with rapidly changing personnel and limited budgets, which would end up being crucial for Team Canada, who had a big tournament coming up.

After failing to secure a spot at the 2016 Olympics due to disappointing losses to Valenzuela and France, the 2019 FIBA World Cup in

China represented Canada's best chance to qualify for the 2020 Olympics. And with a record number of Canadian players in the NBA by 2019 and a championship-winning head coach, it appeared as if everything was finally coming together. "It was crazy because coming off the NBA championship, it was such a huge thing for the country," Phil Scrubb says. "And him coming to the national team, going into the World Cup, I think it was like . . . we're gonna do it this time: We're gonna get all the NBA guys to come and then we're going to make the Olympics."

Unfortunately, as is often the case with Canada Basketball, things wouldn't be so simple.

■

Of the 29 players originally listed on the training camp invite list for the 2019 World Cup, a record 17 were NBA players. But slowly, one by one — whether it was due to the six-week commitment or the significant travel schedule or injuries or contract issues —they dropped out.

The team ended up with just two NBA players on the final roster: team captain Cory Joseph and Montreal native Khem Birch.

The program likely asked for too long of a commitment, with associate head coach Gordon Herbert saying, "You can't be together that long." And they were far too optimistic about recruiting young players in particular, who were never likely to play while still on their rookie-scale NBA contracts without any long-term security. "Shai [Gilgeous-Alexander], a second-year guy, just traded to OKC; Nickeil [Alexander-Walker] is a rookie; R.J. Barrett in his first year," Mike George, the former CIA Bounce co-founder turned Canada's biggest basketball agent, said. "It [was] very unlikely they were playing.

"It really comes down to bad timing and our guys are stupid young."

Nurse took the job expecting to have all of Canada's best players. But he quickly learned that he couldn't force anyone to join the team. "I think it's either in your heart or it's not," he said.

Still, all the program could do was forge ahead with who they had. And after two practices and exhibitions games against Nigeria in Toronto, Canada flew to Australia for a series of exhibition games on the other side of the world. They went 4-3 in exhibition games with Pangos, Scrubb, and a 19-year-old Andrew Nembhard running point, as Joseph was busy attending to a personal matter before eventually joining the team in China the day before the tournament.

Due to a lack of chemistry with the new coaching staff and Joseph joining late; a lack of talent with most of the NBA players not participating; and a really strong international playing field that included being in the "group of death," alongside 6th-ranked Lithuania and 11th-ranked Australia, Canada's hopes of qualifying for the Olympics came to a crushing blow. In fact, the 23rd-ranked Canadians failed to get out of the group stage after losing to Lithuania and Australia by a combined 39 points in its first two games. Canada needed a top-seven finish to clinch a berth in the 2020 Tokyo Games, but finished 21st in the 32-team field. "Obviously when you come in here, we had our sights and goals and dreams on advancing out of this pool," Nurse said. "We knew it was going to be hard."

However, Canada beat Senegal 82–60 in its first qualification game behind a 24-point performance from Joseph. It was the Canadians' first World Cup victory in 17 years, after they failed to qualify in 2006 and 2014 and went winless in 2010. And, more importantly, it was enough to qualify for one of the last chance OQTs the following summer. "Obviously you always want to perform better. But really that is the most wins we've had in a quarter century at the World Cup," said Barrett.

"It looks like our goal of working to get to the Olympics is still very much there."

The next step, however, was trying to host the OQT.

•

Clint Hamilton is a basketball lifer from Armstrong, BC, who was recruited by Ken Shields to join U Vic towards the end of the dynasty. He went on to become the head coach of men's basketball at the University of New Brunswick and then the athletic director at U Vic for 17 years, where the Vikes won 16 national championships.

Hamilton reached out to Glen Grunwald in 2019, when the Franklin Park, Illinois, native was taking over as Canada Basketball CEO. Grunwald moved to Toronto to help launch the expansion Toronto

Raptors in 1994 as vice president of legal affairs and assistant general manager before being promoted to general manager in 1997, when he served on the board of Canada Basketball and met Hamilton.

During their conversation, Grunwald explained that the organization had no plans to pursue a bid to host the upcoming OQT — a travesty given the disadvantages that come with having to win a six-team tournament in a foreign environment in front of hostile fans and suspect referees. Canada Basketball still didn't have the funds to pull off a multi-million-dollar bid, and the government wasn't historically supportive of that sort of thing. But after meeting with a series of local influential individuals in the following weeks, Hamilton decided he might be able to raise the funds himself.

"On a spur I was kind of like holy crap," he says. "The opportunity for Canada, for basketball in our country to have a high profile event in Canada and then have that team win . . . and what that could do for the growth of basketball in our country — it just kind of hit me in a way that I said to Glen, 'Would you be open to a bid from Victoria if I could pull a rabbit out of a hat?'" Grunwald, of course, laughed.

After composing himself, however, Grunwald told Hamilton that of course Canada Basketball would look at a bid if they brought him a viable business plan, assuming that the offer was too good to be true. However, one thing led to another and Hamilton met with a fellow BC native named Scott Lake, who co-founded Shopify in 2006 and was intensely passionate about basketball ever since picking up the game in high school. He followed the Raptors run to the title and then saw Canada disappoint at the recent World Cup.

"I just remember feeling like, Why is that? What is so difficult about that?" Lake says about getting NBA players to commit. "And then just learning that that's like a six-week time commitment through the summer, you're living in China, you're going to some camp — it's not the greatest experience.

"And so that's when I was kind of like, What would we have to do to make it so that NBA players would actually want to come and play for Canada?"

Lake wrote a cheque for a little over $3 million to bid on hosting the tournament in Victoria, BC — the city that in many ways kicked off the

Canadian basketball revolution — showing FIBA that Canada was serious about hosting its first men's basketball tournament since 1994. And after winning the bid, the organizing committee went so far as to purchase the court from Oracle Arena, where the Raptors won their first championship a year before. The group paid $280,000 to bring it home and repaint it, hoping that it would be their lucky charm, similar to the Lucky Loonie that was secretly buried under the ice at the 2002 Winter Olympics in Salt Lake City, where Canada's men's hockey team won its first gold medal in 50 years.

"For the people in Oakland, it was just the floor that was taking up space that they were probably never going to use again," Lake said. "For us, it's the most important floor in Canadian basketball history."

The group wanted to ensure that Canada would have its best possible chance of winning the tournament and qualifying for the 2020 Olympics. By hosting the tournament and selling 27,000 tickets within the first two days of release, they figured Canadian NBA players would show up and play well, receiving thank-you messages from several players who were excited to be playing meaningful basketball at home for the first time since high school.

For a couple of small-town Canadian boys who are passionate about the country and the game of basketball, this tournament was their way of giving back. "It was really that profound love of the game and wanting to see the game grow in our country," Hamilton says.

Plus, after watching Canada fail to secure its best NBA players in tournament after international tournament, they wanted to see Canada's best players compete. "I wanted to see all of those NBA players come and play on a team so that we could actually fairly represent Canada as a basketball nation against the best in the world, instead of our second-string guys against everybody else's first-string guys," Lake says.

What they didn't know is that a few months after winning the bid in November 2019, the world would shut down due to the COVID-19 pandemic.

▪

When the World Health Organization declared COVID-19 to be a public health emergency of international concern on January 30, 2020, everything stopped. Basketball was the least of anyone's concerns until the NBA created a "bubble" in Orlando, Florida, six months later, providing people with a sense of normalcy and entertainment with the first live sporting event since the pandemic began.

However, the Tokyo Olympics were postponed until the summer of 2021, which had significant implications on Canada's OQT and the players who were ultimately available to play. After young stars like Shai Gilgeous-Alexander and Jamal Murray tweeted out their intentions to participate in the OQT following the disappointing 2019 World Cup, neither was able to play once the tournament was postponed, as Gilgeous-Alexander was entering the final year of his rookie-scale contract, while Murray was recovering from a torn ACL he suffered during the 2021 NBA playoffs.

However, the 21 athletes that did participate in training camp was easily the most talented turnout in the history of the national team. And the final 12-man roster featured a record eight NBA players including Joseph, Wiggins, Barrett, Alexander-Walker, Lu Dort, Dwight Powell, Trey Lyles, and Mychal Mulder. It was rounded out by experienced overseas pros Andrew Nicholson, Anthony Bennett, Trae Bell-Haynes, and Aaron Doornekamp.

The turnout was amazing considering what the players had to go through to compete, quarantining in their hotel rooms for the first 48 hours upon arrival in Orlando, Florida, for training camp — where they used the Raptors' temporary practice facility — before flying to Victoria and living in a bubble for several weeks. They underwent regular testing, used masks, and had to stay in their hotel rooms in between practices and games. "Man, that was terrible," RJ says about spending his 21st birthday locked inside a hotel room.

"Living in the bubble for the Olympic qualifier, you could feel that these guys cared," Hamilton says. "It was very demanding on them."

Because the COVID protocols were so strict, Canada had little time to prepare and build chemistry, once again throwing together an all-star team at the last minute. Only this time they had even fewer days to practise, getting together in Florida for three sessions — where some of the players hadn't even cleared COVID protocol in time to participate — before they had three more practices in Victoria.

"No. There's no way we were [prepared]," Nurse says. "We were just under so many COVID restrictions of how we could operate and move and everything was eating into prep time . . . Days were disappearing."

Instead of playing exhibition games like some of their competitors did, Canada had its main team scrimmage against a group of promising young players who were brought into camp, including highly touted NCAA players like Nembhard, Edey, and Bennedict Mathurin — the final cuts who helped Canada's junior team win bronze at the 2021 Under-19 World Cup in Latvia later that summer.

But the true test would come in the opening match against 66th-ranked Greece. After all, there was no getting off to a slow start in an OQT, where only the winner would move on to the Tokyo Olympics. And it was Greece who came out with a quick start against the Canadians, taking a 50–46 lead in the first half after shooting an 8-of-18 on three-pointers. In the second half, however, Canada started switching one-through-five, allowing starting centre Dwight Powell to prove that he could move his feet on the perimeter and keep up with Greece's quick guards, as Canada mucked up Greece's offense and held them to just 41 points and two made three-pointers in the half.

"We have length, guys that can guard one-through-five, and we switched it up in the second half," Alexander-Walker said. "It turned in our favour. Got us out of rotation a bit more. Cut out the threes and we were able to be ourselves."

Wiggins was the best player on the floor in his first game in the red and white since 2015, finishing with 23 points and 6 rebounds. He also had the two biggest buckets of the game, hitting a couple mid-range jump shots in the final two minutes to take Canada home, winning 97–91.

"We knew it was going to be a big learning experience and our first game together with this team against a very, very good team," Nurse said. "I thought we did well to hang in there for the first half."

The following game versus 29th-ranked China was much easier, as Canada ran away with a 109–79 win behind 20 points from Wiggins, 16 points from Barrett, and 12 points and 9 rebounds from Powell.

Through the first two games, it was obvious that Canada's identity lay on the defensive end, with plenty of switchable wings who could guard multiple positions and pressure the ball to force turnovers like Alexander-Walker, Dort, Barrett, and Wiggins. But it also became clear that Canada was small compared to its competition, and as a result, the team's most important player was arguably 6'10" big man Dwight Powell — the one traditional centre on the 12-man roster after Olynyk, Birch, and Thompson all dropped out of the tournament due to contract issues or injuries.

"He's had two really good games," Nurse said. "I think [what he brings is] just his energy and his effort in a lot of facets with his speed, rebounding, physicality, and communication.

"The anchor of our defense and the anchor of our rebounding."

Powell wasn't the flashiest player in the world, but he was always in the right position at the right time, using his footwork to break up lobs in the pick-and-roll, deter shots at the rim, and box out bigger opponents for rebounds. Plus, as one of the most experienced players on the team, after having represented Canada since 2015, he was a leader who constantly communicated with teammates and told them where to be. "I'm way more comfortable [beside him]," Dort says. "Sometimes when I get beat, I can trust him to go get it for me."

The interesting thing is that if the tournament had been held a year earlier as planned, Powell wouldn't have even been able to play because he was recovering from an Achilles tear in his right leg that he suffered in January of 2020. Joining Canada for the OQT was a motivating factor throughout his surgery and rehab process.

"For the Olympics to be pushed back a year, for me, athletically and physically," he said, "it's a massive opportunity."

•

Powell was born in Toronto in 1991 where his Jamaican mother, Jacqueline Weir, raised him.

He played every sport growing up, shifting from soccer to volleyball to cricket to track and field, where he specialized in high jump. Powell was on the 510 Spadina streetcar on his way to a high jump practice at the University of Toronto in grade 9 when he met someone who would change the trajectory of his life.

"I see this kid in front of me who looks great for basketball," Vlad Matevski, who was on his way to a men's league basketball game, said. "We both get off at U of T and I'm going to the second floor where the gym is and he continues up the stairs to third floor."

After two weeks of taking the same streetcar to U of T, Matevski finally asked Powell where he was going, and Powell explained that he had a high jump practice on the third floor. "I'm like, 'What do you mean high jump? There is zero chance you're training for high jump,'" Matevski says. "You should play basketball!"

As a teenager, Matevski immigrated to Canada from Macedonia, where he had been following in his father's footsteps as a pro basketball player since he was 16 but had to stop due to the war. He moved to Toronto with his wife and ended up playing for Toronto Metropolitan University (TMU) before transitioning to coaching the Toronto 5-0 — a club program for underprivileged kids sponsored by the Toronto Police Service — where Matevski transferred his player development knowledge from Macedonia to Toronto's youth.

Matevski gave his contact information to Powell to pass along to his mother, who eventually called him and agreed to send her son to a practice. "I ran him through drills. He almost collapsed," Matevski says. "I told him, 'Listen, you need to be playing basketball.'" At the time, Powell was already being recruited by American prep schools to play volleyball and track and field. But Matevski could see that with Powell's combination of size, footwork, balance, strength, and work ethic, "he's gonna have a bright future in basketball," Matevski said. "And he should make a decision now."

Powell had a crush on basketball from the first time he played with his friends in the park. "The feeling of coming together was — as cliché as it may sound — addicting," he says. But it wasn't until Matevski came along that Powell started to take basketball seriously, making it his top priority just as Matevski was starting the Real Basketball Training group. "I think first and foremost it was his love for the game but also his respect for the game," Powell says of Matevski. "He was a basketball purist, if you will. And his focus was always on the right skills for the right situation regardless of your perceived position or role."

Matevski's training philosophy is holistic, teaching players to learn every position and different skill sets so that they are versatile and understand the game. Powell would practise with Vlad's Toronto 5-0 OBA team and then work on individual skills afterwards. "We worked on everything under the sun, and I think that level of detail made the game so deep for me," Powell says. "It was so interesting because I realized how much better I could get and how much room there was to grow."

After meeting Ro Russell and joining the famous runs at Falstaff alongside Joseph, Thompson, Kabongo, Cadougan, and Ashaolu, Powell started playing against the city's best players and going on regular trips to the United States for AAU tournaments. "Even though he was not as far developed in his basketball career as us yet, he wanted it," Kabongo says. "And he kept coming to the gym, kept putting the work in . . . Every time you saw him, he was adding something else to his game."

Powell transferred to IMG Academy, a prep school in Bradenton, Florida, for grade 10. It wasn't an easy transition, as Powell was living alone for the first time and had to play catch-up to his American counterparts who had been playing basketball since they were kids. But his work ethic was undeniable.

Inspired by his mother, Jacqueline — who left Jamaica alone when she was nine, graduated from Eastern Commerce Collegiate, and went straight to work as a bank teller while going to night school so she could eventually move into the executive ranks — Powell worked harder than everybody else. "That's just how I was raised," Powell said. "My mom instilled in me at a very early age that you can dream big and there is nothing wrong with dreaming big. But once you have goals and you have these things in mind that you want, it's your responsibility to do everything in your power to achieve them."

After a few years at IMG, Powell turned down a scholarship to Harvard in favour of Stanford, where he committed to fulfilling a long-held promise to his mother that he would get a degree before leaving for the NBA. Unfortunately, ahead of his junior year at Stanford, Jacqueline passed away after a long battle with breast cancer.

"It was just me and her, [and her] biggest thing was making sure I had opportunities to be as successful as I wanted to be," Powell said, finding out that she was sick three days before she passed away. "So she kind of went through the whole struggle on her own and kind of kept it to herself."

The Stanford basketball team flew across the country to attend the funeral, and then Powell flew back to California to finish what they had started. He was named the Most Improved Player in the Pac-12 that season before averaging 14 points, 7 rebounds, and 3 assists as a senior. He was drafted 45th overall in 2014 and spent 11 years in Dallas, where he became the longest-tenured Maverick and made over $79 million in his career.

"Everything I do — even before, when she was alive — was to make her proud," Powell said. "Especially now I understand, I'm carrying a legacy for both of us, trying to make sure all the lessons she taught me I'm continuing and walking with her in mind."

Powell dreamed of being an Olympian since he was a kid and was further inspired by teammate and Mavericks icon Dirk Nowitzki — who raved about the Olympic Opening Ceremonies being unlike anything he experienced in his career. Powell got the chance to represent Canada at the 2015 FIBA Americas in Mexico City after his rookie NBA season, barely coming off the bench during their loss to Venezuela.

However, by the time the 2021 OQT rolled around, Powell was Canada's starting centre who, for better or worse, was needed on the floor at all times.

•

Canada topped Group A with a 2-0 record and a plus 36 point differential, resulting in a semifinal matchup against the 11th-ranked Czech Republic. At that point, 21st-ranked Canada was the heavy favourite to win the entire tournament, with a starting lineup of Joseph, Barrett, Wiggins, Lyles, and Powell, and reserves Alexander-Walker and Dort. Czech captain Tomas Satoransky said that Canada is "the second-best team in the world if you would just go by names."

But while Canada was an all-star team made up of eight NBA players, it lacked experience and continuity, with five players making their senior team debuts and only Joseph returning from its previous competition, the 2019 World Cup. "In my mind, we haven't done anything yet," Joseph said. "Yes, we have a talented group of players, but we've got to put it all together."

The Czechs, meanwhile, had nine returnees from the 2019 World Cup, where they finished sixth. Still, they began the tournament with an 87–70 loss to Turkey and followed it up with a come-from-behind 80–79 win over Uruguay, where Satoransky dropped 19 points, 7 rebounds, and 8 assists.

"This is a very experienced European team. Most of them have great size like this, experience, and shooting," Nurse said. "They've played with each other for a long time."

The Czechs started a bigger unit to create a size advantage against the smaller Canadians, inserting 6'6" shooter Blake Schilb and 7'0" Ondrej Balvin into the lineup alongside 7'0" Jan Vesely in the frontcourt, creating a 14-foot frontcourt and mismatch opportunities for the Czechs to attack. In fact, whenever the Czechs saw an opportunity to feed one of their big men in the post, they did so and played off that, usually either getting a layup, free throws, or kicking it out for an open three whenever the Canadians sent a double team.

Despite being allowed about 10 percent capacity (or about 800 fans) to attend the game at the Save-On-Foods arena in Victoria as the first live sporting event in Canada since the pandemic began, it was the Czechs that got off to a 15–6 start before Nurse called a quick timeout. The bench got Canada back in the game towards the end of the first quarter, when Dort forced turnovers on three straight possessions while Barrett and Alexander-Walker provided a scoring punch, finishing the quarter down 29–27.

But the Canadians struggled to contain the Czechs' massive frontcourt, getting out-rebounded 52–39 and blocked six times at the rim in the game. And despite keeping it close for most of the second quarter, they collapsed once Powell picked up his third foul with three minutes left in the half, leaving the game for the offensively-minded Nicholson as the Czechs hit back-to-back threes and ended the half up 52–44.

Canada got back in the game due to strong play from Dort, Alexander-Walker, and Barrett — who played a team-high 40 minutes and finished 23 points, 5 rebounds, 6 assists, a steal, a block, and zero turnovers, refusing to settle for jump shots as he drove to the basket time and again. Plus, the Canadians tightened up their defense with Powell back in the game in the second half, holding the Czechs to just 15 points in the third quarter as they sent fewer double teams to the post and executed their rotations better. "I thought we adjusted really well," Nurse said. "I think that we played the way we needed to play in the second half, but it took us kind of too long to try to adjust."

However, Canada shot just 9-for-37 from three, good for 24 percent. The Czechs, meanwhile, hit 46 percent of their threes, with Schilb out-shooting the Canadians by himself for most of the game, finishing with seven made-threes and a game-high 31 points. "In the second half I thought we had a lot of really good open looks," Nurse said. "And it just didn't bounce our way tonight."

It looked like Canada's hopes of qualifying for the Olympics were over when, with 3:09 left in the game and the Czechs up 83–77, Balvin posted up Powell and was fouled on the shot. After seeing that Balvin was bleeding, the referees went to the video monitor to review the play and determined that after Powell fouled him, Lyles came over to try to block the shot and his elbow made contact with Balvin's head on his way down. It appeared to be unintentional, but the refs called it an unsportsmanlike foul, giving the Czechs four free throws — two for the foul on Powell and two for the unsportsmanlike call on Lyles — and the ball. "There was nothing unnatural about it to me," Nurse said. "Just two guys playing hard and going for a rebound and people getting tangled up."

"It was something that was inadvertent," Barrett says. "I mean, those things are the difference in the game."

All hope appeared to be lost once the Czechs made three of the free throws and went up by nine with just 57 seconds left in regulation.

But that's when something amazing happened. First, coming out of the timeout, Dort hit a deep three. Then after Satoransky made two free throws with 40 seconds left, Barrett came right down the floor and hit a step-back three, 94–88. Then Alexander-Walker stole the inbounds pass and Wiggins drove into the lane for the and-one layup to make it 94–91 with 17 seconds left.

It looked like destiny had finally caught up with the Canadians when Alexander-Walker stole his second-consecutive inbounds pass and threw the ball to Wiggins, who sized up his defender and hit a deep pull-up three with a hand in his face. The Canadians had come to life just in time, sending the game to overtime as the crowd came to a crescendo, sounding much bigger than just 800 people. "I feel like we were in the zone that last minute," Wiggins says. "The way we were connected, the way we were playing."

The Canadians had all the momentum. Not only had they slowed down the Czechs on the defensive end, holding them to just three made field goals in the final 5:42 of regulation, but they also started to finally hit some perimeter shots and had the crowd on their side. The Czechs looked devastated, with Satoransky holding his head in disbelief as the regular time buzzer sounded. "For us it was a little bit of a bad dream the way we finished that game," Satoransky said.

In the opening possession of overtime, Trey Lyles took a charge and Barrett assisted Alexander-Walker on a three before driving to the basket to pick up an and-one, giving the Canadians a quick 99–94 lead with 2:20 remaining. But then history went on to repeat itself, as the Canadians couldn't contain the post or rebound the ball after Powell fouled out of the game late in regulation, with Wiggins getting called for a loose-ball foul on Patrik Auda under the basket, who hit both free throws. And then Alexander-Walker was called for a reach-in on Balvin in the post, who sunk two more free throws.

With the game tied 101–101 and 15 seconds remaining, Satoransky dribbled out the clock for one final possession. With Dort shadowing his every move, Satoransky spun towards the right elbow and soared up for a jump shot with a hand in his face. It looked off, but banked off the top of the backboard and fell through the net with 1.8 seconds left to give the Czechs an unlikely lead.

Nurse called a timeout and drew up a brilliant disguise play. With everyone expecting the ball to go to Wiggins, Nurse told Barrett to throw up a high-arching pass to Lyles as soon as the referee handed him the ball on the sideline, which caught everybody off guard. "I said, 'Just do it, RJ,'" Nurse says. "And he's like, 'No, I don't want to.' I said, 'Just do it, man!' and he made a great play."

RJ threw the ball right into the hands of Lyles, who flared out on the baseline on the far side of the basket and had a wide-open look from about 10 feet out as Alexander-Walker and Dort set screens for him. Lyles rose up and shot it, and the ball went in, spun around the basket, and then went out — with it Canada's hopes of qualifying for the 2021 Olympics.

"A little devastated," Lyles said. "I felt like I let the team down, let myself down. But it happens."

Back in the locker room, the mood was grim. "It was just silent," Herbert says. "Almost like someone had died."

"I was so mad," Barrett says. "I'm like, 'We're in Victoria, the tournament is in Canada, it's perfect.'"

"That was way worse than the Venezuela one," Wiggins says. "That hurt."

Joseph made a speech to the players in the locker room, telling them that even though it might not feel like it, things were trending in the right direction — that as long as the team stayed together and didn't let that loss define them, the future of the program would be bright.

"Yes, it's hurting at the moment, and it should hurt at the moment. But this isn't the end," Joseph says.

"This isn't the last chapter of the book."

CHAPTER 15

THE SUMMER CORE

ON POINT, SANJAY KHURANA

Team Canada superstar Shai Gilgeous-Alexander speaks to the media after committing to Canada's new three-year summer core.

"We gotta kind of flip the script just a little bit to understand this is a real program. This is first class. This is a privilege. This is an honour to play for your country and your national team."
— NICK NURSE

As soon as Canada lost to the Czech Republic, Nurse harped on the fact that it was due to their lack of experience playing together, arguing that chemistry and continuity were key to winning international basketball games. "I think if we can get a group of guys that stick together for some years, that always helps," he told reporters after the game.

Back in the hotel, Nurse sought out Barrett and Grunwald and sold them on an idea. "I just said, 'We've got to get these guys to commit to play together more, or else it just isn't worth doing,'" Nurse says. "'We just cannot continue on the way we've been doing this.'"

Ever since 2016, the Canadian organization had kowtowed to the demands of NBA players, allowing a group of big men to show up late to training camp in 2016, Joseph to miss the entire exhibition tournament ahead of the 2019 World Cup, and some guys to wait until the final days of training camp before finalizing the roster in 2021. It wasn't that any of those individual actions were made in bad faith. In fact, it was probably better to have NBA players show up late than not show up at all given the lack of Canadian talent playing overseas at that time. But the world was getting better at basketball, and gone were the days when you could throw together an all-star team at the last minute and win international tournaments.

Even the Americans learned a similar lesson at the 2002 World Championships, when an experienced Argentina squad led by Manu Ginobili and Luis Scola stunned the United States in the group stage before Peja Stojakovic and Yugoslavia eliminated them in the quarter-final.

Two years later, Argentina sent Team USA packing again in the semifinal of the 2004 Olympics, where they failed to win gold for the first time since 1988.

As a result, USA Basketball chairman Jerry Colangelo led a complete overhaul of the program, asking NBA players to commit three straight summers ahead of the 2008 Games. Led by LeBron James, Kobe Bryant, Chris Paul, and Carmelo Anthony, the "Redeem Team" helped USA return to the top of the international podium, winning gold in 2008 and four straight Olympic basketball titles since.

Spain adopted a similar model once Sergio Scariolo took over as head coach in 2009, bringing together a core group of committed players that returned year after year. They won the FIBA World Cup, four EuroBasket titles, and two Olympic medals during his tenure.

Scariolo understood the importance of creating a culture where the same players return every single summer, giving the veterans the responsibility to teach the young players the way things are done, transitioning from one generation to the next. "Without the help and the contribution of those veterans, who are able to explain to young players who might not understand from day one, why that discipline? Why that togetherness? Why that camaraderie? Why that staying together off the floor?" Scariolo says. "There's a lot of stuff which is basically legacy, which veteran players are translating to the new ones. And the new ones are then in a position where they can bring it to the newer ones. And this is something which we try not to break."

Basketball is like a second religion in countries like Spain, France, Italy, Lithuania, Serbia, Slovenia, Argentina, Brazil, and Australia, where if the national team comes calling, it's almost unheard of to turn it down. "If you start analyzing and being very objective and cerebral about it, maybe you should rest . . . But that's not the way it works," Marc Gasol said about playing for Spain after a long NBA season. "We're humans, and we're moved by emotions."

Canada, on the other hand, has a relatively limited basketball culture and history, especially when it comes to the national team, which became a transient space where players could come and go at will. In other words, it was seen as one of the many options NBA players could do during their summer break.

However, after finishing 21st in the 2019 World Cup and losing to an underdog Czech Republic team in the 2021 OQT on home soil — failing to qualify for five straight Olympics — Nurse and the Canadian team made a significant change to how things were going to operate moving forward. In August of 2021, Team Canada asked for a three-year commitment from NBA players in the summer months.

"Coming out of Victoria last year, we decided to make a systematic change to how we put our teams together," Barrett said. "We determined we need to have continuity and cohesion within our teams.

"We have talented teams; we have talented players. But we need them somehow to be together — the left hand needs to know what the right hand's doing."

The program flew out 17 of Canada's best players to Las Vegas during NBA Summer League, just a few weeks after losing to the Czechs, to pitch them on the idea. And after a big dinner in the private room of Carbone restaurant in the Aria Hotel, Barrett and Nurse spoke about the shift they wanted to see in the program's culture, and the need for a three-year buy-in from their NBA players. "It got really serious and was like, 'Listen, this can't continue like this,'" Nurse says. "We gotta kind of flip the script just a little bit to understand this is a real program. This is first class. This is a privilege; this is an honour to play for your country and your national team."

In the middle of Nurse's speech, Shai Gilgeous-Alexander — who had signed a five-year, $179-million max extension with the Oklahoma City Thunder mere days before the meeting, after establishing himself as one of the best young players in the league — politely interrupted Nurse and stood up. "Coach, before you go on, I just want to let everybody here know that I am 100 percent bought in," assistant coach Nathaniel Mitchell recalls Gilgeous-Alexander saying. "I know I haven't been here in the past. And I know there's a lot of rumblings about where I stand and where I want to be because of the contract and because of me getting an injury, but from here on out, all those things are situated. I'm gonna be a part of Canada Basketball, and I'm gonna be here committed, and I want to get to the Olympics."

Of course, players like Joseph, Olynyk, Powell, and RJ were likely going to commit regardless, just as they had at every opportunity. But it was a big deal to have the best player in the country stop the meeting to commit to the three-year core. "It really helped," incoming CEO Michael Bartlett says.

Nurse had a whole speech planned out, but after Gilgeous-Alexander affirmed such a strong commitment, there wasn't much else to say. Nurse simply laid out the dates of the different competition windows in the coming summers, and the players went on about establishing some ground rules that they wanted to hold each other accountable to, like no showing up late to camp and spending a minimum of three days at each camp if they were not able to compete due to injury or contract status.

Afterwards, Bartlett stepped up to send a message to the players that this wasn't going to be their grandfather's Canada Basketball. Following the work Wayne Parrish put in alongside Nash and Barrett to raise funds in the 2010s — work that was continued by preceding CEOs Michele O'Keefe and Glen Grunwald — Bartlett was taking over at the perfect time to take advantage of corporate Canada's growing interest in basketball.

Together with incoming chairman of the board Brian Cooper, they fundamentally changed the operating model of the organization to an event-based property with an annual Under-23 World Cup called GLOBL JAM played in Canada, which was modeled off Hockey Canada's World Junior Championships. Plus, they partnered with Canadian broadcast giant Rogers Sportsnet and several other Canadian brands that were historically hesitant to invest in basketball.

The organization would no longer be depending on unreliable government funding to support the national teams, boosting the operating budget of the men's team from $500,000 in 2012 to $1.7 million in 2017 to $4.4 million in 2024 despite not getting much more government funding than a decade ago.

Moving forward, Bartlett explained, this was going to be a five-star experience similar to the ones the players got in the NCAA and NBA, with fancy hotels, catered food, chartered flights with families welcome on board, and elite coaching and performance staff. "We're going to promise you brag-worthy experiences," Bartlett says. "We can't pay you, but we can give you memories that will be as good as currency back in your locker room, that you'll be able to say, 'Shit, I just had a great time with Canada Basketball.'"

Nearly all the players committed on the spot, and a few months later, a 14-player summer core was announced, highlighted by Gilgeous-Alexander, Alexander-Walker, Jamal Murray, RJ, Lu Dort, Zach Edey, Dillon Brooks, Joseph, Olynyk, and Powell.

The program had come a long way from allegations of racism and sleeping two to a college dorm less than two decades earlier, with 12 NBA players signing on for a three-year commitment. And while Nurse wouldn't last as head coach beyond 2022, the concept would end up paying dividends down the road. "When your best players are saying, 'I want to be counted here and I don't want to see people trampling on our flag,' that has to impact people," Barrett said. "When you see the players standing up one by one and saying, 'Look, maybe I wasn't here before but from now moving forward I'm going to be here,' it's huge."

On the other hand, for a group of overseas pros who never had a chance to play in the NBA, a fancy dinner in Las Vegas wasn't necessary to determine that the national team was always their first priority.

CHAPTER 16

THE WINTER CORE

LLOYD SCRUBB

Phil and Thomas Scrubb join each other in arms in the living room of their Richmond, BC, home.

"We were selfless enough to understand that was going to take commitment, and that was going to take time, and as much as that sucks that you might have two months less to rest and recover, the idea of standing on the podium and representing your country was worth that."

— MELVIN EJIM

FIBA changed its World Cup qualification method in 2017, creating a ripple effect that ended up advantaging countries with increasingly deep talent pools like Canada.

Whereas in the past teams would qualify for the World Cup by finishing towards the top of the biannual continental tournaments which, in Canada's case, meant the FIBA Americas, the new format sorted eligibility through six qualification windows of two games a piece that would occur throughout the two-year period leading up to each World Cup — itself a qualifier for the Olympics. The newly named AmeriCup, meanwhile, became solely about bragging rights and world rankings.

While the upside was that there were more home games for fans to attend throughout the year, it created the need for a significantly deeper pool of players in order to have competitive rosters in the winter months, when NBA and EuroLeague players are unavailable. Fortunately, by the time this went into effect in 2017 ahead of the 2019 World Cup, Canada was in a position to take advantage.

Gone were the days when Carl English was the only Canadian player in a top European league and where the Canadian basketball passport was one of the worst in the world. In fact, by the late 2010s, Canada's reputation as a basketball country had done a 180 as high-level overseas coaches were actively looking to recruit Canadian players thanks to trend-setters like English, Kabongo, Rock, Nicholson, Bennett, Juan Mendez,

Vidal Massiah, Andy Rautins, Jesse Young, Aaron Doornekamp, Brady Heslip, Devoe Joseph, Jevohn Shepherd, and Kyle Wiltjer.

As the first generation of Canadians who played at a high level overseas, they took their licks learning the European basketball infrastructure and adjusting to the stylistic differences of the FIBA game. "It was really foreign to the guys," Andy Rautins says. "I even struggled as a professional to get used to how they played."

The national team played an essential role in easing this transition for many players, beginning when Maurizio Gherardini started working with Canada Basketball in 2007. Gherardini saw that Canadian kids grew up watching the NCAA with its 30-second shot clock and the NBA with its isolation-based game, simultaneously developing habits in an American AAU system that often catered to one or two players dominating the ball instead of learning how to play a role in a movement-oriented system alongside other good players. He was adamant that Canada had to move away from the American developmental model and closer to the rest of the international basketball world if they wanted to catch up.

"They were trying to basically copy what was happening in the US but not really understanding that it's a different country, different systems, different resources — everything is different," Gherardini says.

Canada had only recently adopted FIBA rules in 2005 — a significant step to standardize rule sets across the country — with no defensive three second rule, 10-minute quarters, a maximum of 5 personal fouls, and a short, 24-second shot clock that forced players to develop creative ways to score. Gherardini helped recruit experienced tactical coaches Michael Malone, Kelvin Sampson, and Renato Pasquali to help internationalize the federation by teaching Canadian players and coaches the fundamentals of FIBA basketball, which tends to favour a more democratic style where the system creates the advantage rather than the player. "There's a lot of iso-ball, 35 second clock, you have plenty of time to dribble, dribble, dribble and try to make a play out of it," Andy says about North American basketball. "As opposed to the European guys, where the ball might touch the ground once in a half court possession, because it's being swung from side to side."

Pasquali would leave Italy every two months to travel to different Canadian cities and run clinics for coaches, teaching them international concepts like quick decision-making and reacting to defensive coverages instead of the old-school one-on-one drills that Canada's national coaching certificate previously taught.

"Basketball, yes, you have to be able to have those skills individually, but they have to play inside the system," Pasquali says. "One thing that we are trying to teach them is that pick-and-roll is an action that has to be played with five players, not with two."

Over time, Gherardini and Pasquali introduced countless Canadian players to FIBA concepts through Team Canada training camps, individual workouts, and even implementing it into the grassroots ecosystem through coaches clinics. They also helped players understand that while the NBA was for a tiny percentage of athletes, there were million-dollar contracts to be made in overseas, FIBA-sanctioned leagues.

As players developed in grassroots clubs and got FIBA knowledge through Canada Basketball, Canada's overseas complement began to fill out.

"I think we definitely expanded and improved the technical equation and the growth of basketball at every level," Gherardini says. "We all witnessed a very, very exciting process."

■

The only problem was that when Canadian players returned home in the summers, they had no place to train. "I'm going to Falstaff and trying to find different gyms," Rock remembers. "Reaching out to janitors."

In an effort to help their growing pool of athletes, Canada Basketball opened a national training centre out of Humber College the same year that FIBA changed its qualification format in 2017.

General manager Rowan Barrett wanted to give all of Canada's best athletes the opportunity to do everything under one roof, hiring player development guru Nathaniel Mitchell to run the basketball training and organize the schedule, as well as a strength and conditioning coach and a physical therapist to all work together. It created a more holistic system that was better for the athletes' development and also gave them more reason to trust Canada Basketball — which needed to grow the player pool for the crucial winter windows.

"I knew from my playing days, from the very beginning, if we're going to be able to compete, we're going to need to have more players," Barrett says. "It's given them a home base and it's also given them an understanding that Canada Basketball cares about me and my development."

It also became a training ground for the next generation of Canadian coaches, as Mitchell made it his mission to get as many up-and-coming coaches in the building and to give them opportunities to work with high-level athletes like Gilgeous-Alexander, Nembhard, and RJ. "Nate Mitchell has been instrumental for not only me, but a lot of other Canadians trying to grow in the basketball world," says Kareem Elliott, who got a job with the Raptors after the national training centre. "He just allows you to be in a lot of gyms with high level athletes, high level execs, and allows you to learn, to grow . . . but also learn from him and learn from like-minded individuals."

The program graduated a ton of Canadian coaches to do bigger and better things including Sheldon Cassimy, head coach of the Canadian Elite Basketball League (CEBL)'s Hamilton Honey Badgers; Joel Anthony, owner of the CEBL's Montreal Alliance; Matthew Gray, assistant coach for the Raptors 905; Ryan Schmidt, assistant coach of the Atlanta Hawks; Myck Kabongo, assistant coach with the Salt Lake City Stars; and Tobi Owotomo, athletic therapist for the Oklahoma City Thunder.

Mitchell played point guard at Oakwood Collegiate before becoming a coach, developing the skills of fellow Canadian athletes before getting a job with Team Canada in 2016. He always saw it as part of his responsibility to give back to the game by helping the next generation of Canadian coaches. "I'm about promoting growth," he says. "I wanted to bring in all those guys, kind of teach them how to do player development. Because I felt like it was going to make us stronger, to help as many athletes as possible."

■

Nobody has played more basketball for Team Canada over the past decade than Phil and Thomas Scrubb.

The brothers, who were born in Richmond, BC, in the early 1990s to former U Sports basketball players Lloyd and Diane Scrubb, followed in their parents' footsteps. They started playing basketball on a Fisher-Price net in their garage and outside on the driveway, where they would go two-on-two against their parents.

The Scrubbs were fortunate to be born a decade after Nash, when the basketball scene in BC was exploding due to the birth of the Vancouver Grizzlies in 1995. They played in a weekly Jr. Grizzlies Camp, the Steve Nash Youth League (which was started by the Grizzlies and funded by Nash), and a summer league run out of a community centre in Richmond before graduating to the provincial team and AAU tournaments in nearby Seattle.

"We were kind of playing all the time, and we met a bunch of people there who liked basketball," Phil says. "It was just kind of good timing where basketball for me and in Vancouver and Richmond, it was just everywhere."

After high school, Phil and Thomas were both recruited to Carleton University by head coach Dave Smart, who was beginning to build a dynasty in the Canadian capital of Ottawa, Ontario.

Smart played point guard for Nepean High School in Ottawa before suffering a leg injury ahead of his freshman year of college, when he started coaching the basketball team at Nepean. "I really liked it, and I didn't really want to go back to playing," Smart says. After about three years of coaching at the high school level, Smart co-founded the Ottawa Guardsmen — a club team built around a strong group of players from Nepean who needed extra practice outside of school, including Shawn Swords.

Smart eventually did return to play at Queen's University, in his hometown of Kingston, where he was a three-time Ontario university all-star and led the country in scoring, averaging 29 points per game in 1992–93. But he continued to coach, simultaneously working as an assistant coach on the Ontario provincial team and turning the Guardsmen into a summer AAU program that brought all the best players in the Ottawa region together.

Smart gained notoriety in the community and was recruited to be an assistant coach of Carleton University in 1997 at 30 years old. The program had struggled for most of its existence, suffering six straight losing seasons by then. In his first year as an assistant coach, four players quit the team. "Some guys just didn't want to work," Smart says. "That's not what they signed up for."

Carleton slowly improved after he took over as head coach in 1999. And by Smart's fourth year in charge, the Ravens won the first of five consecutive national championships. "The selfish talk, the selfish attitude, it just wasn't accepted," he said about his philosophy. "It's ironic because I was being selfish: I wanted to win, so I wanted them to be a team-first, hardworking group so we had the best chance to win."

Carleton's initial success was built on the strength of Smart's familial connections, as nephews Rob Smart, Mike Smart, and Aaron Doornekamp led the team alongside a group of players Smart had nurtured with the Guardsmen. By the time Phil and Thomas joined the fold in 2010, the Ravens had won national championships in six of the previous eight years. And it was a difficult adjustment for the BC natives to get used to the higher level of competition. "Once I got to Carleton, I realized that wasn't enough and I had to kind of change my approach to basketball after that," Thomas says.

"The culture there is very demanding," Phil says. "Your skills have to raise to the level of university sports . . . and at the same time, playing at such a high intensity with Carleton."

But that was also the selling point for the Scrubb brothers, who were told during the recruiting process that it was going to take a lot of hard work to play there, but that it could ultimately help them become pros. "What we tell recruits is 'If you don't want to work hard, don't come,'" Smart said. "If you don't like hard work, it's going to be a horrible situation."

Similar to Ken Shields's 1980s U Vic teams — the only other comparable dynasty in U Sports men's basketball history — Carleton was built through attention to detail and demanding practices, where Smart's philosophy was to turn everything into a competition. "You walk into our practice and guys are screaming at each other, guys are kicking balls if they lose," Smart says. "People are going, 'Oh, this isn't fun.' And it's like, What do you mean? For competitive people, this is the most fun in the world."

Smart believed in keeping score for every drill. Whether the guys were shooting before practice or playing one-on-one afterwards, the coaches would always keep score and raise the stakes so that guys were competing with 100 percent speed and intensity, giving them different incentives to win even the silliest of drills. "It was just the constant fight to win in everything," Doornekamp says. "And it was sort of ingrained into you by the older guys because when you got there, you're like, 'Wow, this is crazy.' But everyone's doing it. So it seemed like, 'I either gotta do it or I gotta get out.'"

"You literally figured out how to win," he says, noting that losers would do sprints or push-ups. "So when you're doing that in every practice, the games sort of become a lot easier."

The Ravens won five more consecutive championships behind the strong play of point guard Phil and big man Thomas, who developed a nasty two-man game after playing with each other since they were boys. The Ravens regularly blew out Canadian universities and even became the first Canadian university to beat a number of mid-major NCAA Division I colleges.

Phil compiled a 102-3 record in his four years at Carleton, winning U Sports Rookie of the Year and the U Sports Most Outstanding Player award three times. Thomas had the same record and won the U Sports Defensive Player of the year twice. They inspired the next generation of Canadian players to stay home before going pro. "Every player that goes pro from a U Sports school inspires the next," Phil says. "As long as people keep seeing that every year, then I think U Sports will keep having great players come out and represent it."

It culminated in arguably the best dynasty in U Sports history, with Smart leading the Ravens to 13 national championships and an overall record of 591–48, second only to Coach K at StFX. Carleton has won 17 of the last 22 titles, despite Smart leaving in 2019.

The Ravens also crucially forced their U Sports competition to catch up. As a matter of fact, by the middle of Smart's Carleton tenure, Rana was building a mighty program of his own at TMU in downtown Toronto, where he won two provincial championships while producing several players who went on to play for Canada and in the professional ranks. "I think it's essentially the genesis of where U Sports is today," the head coach of McMaster University, Patrick Tatham, says about Carleton. "It kind of made every other coach be like, 'I gotta get better.' Because you were getting dusted by 30, 40."

■

Both Smart and Rana also became key figures on the Canadian national team. Smart was an assistant coach under Rautins and Triano for most of the 2010s, while Rana built up the age group programs before being promoted to the interim head coach of the senior team from 2017 to 2019.

As the qualification format changed in 2017, Canada needed more players to be available during the winter months. And while NCAA schools weren't going to allow their players to leave in the middle of the season, U Sports schools had no problem doing it. "To get Canada Basketball to understand that U Sports players were actually pretty good and could handle themselves, that wasn't easy," Rana says. "There was a belief that those players wouldn't be good enough."

U Sports players like Phil and Thomas Scrubb, Aaron Best, Conor Morgan, and Kaza Kajami-Keane were identified by Canada Basketball thanks to Rana and Smart, working their way up the youth system to the senior team in time for qualification for the 2019 World Cup. Thirty-five different players helped Canada finish first in the Americas in qualification, with a 10-2 record and plus 282 point differential. The majority of them came out of U Sports schools like Carleton and TMU, including the Scrubb brothers, who played in 8 of Canada's 12 games during that qualification cycle.

"They're completely dedicated to the national team program and always have been," Triano says. "Anytime we ask them to do something, they're there."

Unfortunately, despite proving that players could have long, successful pro careers coming out of U Sports schools, there are significant barriers to the Canadian university basketball infrastructure that have stunted its growth in recent years. For starters, certain provincial bodies like the Ontario University Association (OUA) cap financial assistance at $5,000 per student each year, failing to compete with Division I schools that cover the full cost of tuition and board. Plus, Canadian schools tend not to invest much into their sports, creating lackluster fan environments and limited media exposure.

With the introduction of the NCAAs transfer portal and Name Image and Likeness (NIL) deals that enable student-athletes to make millions of dollars, Canadian players can now be plucked out of U Sports schools by NCAA teams at any stage in their careers without having to redshirt, making significant money when they do. While it's great for the players, the quality of U Sports basketball is suffering as a result.

▪

Following the 2021 OQT and the meeting in Vegas, a demand was made for an official three-year core of overseas players for the winter windows. They would play an important role in boosting Canada's world ranking and helping it qualify for the 2023 World Cup. With a compliment of Canadians playing in some of the best overseas leagues and the national training centre to come back to, 31 players suited up for Canada across its 12 qualification games between 2022 and 2023. Phil and Thomas were the only players to play all 12 games; Melvin Ejim played six, and Kassius Robertson, Kyle Alexander, and Trae Bell-Haynes were also important players.

It was physically and mentally gruelling to leave their pro clubs in Europe and to fly across the world to Canada, immediately go into training camp, play two games around the Americas, and then fly right back to their pro teams. But the commitment of winter core members like Phil, Thomas, and Ejim set the tone for what kind of sacrifices were needed in order to succeed. In fact, Thomas delayed his honeymoon upon getting invited to the 2019 World Cup, after all the NBA players dropped out, while Ejim watched his wife give birth to his son via Facetime at the same tournament.

The 6'7" wing grew up in Brampton to parents of Nigerian descent, playing soccer until his uncle, David Omoghan, took Ejim and his brothers under his care, not wanting them to fall into the same gang-related activity that he had. So, he instilled some structure into their lives, teaching them how to play basketball by bringing them to the local YMCA to play against adults.

"They kind of have a way there. They want to play where you got to help them out," Ejim says. "You got to understand the game and I think it really taught me a lot."

But it wasn't until he was introduced to the Malton Mavericks program run by Mike George that he started to take it seriously. "That really changed my life because that's when I got introduced to what real basketball was," Ejim said. "How to work in basketball, how to appreciate basketball, how to be part of a team."

In between his freshman and sophomore seasons at Iowa State, Ejim joined the Nigerian national team that had been recruiting him since he was a kid due to his family's roots. But he realized that the federation was lacking the funds to treat its athletes professionally. After being invited to play for Team Canada at the FISU Games the following summer and at the Pan Am Games and FIBA Americas in 2015, he saw that the Canadian organization was far ahead when it came to resources, coaching, and professional standards. He took advantage of the national training centre every summer, helping Canada qualify for the 2019 and 2023 World Cups.

"I got to see how that organization was run and the importance that they put on their players and the importance on developing," he says. "They were really invested in my success.

"And I think that I reciprocated that with my commitment."

Canada went 11-1 with a plus 351 point differential in qualification for the 2023 World Cup, finishing number one in the Americas after beating Team USA twice. Those wins helped the program climb up from 21st to 15th in the FIBA world rankings entering the tournament.

"You had a lot of guys who felt the importance of representing Canada, and really getting back to that world stage," Ejim says. "We were selfless enough to understand that was going to take commitment, and that was going to take time, and as much as that sucks that you might have two months less to rest and recover, the idea of standing on the podium and representing your country was worth that."

Meanwhile, the winter core also proved that great basketball players exist outside of the NBA — guys who went to Canadian schools and became great pros making good money in competitive leagues overseas. "I think sometimes we kind of lose track of how good of players our non-NBA guys are," Powell says. "We have some amazing Canadian-European pros that have contributed at every single level and every single competition and are why we are where we are right now. In a lot of situations, I lean on those guys."

And while only a select number of those players make the final roster for summer competitions like the World Cup and Olympics, the winter core deserves a lot of credit for helping turn around the national team.

"It's a whole country," RJ says. "Even the players that do the work getting us in position to even go to these tournaments — it's everybody. It's not just a small group of people."

CHAPTER 17

HISTORY IN THE MAKING

ASSOCIATED PRESS

Kelly Olynyk, RJ Barrett, Shai Gilgeous-Alexander, Zach Edey, Lu Dort, Nickeil Alexander-Walker, and Dillon Brooks pose with bronze medals after beating Team USA at the 2023 FIBA World Cup.

"It's about proving that Canadian players can compete at the highest level. I want to make an impact not just on the court but by helping elevate the national program. That's how legacies are built."

— SHAI GILGEOUS-ALEXANDER

When Nick Nurse signed an extension with Canada Basketball in August of 2021, it was assumed that the Iowa native would at least fulfill his contractual obligation until 2024. But following a disappointing season with the Toronto Raptors in 2022–23, when they finished ninth in the East and failed to reach the playoffs, the Raptors decided to part ways with their head coach after five seasons at the helm.

Nurse landed a new job as the head coach of the Philadelphia 76ers later that spring, pushing him to step down from his post as head coach of Canada. "I just knew how busy it was going to be," Nurse says.

"I probably could have demanded that I could do it," he adds. "But I just didn't feel like it was the right thing to do for me or for the Canadian team or for the Sixers."

In the end, Nurse was on the bench for 19 games with Team Canada, finishing with a 12-7 record. His insistence to demand a three-year commitment from NBA players was a massive step forward for an organization that had a history of short-term thinking, ultimately helping wrangle commitments from some of Canada's best players. "That was a big vision. And a vision takes a plan, and a plan takes a lot of work," Nurse says. "And to not be there to see the qualifying moment or be a part of it . . . that's hard."

As Nurse's time with the Raptors was beginning to wind down, general manager Rowan Barrett started to search for experienced FIBA coaches to join his staff and potentially succeed Nurse. And on June

27, 2023, Canada announced that Spanish international and Sacramento Kings associate head coach Jordi Fernandez would be taking over.

With just 59 days remaining before the 2023 FIBA World Cup, Fernandez had his work cut out for him. "It almost came out of nowhere," said Fernandez, who originally interviewed to be Nurse's assistant before the head coaching job opened up. "I told him it would be an honour for me to be able to be a head coach to a team like this.

"I felt like this could be like the opportunity of my life."

•

Fernandez was born in 1982 in Badalona, Catalonia — an autonomous region in northeastern Spain that is widely considered the European capital of basketball. "It's the number one sport over soccer," Fernandez says. "So that's why I fell in love with basketball."

When he was 13, Fernandez participated in a "fire run" — a frantic Catalan celebration that consists of a procession of people dressed as fire-breathing monsters and dragons led by horned devils emitting fireworks and chasing people in the streets. Spectators can choose either to run away from the creatures or challenge them. And Fernandez — always the thrill seeker — challenged a fire-breathing monster and burnt his right hand.

A few days later, during the final seconds of championship game of the Under-14 nationals as the point guard of Badalona's best club, Joventut, Fernandez drove to the basket and got fouled, giving him an opportunity to ice the game at the free-throw line. But after missing the first, Fernandez unraveled the bandage that was covering his burnt shooting hand, tossed it aside, and fought through the pain to sink the final free throw for the win.

"Everyone's competitive nature is different," Fernandez says. "For me, it's [about] sharing with everybody else, with my teammates, having a team that was connected . . . We have common goals as a group, and everything we do, we have some sort of identity which helps your competitiveness."

Fernandez played at Spain's highest level until he was 15, when he transitioned to coaching — a natural adjustment for the 6'1" point guard who always used his voice to organize people on the floor. When he was 19, Fernandez went to school for sports science, and as part of his degree, he spent semesters in Norway and the Netherlands. He had little money, didn't speak English, and worked at different bars and bounced around different hostels to get by.

"Once I went through that year, I felt like I could do anything," Fernandez said. "It was the growth of that experience, having to figure things out. You don't know how much you can learn until you push yourself to the limit."

After working with a number of youth clubs throughout Europe, Fernandez landed an internship at Joe Abunassar's Impact Basketball development program in Las Vegas in the summer of 2008. He paid his own way there and started from the ground up, rebounding for the athletes, cleaning the gym, and working with the younger campers. "I didn't do it because I wanted to work in the NBA," he says. "Everything was learning and excitement and growing and pushing to higher levels and learning things about player development that was not done in Europe."

One thing led to another and Fernandez landed a job as a player development coach for the Cleveland Cavaliers in 2009, leaving Spain for good and beginning the long, arduous task of climbing his way up the NBA coaching hierarchy. He worked with everyone from G Leaguers trying to make it into the NBA, like Danny Green, to NBA All-Stars, like Kyrie Irving, Shaquille O'Neal, and LeBron James, getting through to players because he knew what he was talking about, could communicate effectively, and, like many of them, had come from the ground up.

"The thing that makes Jordi the most special is the ability to connect," Mike Brown, who hired Fernandez in Cleveland, said. "His ability to build relationships is just unbelievable."

"He listens to you and what you have to say," Jamal Murray says. "It's not his way or the highway."

After surviving five head coaches and three general managers in Cleveland, Fernandez became head coach of the Canton Charge G League team before leaving to work as an assistant coach in Denver and Sacramento. He coached Canadian NBA players Murray and Trey Lyles, but the most attractive part of Fernandez's resumé for Canada Basketball was his experience coaching internationally in the summers.

Fernandez was indoctrinated in the Spanish basketball system, working with youth clubs in Spain before coaching the junior national team in 2013 and then working as an assistant coach on the senior men's team between 2017 and 2019, when they won the FIBA World Cup and climbed to number-one in the world rankings. "He's steeped in FIBA," Barrett said. "He understands this game very, very well. He's gonna understand the officiating, he's going to understand the other teams, the systems they've learned, he's going to understand those countries."

Working with the Spanish federation taught Fernandez how to build a sustainable winner by creating a culture where everybody sacrificed for the flag and the veterans passed down that understanding to the young players. Even during years when certain NBA players couldn't play due to injury or contract, they kept winning because "the rest of the group kept fighting, kept working," Fernandez says. "There was success, there was adversity, but they continue. They kept fighting, and that's what gives you a window of many years of success."

"They built the number-one program in the world because they cared about it," he added. "Were they talented? Yes, but the number-one thing was how they created a team."

■

The first thing Fernandez did upon getting the Canada job was call each of the summer and winter core players and introduce himself. And once 18 of the best Canadians got together on the court on August 1, 2023, for training camp in Toronto, Fernandez preached the need for the players to buy in to their roles so that they could achieve something that was bigger than any one individual.

"It's hard to take over a group of players who already know each other," Gilgeous-Alexander said. "He did a great job connecting with the guys and earning our trust."

It wasn't the first time Canada entered a tournament with several NBA players. But what was different in 2023 was the level of role definition and buy-in. "In '15 we had talent, but it took some time for guys to accept the role," former assistant coach Dave Smart says. "It is not easy:

You're in the NBA, and you're one of the first [Canadians] to be in the NBA . . . And then you come back in your national team, and you don't want to be coming off the bench when you're already sort of trumpeted as an NBA guy.

"So, I just think it goes in stages."

Canada had a clear style of play that emphasized speed and playing in transition, while getting paint touches and ball-reversals in the half court. They finished with the second-best offense in the 2023 World Cup, averaging 99 points on 50 percent shooting and 40 percent from three. And once Cory Joseph and Jamal Murray went home due to injuries at the end of camp, Canada had a clear hierarchy, too, with Gilgeous-Alexander at the top of the food chain, organizing the offense and taking the most shots; Barrett and Dillon Brooks on the wings, feasting on mismatches and in transition; Olynyk and Powell filling in the gaps and acting as leaders; and Alexander-Walker and Dort coming off the bench to wreak havoc on the defensive end. Phil Scrubb, Melvin Ejim, Zach Edey, Trae Bell-Haynes, and Kyle Alexander rounded out the roster.

"We all knew our roles, played our roles. And it was something that we didn't have in the past," Olynyk says. "Everybody knew what they had to do, did it to the best of their abilities, and trusted each other 110 percent that we would be on the same page and be out there competing for each other.

"I think that mutual connection and that mutual respect and trust was something that I don't think we've had in previous years."

It helped that this was a group of long-time friends, composed primarily of Toronto-area-raised hoopers that were born between 1996 and 2000. Most of them had played with or against each other growing up in the school system and the OBA. Plus, Alexander-Walker and Gilgeous-Alexander are first cousins, Phil and Thomas Scrubb are brothers, Brooks and Barrett grew up in Mississauga, while Olynyk, Powell, and Ejim had been playing together for Canada for nearly a decade.

"You know everyone that's in the building," Brooks said. "It's a family environment."

Following a week-long training camp in Toronto, the team hopped on a plane to Berlin, Germany, to begin a five-game exhibition schedule to get prepared for the World Cup. They played cards the entire flight, eventually downloading UNO on their phones and continuing to play whenever they were on busses to practices or hotels.

When they got to Grenada, Spain, for the rest of their exhibition games, Fernandez took them on a walking tour and handed out a list of local restaurants and dishes to try in the city, organizing team dinners where the players all sat together away from the coaches. "He wanted to keep the guys together," Phil says. "He wanted us to constantly be together as a team and a unit."

When the team got to their hotel, they started playing Ping-Pong, cards, and *Mario Kart* on a Nintendo Switch with a big projector in the games room, talking trash and getting into heated arguments "pretty much every time," Mitchell says. "I think when you bring high-level competitors, no matter what the game is, nobody wants to lose," noting that Alexander-Walker and Brooks were especially bad losers.

"A lot of times it got really heated, but that's kind of the name of the game. And I think that's also why that summer's team gelled so well, because those little conflicts kind of help build character and help you understand who you're with."

It was immediately clear how much that comradery translated to the court as Canada beat New Zealand and Germany to win the DBB Supercup exhibition tournament Hamburg before beating Spain in Grenada. "It helps a lot," Gilgeous-Alexander said. "There's a relationship. So in the game, if you yell at a guy, you know it's coming from a great spot. It's camaraderie at the end of the day and the greatest teams have that."

"Everybody has been talking about how talented we are, but that's not the definition of a team," Fernandez said. "These guys have approached every single day since August 1 to build a team."

■

Canada had several obstacles to overcome if it was going to come out of the World Cup with a medal or Olympic berth. Aside from having a brand-new head coach and a roster lacking international experience, Canada fell on the wrong side of the bracket due to its lackluster 15th world ranking.

Placed in Group H alongside France, Latvia, and Lebanon playing in Jakarta, Indonesia, they happened to fall on the same side of the bracket as powerhouses like Germany, Australia, Slovenia, and Spain — teams they would have to beat in order to make it to the knockout stage. On the weaker side of the bracket playing in Manila, Philippines, were the United States and the Dominican Republic, who each posed a threat to Canada's goal of finishing in the top two from the Americas teams in order to qualify outright for the 2024 Olympics.

Canada wouldn't have any time to ease into the tournament, either, with the opening contest being marked as the matchup of the group stage as Canada took on number-five-ranked France — a team that won silver at the 2021 Games and the 2022 EuroBasket and had not lost to Canada at the senior level since 1984.

Despite being without teenage phenom Victor Wembanyama, France was stocked full of NBA players such as Rudy Gobert, Nicolas Batum, and Evan Fournier, who helped them jump out to an 18–14 lead after one quarter, holding Gilgeous-Alexander scoreless after missing his first five shots.

Canada's only bright spot of the first quarter was Brooks, who set a tone with his defense and had a pair of huge dunks to get his teammates fired up early. And Canada started to turn things around in the second quarter after Gobert elbowed Olynyk in the face and was assessed an unsportsmanlike foul, forcing the French big man to take a seat on the bench. Canada went on a quick 10–3 run, with Alexander-Walker and Dort creating turnovers that enabled them to get out on the break, providing a spark for the Canadians, who went into the halftime break up 43–40.

What happened in the third quarter was only possible because for the first time since Steve Nash led them at the 2000 Olympics, Canada finally had a superstar. And by the time the 2023 World Cup began, 25-year-old Gilgeous-Alexander had established himself as one of the best players in the world, coming to life in the third quarter as he blew past his defenders, knocked down mid-range jumpers, and made all six shots he took in the quarter, outscoring the entire French team by himself 13–8. He finished the game with a game-high 27 points,

13 rebounds, and 6 assists. Canada's defense also ratcheted up its intensity and they outscored the French 52–25 in the second half and ran away with a 95–65 win.

"You guys can see here a guy that is gonna be the MVP of this World Cup," Fernandez said after the game.

"We'll see," Gilgeous-Alexander said. "It's not my main focus, obviously. The gold medal is my focus, but if that comes with it, I'll be happy; if it doesn't, I won't care."

It had been seven years since Gilgeous-Alexander was last with Team Canada in Asia playing a crucial game against France. Only in the 2016 Olympic Qualifying Tournament in Manila, he never got on the floor. "I was really young. I didn't play a minute in a game. I was pissed about it," he said. But he learned how to be a pro and was inspired to come back and represent his country nearly a decade later.

•

After landing at his dream school Kentucky for college, Gilgeous-Alexander was the lowest-ranked recruit in a seven-man class — a four-star prospect and the 43rd overall recruit in the class of 2017.

But when he entered Kentucky's starting lineup in January, after coming off the bench for the first 15 games of the season, the 6'6" point guard immediately became the team's best player, leading the Wildcats to an SEC tournament championship and MVP. "I've been the underdog in most of my career," Gilgeous-Alexander said. "So outcomes never came right away. I had no choice but to work hard and trust it and just kind of let it play out."

After the SEC tournament, Gilgeous-Alexander's NBA Draft stock shot up from the low 20s to the lottery, where he was selected 11th overall by the Charlotte Hornets in the 2018 NBA Draft before being traded to the Los Angeles Clippers. There, he earned the starting job 10 games into the season as a rookie on a 48-win team. However, after his rookie season, Gilgeous-Alexander was traded to the Oklahoma City Thunder in a deal that landed both Paul George and Kawhi Leonard on the Clippers — one that had massive ramifications for his hometown

Raptors. And while the Clippers clearly didn't believe in his talent, Gilgeous-Alexander looked at it as an opportunity to be the face of his own franchise. "I'd say it worked out in my favour," he said.

In his first season with the Thunder, Gilgeous-Alexander was able to pick the brains of veteran point guards Chris Paul and Dennis Schroder, doubling his scoring total to 19 points a game while helping lead the Thunder to a 44-28 record. But it wasn't enough to advance past the first round of the playoffs, and the Thunder traded away their veterans and went into a multi-year rebuild following the 2019–20 season. All the while, however, Gilgeous-Alexander continued to focus on improving as a player and a leader. And by the time the 2023 World Cup rolled around, he was coming off an impressive 2022–23 season where he averaged 31 points — the most ever by a Canadian — 5 rebounds, 6 assists, 2 steals, and a block on 51/35/90 shooting splits, finishing fifth in MVP voting. Only one other NBA player had averaged those stats for an entire season before. His name: Michael Jordan.

"I want to be one of the best point guards to ever play," Gilgeous-Alexander said. "I'm not playing this game just to be a good basketball player. I want to be one of the greatest to ever play."

Former Team Canada head coach Triano tells a story about when the team got on the bus one morning to go to practice in Manila and Gilgeous-Alexander wasn't there. So, in order to send the teenager a message about sleeping in, the bus left without him. Or so they thought. When they arrived at the gym, Triano learned that the young point guard had been waking up early each morning to get up shots with assistant coach Nathaniel Mitchell. One day, general manager Steve Nash even joined and practised balancing drills with the young point guard. "I had no idea the player he'd turn into," Nash said. "His work ethic and focus are outstanding, and he's proof that you never know what's possible unless you commit wholeheartedly with vision and go after it every day."

Gilgeous-Alexander and Mitchell formed a connection that lasts to this day, working together each summer, when Mitchell will meet Gilgeous-Alexander and a SUV full of his closest childhood friends in Hamilton-area gyms six times a week. Mitchell will put him through dynamic drills while his friends defend him. Then they will go to local weight trainer Nem Ilic's converted two-car garage to weight train in what has appropriately been dubbed "Shai Camp."

"It's like I'm addicted to the feeling of getting better," Gilgeous-Alexander said, working just as hard today as he did when he was an unknown high school prospect in Hamilton trying to get to the NCAA.

"I like failing. I like being bad at something, or not being where I want to be, and getting worse at it, to then get better at it," he added. "I like breaking things down. And then going crazy on it."

FIBA became a big part of that addiction for Gilgeous-Alexander, as the slower pace, increased physicality, and lack of defensive three-in-the-key rule presented a new challenge for the basketball monk — one he wouldn't otherwise get in the summer months. And after being overlooked his entire career, Gilgeous-Alexander felt a responsibility to not only prove himself worthy of being on basketball's biggest stage, but to help prove that all of Canada belonged there too.

"Being part of Team Canada is such a big honour for me, and I take it seriously," Gilgeous-Alexander says. "It's not just about what I accomplish personally — it's about helping grow the program and inspiring the next generation of Canadian players.

"It's about proving that Canadian players can compete at the highest level. I want to make an impact not just on the court but by helping elevate the national program. That's how legacies are built."

■

Canada followed up its dominant win over France with a 128–73 dismantling of Lebanon and a 101–75 win over Latvia, finishing with a 3–0 record at the top of its group for the first time ever at a World Cup, while leading the entire tournament in point differential at plus-111.

The team's early success set them up for a second-round matchup against the 13th-ranked nation, Brazil. Not only would a win catapult Canada over Brazil, a fellow Americas team, in the seeding, but it would also guarantee them a spot in the knockout stage. However, despite having zero NBA players, Brazil dictated the style of play from opening tipoff, setting the tone with a high level of physicality and by dominating the rebounding battle, winning the opening quarter 16–13. The underdog Brazilians knew they had to get creative to beat Canada, so they walked the ball up the floor, didn't turn it over, and only shot when the shot clock was winding down, holding Canada to just nine fast-break points — by far a tournament low.

Still, Canada led late in the third quarter until the Brazilians found another gear against Canada's lackluster bench and scored 13 straight points to take a 53–52 lead. And after the starters re-entered the game and Gilgeous-Alexander hit a tough jumper to retake the lead, Canada started playing tight, over-dribbling, and not trusting the pass, with guys standing around as Gilgeous-Alexander went one-on-one. They finished with just 65 points on 33/27/88 shooting splits along with 10 assists and 9 turnovers.

"Offensively, we were not willing to do anything for each other: space the floor, move the ball, move bodies," Fernandez said. "And when you play like that, it's really hard to win.

"I thought we played the right way throughout the tournament and today we didn't."

After Powell fouled out late in the fourth quarter, Canada went small to close out the game and were hurt for not having a big man on the floor. Brazil's 5'10" point guard Yago Santos sped past world-class defenders Brooks and Dort, getting into the unguarded paint for back-to-back layups in the final minute to give Brazil a 69–65 win.

"Shai has to score, defend, and play-make, and he didn't. And I can go down the line," Fernandez told the media after the game. "Kelly has to play-make, rebound, and score efficiently — he didn't.

"We own it, we'll watch it, we'll learn from it, and we're gonna come really, really, really aggressive and ready to fight the next game. That's how life is."

It was human nature for Canada to take its foot off the gas against a lower-ranked Brazil team, but the loss raised the stakes for Canada's final group stage game against Spain a couple days later: win and you're in the Olympics for the first time since 2000. Lose and you go home without an Olympic spot. "I think we all embraced it," Mitchell says. "That just turned this game into must win and we're in. And so it raised the stakes."

All Canada had to do was beat Spain: the top program in the world and the reigning world champions and European champions, who had not lost to Canada since 1974. But after decades of heartbreaks and disappointments, Canada finally understood how to approach an opportunity of this magnitude. And they had a newfound level of calm and confidence stemming from their continuity, star power, and past experiences.

"I felt more confident in the confidence of our group," Powell says. "I think we had such a clear image in our head of past failures and didn't take them as things to be sad about or to lament over, but rather motivations and lessons.

"We were able to lock in when it was time to lock in, and that was a really cool feeling."

•

Canada versus Spain did not lack for storylines: it was NBA talent versus international experience, Jordi Fernandez versus his former team and boss, and the up-and-coming 15th-ranked Canadians versus the long-established number-one program in the world.

"You do this job for games like this," Fernandez said. "And that's the fun part."

Unsurprisingly given the stakes, both teams opened the game with a do-or-die intensity: picking up their opponents at half court, pressuring the ball, embracing contact on both ends, diving on the floor for loose balls, and executing at a high level.

After becoming spectators to Shai's one-on-one greatness for parts of the Brazil game, Canada's game plan was to let Brooks and Barrett take advantage of mismatch opportunities early. And when Brooks got the small 19-year-old Spanish point guard Juan Nunez on him in the post on the first possession of the game, he put him under the basket and scored the floater and the harm.

But Canada fell into an early 18–12 hole after some foul trouble helped Spain get into the bonus early, with Brooks having to sit on the bench with two fouls. Canada responded with a 9-0 run of its own as Barrett was relentless attacking the rim, scoring 11 of Canada's 21 total points in the opening quarter.

The Spaniards won the physicality battle in the second quarter, outmuscling the Canadians for loose balls and offensive rebounds while Canada got into deeper foul trouble, as Brooks and Barrett both picked up their third fouls and had to sit — several of them questionable calls that all seemed to be going Spain's way. So, down 36–33 with 3:11 left in the first half, Fernandez called a timeout. "Forget about the refs. We are getting fucked. And it's okay," he said.

"Let me do the bitching, and I'm gonna stop. But if we believe and we stay with it, we'll be okay."

However, the half ended about as poorly as it could have for Canada. Despite Gilgeous-Alexander and Barrett combining to score 24 of Canada's 38 first-half points, Canada couldn't defend the paint or come up with rebounds, as Spanish big man Willie Hernangomez scored 18 points in the first half alone. Meanwhile, veteran wing Alex Abrines made three key three-pointers to give Spain a 48–38 lead going into the break.

Still, as Fernandez waited for his team to go into the locker room, he remained calm and optimistic. "Our hope was that at some point the favourite team would choke and have the bad feeling of not being able to close the game," Scariolo said. "But every time I watched their bench . . . he was in full focus and control. He was not giving any sign of pressure — that was bad feedback for me."

To start the second half, Canada made an adjustment by starting Lu Dort in place of team captain Kelly Olynyk, sliding Brooks up to play the power forward while Dort defended Spain's shifty ball-handlers. And he immediately made an impact by taking a charge on a Spanish player before the ball was even inbounded to give Canada the first possession of the half.

Born in Montreal North to parents of Haitian descent, Dort played for the Adidas-sponsored Brookwood Elite AAU program before bouncing around various prep schools and landing a scholarship at Arizona State. He looked up to Raptors star DeRozan growing up and was a scorer in high school and college, using his 6'4", 220-pound frame to bully his way to the basket. But after going undrafted in 2019, Dort realized that defense would be his calling card in the NBA. He signed a two-way contract with the Thunder before eventually turning himself into one of the best three-and-D players in the world, singing a five-year, $83-million contract in 2022.

"We did think he was the X factor," Mitchell says. "We just wanted him to be a dog — defend guys, lock guys up, make catch-and-shoot threes. I think he did that at a high level, and it gave us the flexibility if we wanted to start small."

With Dort in the starting lineup, Canada began to switch almost every ball screen and took the Spaniards out of their beautiful ball-movement-oriented offense. In fact, while Spain came into the game averaging a tournament-leading 203 passes per game (compared to 137.5 for Canada), the switching slowed them down and enabled Canada to surge out of the half with a 17–4 run to tie the game at 52 within the first five minutes of the third quarter.

Finally, the tables had turned, and the basketball Gods seemed to be on Canada's side in the referee department, too, as Spain picked up six fouls within the first three minutes of the second half. Scariolo added to the problems as he picked up a technical foul, asking the referees if somebody called them at halftime to change how they officiated the game. "Why are you going after us?" he asked, as Fernandez smirked from the opposite bench.

The game continued to go back and forth, with the two sides putting their bodies on the line and playing with pride that only representing your nation can inspire. Spain retook the lead after Dort picked up his fourth foul and had to sit, allowing Spanish captain Rudy Fernández to get loose and knock down a three. But Olynyk came off the bench and hit back-to-back threes of his own to give Canada the lead. "I think just having all that experience, knowing that it's nothing personal," Olynyk says about his mindset coming off the bench. "Your number's still gonna be called; you got to be ready."

Memphis Grizzlies forward Santi Aldama started to get going in the second half, hitting back-to-back threes before finishing a massive dunk in transition. He led a Spanish bench that outscored Canada's reserves 38–8 in the contest, highlighted by an 11–0 run to close the third quarter up 73–61.

But Canada wasn't going home without a fight. Despite being down 12 to open the fourth, Brooks hit a pull-up three with a defender in his face to begin the quarter. The next possession down, Gilgeous-Alexander was fouled on a three-point attempt of his own, going to the line for three free throws. Then Brooks hit another three before driving down the lane and scoring a layup, cutting the lead to 78–71.

After Gilgeous-Alexander found his cousin Alexander-Walker for a corner three-pointer that made it 78–74 with 3:30 left in the game, nobody could score for the next few possessions as Canada turned it over twice and Spain's heavily contested looks went in and out. And in the final two minutes, it was time for Gilgeous-Alexander to take over.

First, Canada's point guard gallivanted his way into the lane, using a nasty right-to-left crossover to get his defender off-balance before getting all the way to the rim, where several Spanish defenders converged on him. He scored the layup and the free throw after Hernangomez fouled him, bringing Canada within one with less than two minutes left.

After that shot, Hernangomez was fouled by Barrett following an offensive rebound, making two pressure-packed free throws to go up 80–77 with 1:20 left. But Gilgeous-Alexander came down the floor, saw Spain's defenders converge on him again, and passed the ball to Brooks for a deep three to tie it at 80, with Brooks skipping back down the court.

Canada's defense reached a different level in the deciding minutes, holding Spain to just 12 points in the final quarter as special players took turns making special plays — instantaneous reads that won't show up in the box score but are a result of good coaching and countless hours of playing and studying film.

After making the biggest three of his career, Brooks saw that Alexander-Walker got tripped on a high-ball screen, hitting the deck around centre court. And instead of staying with his man, Aldama, who passed the ball, Brooks sprinted to the open basket to cover rolling big man Usman Garuba. He then left him to help on Abrines, who caught the ball in the corner and drove past Gilgeous-Alexander towards the rim. But Brooks was there first, forcing Abrines to step out of bounds on the baseline.

He finished with 22 points and the biggest defensive stop of the game. "He was big time," Gilgeous-Alexander said. "I would say he played the best basketball in the tournament in the last quarter, and he came up when we needed him most.

"That's what big time players do, that's what leaders do."

Despite not taking a timeout, the Canadians knew what they wanted to do following the turnover. With the game still tied at 80, Gilgeous-Alexander dribbled the ball up the court before Brooks came to set a hard screen for him, making Spain switch its best defender, Alberto Diaz, off of him while Brooks's defender, Victor Claver, moved on to Gilgeous-Alexander. "With all the switching and all the hitting that they were doing to get the ball out of [Gilgeous-Alexander's] hands, that simple play, it just put a guy that I felt was more favourable for him," Fernandez says.

"He got the matchup he wanted, and he was in rhythm. And obviously it was a simple shot, a simple play for him."

With 43 seconds left in the game, Gilgeous-Alexander sized up Claver at the top of the arc with the floor spaced around him, crossed over from his left to his right hand while pushing his left shoulder into Claver's chest to create space. Claver fell deep into the paint as Gilgeous-Alexander stepped back and swished a wide-open two-pointer. It was instantly one of the biggest shots in Canadian basketball history, giving Canada an 82–80 lead that they would not surrender after Gilgeous-Alexander added six straight free throws to win the game 88–85.

The win sent Canada through to the knockout stage and, more importantly, its first Olympics in 24 years.

"There was a lot of adversity," Gilgeous-Alexander said. "But I think our group just wanted it a little bit more. We knew what was at stake and we were willing to do whatever it took. And we ended up getting it done."

The deciding shot was one Gilgeous-Alexander has made thousands of times in his career, and it perfectly encapsulates how his game is predicated on balance. Like a ballet dancer, he is always at a balance advantage over his defender, even when he dances with the ball and makes contact with his shoulder or arm, knocking defenders back and, crucially, making them lose their balance while he is strong enough to maintain his own, rise up perfectly straight, and swish a jumper.

"Even at this incredible level, you still see great players who don't have the type of brakes or balance that Shai does," Nash said. "And for someone with his frame, his skill level and feel, to be able to add the different gears, the brakes, the balance, and that dexterity, it just opens up a world for him."

"I think my advantage comes from not knowing what I'm going to do," Gilgeous-Alexander said. "Unorthodox. Offbeat. Slithery. Being unpredictable and doing things that are not seen a lot."

For the third time in five games, Gilgeous-Alexander outscored the entire opposing team in a quarter, doing it against France, Latvia, and in the deciding fourth quarter against Spain, 13–12. He finished the game with 30 points, 4 rebounds, 7 assists, and 3 steals.

"He was amazing," Brooks said. "He was composed all game. They were throwing everything at him: from box-and-one to double teams. He was patient in getting his buckets and finding guys with assists."

"Shai, he just did MVP things at the end to will us to the finish line," Olynyk says.

When the final buzzer sounded, Gilgeous-Alexander embraced his cousin, Alexander-Walker, before his AAU teammate, Barrett, ran up and celebrated with them. "Getting to do it with family and having the opportunity to do something that Canada has never done . . . it's huge," Alexander-Walker says. "Not many families can say that they've done it together."

Meanwhile, long-time veterans like Olynyk, Ejim, Kyle Alexander, and Phil Scrubb could barely watch the end of the game from the bench, covering their eyes with their shirts and towels. But they all shared a big hug as the final buzzer sounded before taking to the court to celebrate with the support staff, who had been there as long as anyone. "That released a lot of pent-up emotion," Olynyk says. "It was one of those moments where you're just so elated, so ecstatic and blissfully happy and not just for yourself, but for everybody who's been through the ringer and been through everything in the past 23 years."

"It had just been such a long, long journey," Phil says. "And it was like the tournament wasn't done, but it felt like we had really accomplished something."

Mitchell, meanwhile, stayed on the bench when the buzzer sounded, taking a few minutes to collect himself while everyone celebrated around him. He was having trouble believing that it was real — that they finally did it. Eventually, he got up and hugged a few of the players before seeing Gilgeous-Alexander making his way off the court. "And Shai was not even smiling, jumping around," Mitchell says. "He's just like, 'I want to win this.'"

As Gilgeous-Alexander filtered through the media zone on his way to the locker room, he couldn't help but smile. "We are a part of history," he said. "It's something that is almost indescribable." But before heading to the locker room, he made his feelings very clear. "We wanted to go to the Olympics and we wanted to get gold in this tournament," Gilgeous-Alexander said.

"Half of our job's done."

CHAPTER 18

DILLON THE VILLAIN

DIANE BROOKS

A young Dillon Brooks surrounded by basketballs inside his Mississauga home.

"I've just got to keep playing with emotion and live or die by it."
— DILLON BROOKS

Canada flew from Jakarta to Manila, Philippines, for the knockout stage of the World Cup, starting with a quarter-final matchup against seventh-ranked Slovenia.

The plan was to slow down Slovenia's lone NBA player, Luka Doncic, at all costs, giving Dillon Brooks the primary responsibility of guarding him and wearing him down as the game went on. Doncic had a strong first half as he targeted Canada's weaker defenders on switches and finished with 17 points on 5-of-12 shooting, double the amount of shots any other Slovenian took. Slovenia also made 10-of-17 threes in the half, going into the break tied at 50.

Canada never had trouble scoring on the older and slower Slovenian team and, in the second half, it ratcheted up its defense and started forcing turnovers to propel the offense, winning the third quarter 30–21 and forcing 10 turnovers for 23 fast-break points in the game. "We gave them too many opportunities to score from the fast break and this is where they made this advantage," Slovenian head coach Aleksander Sekulić said. "We knew that they're a very dangerous team in this — they have the ability, they have the athleticism, and this is where they made this advantage."

RJ had 24 points and 9 rebounds while Gilgeous-Alexander finished with 31 points in addition to pulling down 10 rebounds, 4 assists, and 2 steals. He became the first Canadian with back-to-back 30-point games in a World Cup.

But it was Brooks who helped turn the game after scoring 14 points on 5-of-7 shooting and slowing down Doncic. Known for getting under the skin of his opponents and occasionally going over the line with some of his antics, Brooks did everything possible to make life difficult for

Doncic. And while he has struggled with that balance for much of his career — getting into trouble for going overboard and paying for it with technical fouls and suspensions — he toed the line perfectly against Slovenia, being physical enough to frustrate Doncic while staying out of foul trouble, holding Doncic to just 9 points on 3-of-8 shooting in the second half. In fact, Doncic got so frustrated that he was ejected after picking up two unsportsmanlike fouls late in the fourth quarter, gesturing to FIBA officials sitting courtside that the game was rigged. "I think Dillon played great," Doncic said. "He was very physical, like he always does. A lot of people don't like him, but I respect him for what he does."

Canada ran away with the 100–89 win, moving on to the semifinals of the World Cup for the first time in program history, where they matched up with Serbia — a storied program that was ranked sixth in the world after finishing as runners-up of the 2014 World Cup, 2016 Olympics, and 2017 EuroBasket. And despite missing key players like reigning NBA MVP Nikola Jokic, Serbia was one of the most talented and experienced teams at the tournament, with several NBA and EuroLeague players and an illustrious history that includes two World Cup titles, three EuroBasket titles, and two silver medals at the Olympic Games.

Canada was at a rest disadvantage after flying in from Jakarta and having one day off before the game, while Serbia stayed in Manila and had two days to recover. It showed early as the Serbians took a 23–15 lead into the second quarter, as Serbia had Canada scrambling on defense with rapid ball movement and perfect half-court execution. And they exploited Canada's lack of depth, outscoring a bench-led unit by 10 in the first half, when the Canadians found themselves down 52–39.

Canada stayed in it with a strong performance from RJ, who had 23 points on 8-of-14 shooting. But nobody else managed to step up after Serbian guards Stefan Jovic and Dejan Davidovic took Gilgeous-Alexander out of the game, holding him to just 15 points on 4-of-8 shooting along with 9 assists.

Serbia forced the other Canadians to make decisions with the ball in their hands and they struggled, highlighting the lack of trustworthy ball-handlers on the team. Alexander-Walker, RJ, Olynyk, and Brooks all turned the ball over at least twice, allowing Serbia to take advantage and score 18 points off turnovers. "We demonstrated one more time that we can play defense, that we can play transition offense," Serbian head coach Svetislav Pesic said. "The very important point in preparing the game was to take away points from transition."

Serbian captain Bogdan Bogdanovic caught fire in the second half, finishing with 23 points, 4 rebounds, 3 assists, and 3 steals. And it was a well-rounded attack from Serbia, who had all 10 players contribute, playing a nearly perfect game for the entire 40 minutes as they shot 62 percent from the field and 45 percent from three while winning nearly every major statistical category in what ended up being a lopsided 95–86 victory. "Credit to Serbia. They played a great game," RJ said. "They played hard, they played physical, they're very well coached and disciplined."

The win highlighted the contrasting basketball styles and cultures of the experienced Serbians versus the more talented Canadians, who were still getting used to the increased physicality and different rules of FIBA basketball. That fact was highlighted earlier in the competition when Gilgeous-Alexander was walking back to the court after a late-game timeout against Spain, and he asked his coaches, "Yo, do we have any timeouts or no?" Everybody looked confused until Fernandez realized the mistake, telling Gilgeous-Alexander that it didn't matter because players cannot call timeouts in FIBA.

"The team didn't have experience," Fernandez said. "When we say that we were one of the favourites, that's just the opinion of some people, the media. That was not realistic. We had a very young group of players who had never played together or in a World Cup.

"Playing at the FIBA level was very challenging against teams that know each other."

Canada had almost zero fans travel to Manila, with most failing to realize the importance of the tournament until it was too late to show up and support the team in person. Serbia, on the other hand, had thousands of supporters fly east to cheer on their team. After all, basketball is the national sport of Serbia; it played a major role in the rebuilding of the country following the war that broke up Yugoslavia. "We never give up. We fight till the end. It's in our blood," veteran Marko Guduric said. "We are proud of our country and we represent our families, our people. And you see the crowd that we have here and I cannot imagine how it is now in Serbia." Until Canada develops a similar culture around basketball, it will be impossible to reach our ceiling.

Despite the loss, Canada was excited for the bronze medal game against continental rivals Team USA, who lost to Team Germany in the semifinals despite being the only team with 12 NBA players.

▪

Sports psychologist Peter Jensen had worked with Canadian athletes for decades, including a stint with Hockey Canada at the World Junior Championships in 2014. The Canadians were eliminated in the semifinal and went out drinking after the game, not taking the bronze medal game seriously since Hockey Canada's mandate was always gold medal or bust. They lost the next day to Russia and finished fourth, regretting the decision to not take the game more seriously, with one player later telling Jensen, "You know what I wouldn't give now for a bronze medal?"

Before the game against Team USA, Jensen shared that message to the Canadian players. "You don't want to have that regret," he says. "Is it hard to get up when you were planning on playing for the gold at the World Championship? Yes, it is hard, and you will get over that. You will get over having to get up and play hard in this game. But you will never get over the regret."

Despite coming into the game with a 0–12 record versus Team USA at senior international competitions, the labels that had been given to prior generations of Canadians no longer held any weight; this group of Canadian athletes could not be called soft, afraid, or lacking for confidence, as they genuinely believed they could take down the juggernaut Americans on one of basketball's biggest stages. After all, this group of Canadians had been going down south and proving themselves against American AAU and prep teams since they were boys.

Canada put its foot on the gas from the opening tipoff, getting off to an 8-0 start after Brooks scored the first five points of the game and

Gilgeous-Alexander had four assists in the opening six minutes to take a 35–25 first quarter lead.

But Team USA would not go away quietly. Despite sending a B team and missing Jaren Jackson Jr., Paolo Banchero, and Brandon Ingram due to an illness, its depth of NBA talent was evident as Jalen Brunson and Anthony Edwards came out of the gate firing to combine to score 18 first-half points. Meanwhile, Tyrese Haliburton and Austin Reaves gave them a huge boost off the bench at the end of the first quarter and the start of the second, going on a 19–2 run and outscoring the Canadian bench 23–8 in the first half.

Team USA got its first lead of the game at the 7:47 mark of the second quarter, when a Cameron Johnson three-pointer put it up 38–36. But it wouldn't last long, as Canada stormed back behind a master class of shot-making by Brooks and Gilgeous-Alexander, who combined to score 22 straight points for the Canadians to put them up 58–56 at the half. "We tried everything [on Gilgeous-Alexander]," Team USA head coach Steve Kerr said. "When we doubled him, Brooks was making threes. When we didn't, he was making his pull-ups. So, give those guys credit. They both play great."

Canada took control in the third quarter, outscoring the Americans 33–26 behind 11 points from Gilgeous-Alexander, going up 91–82 at the end of three. But the USA bench once again dominated in the fourth, going small without a centre on the floor as they used their speed and athleticism to spread out the Canadian defense, retaking the lead with a Mikal Bridges three with two minutes left in the game, 102–100.

The next time down the floor, Gilgeous-Alexander drove into the paint and saw that the Americans were starting to double-team him. He passed to Brooks, who hit a deep three — his seventh of the game. Then Brooks drove on the smaller Reaves and got fouled, going to the line for two free throws. And after Gilgeous-Alexander hit another mid-range jumper, Brooks came up with a defensive rebound and made two more free throws, giving Canada a 111–107 lead with 10 seconds left.

USA chose not to take a timeout and ran down the floor, with Reaves missing a floater over Brooks. However, Bridges came up with the rebound and was fouled by RJ with 4.2 seconds left in the game.

There was only one very unlikely way for Team USA to force overtime, and Bridges executed it to perfection. After making the first free throw, he purposely missed the second, with the ball bouncing to the right corner near the three-point line. Bridges sprinted to the ball after no Canadian boxed him out, picked it up, and fired up a fade-away three-pointer to tie it at 111 and send the game to overtime.

The Canadians didn't know what hit them. But in the huddle between regulation and overtime, Gilgeous-Alexander said that it was no fluke Canada led for most of the game, while Olynyk told them that they should feel lucky that they get to play five more minutes together before the tournament came to an end. "If someone was like, 'You got five minutes against USA to win bronze.' I mean, we would have taken that instantly," Olynyk says. "We're blessed to be able to play for five more minutes. And I think we're the more connected team at the moment, the better team.

"Our goal was to just go out there and play five hard minutes and win a bronze medal for our country."

Gilgeous-Alexander scored the first seven points of overtime, hitting a mid-range jumper and then a step-back three where he dropped his defender, Bridges, to the floor, smiling as he backpedalled down the court. He finished with 31 points and 12 assists in the game.

Brooks hit a floater to take a 121–115 lead with 1:15 left before Gilgeous-Alexander found RJ at the top of the arc, who struggled all game before hitting the biggest three-pointer of the night as Canada made history, winning 127–118.

Canada picked up its first ever medal in a World Cup and just its second ever medal in an international competition, with its last one coming 87 years prior on the muddy court at the 1936 Olympics. Canada went 6-2 at the World Cup, beating the number-one-ranked nation in the world, Spain; number two USA; number five France; and number seven Slovenia — a murderers' row of the best basketball teams in the world.

"It's special," Olynyk said. "You've got a great group of guys that came together, fought for each other, fought for our country, represented our country with pride, with passion every day."

"Everyone put their pride aside to play for each other and play for one big goal," Alexander-Walker says. Gilgeous-Alexander led the Canadians throughout, averaging 25 points, 6 rebounds, 6 assists, 2 steals, and just 1 turnover over the course of the eight-game tournament as he led Canada in every major statistical category and was named to the All-Tournament first team.

"I've been around greatness," Fernandez said. "I've been around LeBron. I've been around [Nikola Jokic] . . . I know Shai is at that level."

But nobody had a more redeeming tournament than Brooks, who was coming off a down year in the NBA and completely rewrote the narrative surrounding his career. After his Memphis Grizzlies lost to the lower-seeded Los Angeles Lakers in the first round of the playoffs, the team scapegoated Brooks for the disappointing postseason after he got in an altercation with the world's most famous player, LeBron James. As a result, Brooks was booed by the basketball-crazed fans at the start of games in Jakarta and Manila before proving a lot of doubters wrong as a hyper-efficient scorer and versatile defender who made history against Team USA, scoring 39 points — the most points a Canadian has ever scored in a World Cup game.

When the game was winding down, the same fans got on their feet and praised Brooks with "MVP" chants, falling in love with his hustle and heart after seeing what he was capable of in a different basketball environment. "They did the same thing in Jakarta," Brooks said about the boo's turning into "MVP" chants. "It's just an amazing feeling to be recognized during the game. But I just never took it for granted."

After celebrating the win as a team, Brooks and RJ conducted a courtside interview with Canadian broadcaster Sportsnet. Brooks had a big Canadian flag flung over his shoulders and a bronze medal hanging around his neck when he looked into the camera and sent a message to his friends back home, saying: "Sauga City, stand up!"

▪

Dillon Brooks was born in Mississauga, Ontario, in 1996 where his parents Wayne and Diane raised him before splitting up when he was a teenager. Diane would take a GO bus to work in a bank in Toronto every day before coming home to take care of Brooks and his younger siblings, Jax and Brandi.

Growing up with a learning disability, Brooks felt insecure at school until he discovered basketball at age 10. The sport gave him an avenue to expend his copious amounts of energy, and he immediately excelled in it, gaining confidence as one of the best players on the court. He went to Raptors games with his aunt and stayed up late reading the programs he took home under a giant Dwyane Wade poster in his bedroom, spending most of his time playing basketball at the local YMCA.

Brooks started playing with a group of friends known as the Mississauga "Wolfpack." And while you couldn't always see the relatively pudgy and raw Brooks dominating the game when he was young, you always heard him: talking trash, yelling, cursing, arguing every call, and kicking the ball into the stands if he wasn't happy. "That's the one thing about Dillon that everyone knows," his friend Allan Anderson said. "His passion."

Eventually, the Mississauga boys got older and started going off to prep schools in the United States and eventually to NCAA colleges. But they would return home each summer and bring that American dog-eat-dog mentality back to the YMCA, teaching the younger guys the way. "Bringing back that same grit that they learned up there," says Jalen Poyser, who grew up with Brooks. "Showing us that you got to be a dog everywhere you go, no matter what gym you go into."

The group of friends, including Anderson, David Tyndale, Naz and Elijah Long, and Brooks grew close through a shared passion of basketball, working to make each other better so that all their dreams could come true. "It's a bunch of my friends that just love playing basketball, love competing," Brooks says. "We love each other, we want to see good in each other, and a lot of us, older and younger, made something out of basketball.

"That friendship, the camaraderie, that competitiveness made us sprout into making this basketball thing a lifestyle and making it an occupation."

Brooks eventually started playing organized basketball with the Brampton Warriors before the program merged with CIA Bounce to give the athletes better exposure on the EYBL Circuit. He was a natural scorer, using his overpowering size and strength to get to the rim and score in the mid-range. But he had a tough time controlling his emotions in practices and games, as he wanted to win so badly that he would easily get frustrated when things weren't going his way.

"He kind of always had that edge about him," Poyser says. "He didn't like losing at all." It wasn't just on the basketball court, either, as Brooks once broke one of Jalen's PlayStation controllers after a losing game of *NBA 2K*.

Brooks got that fire from his father, Wayne, a former boxer turned construction worker who came from East Preston, Nova Scotia — a historically Black town on the eastern shore of Halifax. Brooks would visit in the summers, when he and his cousin Gentrey Thomas would drive around town looking for pickup games. The basketball there was more rugged, as Brooks remembers playing on the outdoor tarmac with people talking trash from the sidelines as their pit bulls barked, instilling a sense of toughness in him.

"I got to see my family, my roots," Brooks said. "Seeing where my dad was from, the grind he went through. It taught me that you always have to go get what you want."

■

After growing up watching Vince Carter dominate the NBA with his God-given athleticism, Brooks was inspired to one day play in the league. However, despite always being taller than his peers, he was a pudgy kid with a sweet tooth and was never going to be able to run or jump like the world's top ballers. He figured that he had to find an edge that would help him get to the NBA, tapping into his competitive side by learning how to play extremely hard every time he stepped on the court, doing everything possible to gain a mental edge.

"He's just wired that way," Houston Rockets general manager Rafael Stone says. "I think he's an extraordinarily competitive guy and tough guy . . . It's a talent. I think there are lots of people who'd like to play as hard as Dillon, but they don't have the capacity to."

Brooks went to Father Henry Carr for high school, waking up at 6:30 a.m. to take three TTC buses from Mississauga to Rexdale every morning. Head coach Paul Melnik built the program into a powerhouse by instilling a defensive mindset into his teams. And while Brooks struggled to shoot and handle the ball in his early days, coming off the bench and playing sparingly in his grade 9 season, he always loved the game and played extremely hard, which was perfect for Melnik.

"I wouldn't call [Brooks] a villain in high school, but he was *that* guy," Melnik said. "You couldn't watch us play and not take note of him. If you were a parent on the other team, you probably didn't like it. He was giving it to you and your kid, and letting you know about it."

After working on his jumper in the YMCA with the Wolfpack every day that summer, he came back better and started every game for the junior team in grade 10, losing just one game all season before winning the city championship. Brooks hit a growth spurt in between grade 10 and 11, jumping up to the senior team that went all the way to the OFSAA finals before losing to St. Mike's.

He also started playing against better competition on the AAU circuit with CIA Bounce. But his emotions continued to get the best of him during an EYBL game in Virginia during his grade 11 year, when Brooks got so upset with a foul call that he started to get emotional and play poorly. "Every tournament, I would get so upset and so out of control where I'd take myself out of the game," Brooks says. Head coach Tony McIntyre grounded him in his hotel room after the game until he could find a way to better control that rage. "You can't just tell me this is something that happens," McIntyre said. "Your temperature has to rise. There has to be a feeling. There has to be something that you feel is a trigger — so you can let me know when it's happening and I can help you."

It was the first time that Brooks would have to recognize all the energy and emotion that built up inside of him on the court and come up with a strategy for how to quell it. One idea he and McIntyre came up with was a safe word that Brooks would use whenever he felt his emotions boiling up so the coaches could pull him out of the game and calm him down. "And that worked a lot," Brooks says. "With each coach, I'd get better and better with it."

Brooks left Father Henry Carr after three years to go to Findlay Prep. But he was stuck behind highly rated prospects Kelly Oubre Jr. and Rashad Vaughn and averaged just eight points a game in his junior year. He was growing frustrated after not getting any attention from good NCAA schools, struggling to decide whether he was going to return to Findlay or reclassify and go to college. But that summer on the EYBL Circuit for CIA Bounce, everything finally came together, averaging 17 points and 5 rebounds a game at Peach Jam. "He just had all that pent-up energy [from not playing at Findlay]," Findlay Prep assistant coach Rodney Haddix says. "And he already had a lot of energy."

Later that same summer, Brooks led Canada's Under-18 team as its top scorer at the 2014 FIBA Americas, averaging 25 points on the way to a silver medal. After improving his stock among NCAA coaches, Brooks reclassified and joined the Oregon Ducks in 2014. "When Dillon was coming up as a young player, I don't think anybody thought but him that he was gonna be a high major player," says Oregon assistant coach Mike Mennenga. "He literally willed it to happening."

Brooks went to Oregon with 17 percent body fat and dedicated himself to the gym, cutting out sweets and fast food and remaking his body in order to thrive in Oregon's fast system. By the end of his junior season, Brooks's body fat was down to 8 percent and he was averaging 16 points, 3 rebounds, 3 assists, and 1 steal on 49/40/75 percent shooting splits to win the Pac-12 Player of the Year before leading the Ducks to the final four of the NCAA tournament.

"I just think he loves the game, and I think he loves playing ball, and he loves being in the gym," Mennenga says. "You take the game away from Dillon and he'd be a fish out of water."

■

Brooks was a good defender at Oregon, but he didn't truly embrace the role until he was drafted 45th overall by the Memphis Grizzlies in 2017. His first NBA coach, David Fizdale, told him that he was going to need to be a standout defender to stick in the league. And Brooks took it to heart, studying film of his opponents for hours at a time and working diligently in the weight room to add muscle, while putting his ego aside to grow to love his new role as a star-stopper.

"It's not a job everybody wants," Brooks says. "That's what makes me different. Guys don't like dealing with the physicality. They don't like to get bumped. They don't like having someone in their space all night."

Brooks thrived by tapping into the same emotional energy that got him in trouble when he was young. In fact, his ability to motivate himself to always play with 110 percent intensity enabled the pudgy four-star recruit from Mississauga to become the longest-tenured player in Memphis and earn more than $120 million in his career. "It's been a hassle all of my life to figure out how to channel it and find ways to put it to great use," Brooks said. "I feel like I've found a way and I have to bring it every day. I can't pull it back because I've tried that already and it hasn't worked to any good extent. I've just got to keep playing with emotion and live or die by it."

The Grizzlies relied on Brooks to do the defensive dirty work for six seasons, vaulting up in the standings from 22 wins in 2017–18 to 51 wins in 2022–23. "You absolutely have to have that person," Grizzlies head coach Taylor Jenkins said. "He definitely draws a lot of attention, and it can seem very selfish and individual, but it's not.

"For the program we're building here, DB's the guy who epitomizes it."

However, Brooks's fiery persona also got him in trouble. In between spats with Duke's Coach K, Cleveland Cavaliers guard Donovan Mitchell, a courtside camera man, and LeBron James, who he called "old" in the middle of their playoff series, Brooks picked up the "Villain" nickname.

"Everyone can't be the hero," Brooks said. "I'd rather be what was chosen for me."

"That's what makes him who he is," Melnik says. "Without that energy, he's not in the NBA. You don't get better without that desire, that energy, that . . . persona."

However, as soon as the Grizzlies lost to the Lakers in the playoffs, management leaked to the media that Brooks, an unrestricted free agent, would not be back "under any circumstances," scapegoating him for the loss. But despite fans taking to Twitter to joke that he would have no other choice but to play in China, Brooks signed a four-year, $86-million contract in Houston that offseason before joining Team Canada at the 2023 World Cup. He once again used the Canadian national team to redeem his reputation as one of the best players in the world, averaging 15 points, 3 rebounds, 3 assists, and 1 steal on 59/59/79 shooting splits while defending the opponents' best players throughout the tournament before dropping 39 points in a historic win over USA.

"I always try to prove people wrong," Brooks says. "People forgot that before that year I was averaging 18 points a game, scorer mentality, dog, play both ends of the floor, and I feel like Memphis kind of drowned that out of me.

"But it made me grow as a man and get in the gym more and be able to showcase my talents."

It was an amazing turnaround for a player who hadn't played with Canada since 2015; he was the lone player from the summer core to skip out on a training camp in 2022 until he saw all his childhood friends show up and was motivated to join them and make history. "As a team, we wanted this," Brooks said. "This bronze medal, to do something that hadn't been done, to keep creating history.

"It's a great stepping stone for us as a ball club, as a country, and we all just wanted to make our country proud." For Brooks and the rest of the Canadian team, the cherry on top was that they got to prove a lot of people wrong along the way.

CHAPTER 19

THE PREP SCHOOL BOOM

MARK PETERSON AT ATHLETE INSTITUTE

Jamal Murray dribbles up the court during his historic season at Orangeville Prep.

"When you stay in Canada, you just have to work harder to get noticed. Going to the US is what everyone else is doing. There always has to be an outlier. I guess that's me."

— JAMAL MURRAY

Roger Murray and his family followed a long line of immigrants out of Jamaica for the Greater Toronto Area when he was nine, settling in Kitchener, Ontario, one hour west of Toronto. He ran track and field and dabbled in basketball but never had the time to specialize in sport, going to work before having two kids, Jamal and Lamar, with a Syrian-Canadian named Sylvia.

As a young boy, Roger discovered Bruce Lee, the 5'7" mixed martial artist who never backed down from a fight or showed fear against his larger opponents. "I saw him as almost superhuman," Roger said. "I wanted to know more about how he got so strong mentally. No matter who was standing in front of him, he was never afraid."

Roger began reading books on kung fu and incorporated Zen Buddhist and Taoist philosophies into his life as he settled in a new country, practising martial arts and training his mind to thrive under pressure and overcome adversity. Not only did it help him, but it also gave Roger a blueprint to fatherhood, promising himself that when he had kids, he was going to help them become the very best at whatever they wanted to do. "It happened to be basketball that he loved," Roger said. "Jamal could play for hours even when the ball was as big as he was."

Jamal was born in 1997 and had a basketball in his hands by the time he was two, starting on a Fisher-Price net in his home before playing pickup against top-ranked high-school- and college-aged players since he was 12. He even joined Roger's men's league games because of the lack of youth programming in the Kitchener-Waterloo area. "He was pissing me off," says Jeff Lyle, who played against Jamal in the men's league. "Because he was quick. I couldn't catch him."

But the hardest work was reserved for when the rest of the players cleared the court, when Roger and Jamal would spend countless hours working on physically and mentally taxing drills designed to make Jamal more tough and prepare him to deal with adversity. The stories about Roger and Jamal became the stuff of legend in the Kitchener-Waterloo area: how Roger would have Jamal balance cups of hot tea on his knees while sitting in a squat to learn how to deal with pain; how Jamal would shoot from his knees with a blindfold on, or from half court without jumping to hone his form; how he would do push-ups and run hills in the snow to get used to different conditions; and how he would have to make 30 free throws in a row while Roger pushed him around and talked trash to him, starting over if he missed one.

"It's less about basketball, more about you as a person and how you deal with whatever you're talking about," Jamal says. "How do you deal with pain, physical, emotional, mental — how do you handle that?

"It was just everything that I learned back then helps me now as a man today. And, obviously, during the game. But those are more life lessons for me."

Roger wanted his son to understand that it was mind over matter. That — as Bruce Lee taught him — humans put physical and mental limits on themselves. But as Roger put it, "Why not do more?"

•

Every evening after school, Roger and Jamal would go to the Stanley Street playground across the street from their house and Jamal would put up countless shots on the double-rims that honed his shooting form. "Ever since I can remember that I've known him, he's been training," says Miro Iliev, who befriended Jamal in grade school. "He was always on the court with his dad doing some type of unorthodox drill."

Iliev would join them on occasion, playing one-on-one against Jamal. But Roger would restrict his son in order to make it more fair, telling him to only dribble once before shooting or to only score with his left hand. "It kind of felt bad being on the other side," Iliev says. "I'm guarding Jamal and I can score any way I want, but Roger's telling him, 'Jamal, you can only hit bank shots,' and he's still beating you."

At home, Jamal wasn't given a cellphone or any new gaming systems like most teenagers. Instead, his parents made sure their oldest son got A's in school in addition to working on visualization, breathing, stretching, and meditation techniques that helped lower his heart rate to 34 beats a minute. "I didn't let him hang out with kids at the mall, either," Roger said. "Kids waste so much time these days. They cheat themselves. I wanted everything he did to have a purpose."

"My brain doesn't need that junk right now," Murray said. "Basketball is what fills my brain."

Sylvia, like many mothers of Canadian basketball players, played an equally important role in her son's life behind the scenes. She would keep the house in order, the table full, and make sure that Jamal's academics were on point while acting as a nurturing presence that Jamal could always go to for support in order to balance Roger's tough coaching.

But Roger made it his full-time job to train his son, becoming his best friend, his biggest critic, and his coach. "I stopped my life for this kid," Roger said.

"My dad knows me better than anybody else," Murray said. "He probably knows me better than me."

By the time Jamal walked into Grand River Collegiate Institute for high school, he was a tall and lanky point guard who could shoot from anywhere inside half court. But what amazed teammates like Iliev and Chuder Teny was how seriously he took the game, finding a quiet spot to meditate and visualize the moves he would make before games and then executing them when the pressure was on.

"His attitude was just different," Teny says. "There is nothing that could really budge him or anything. He was always mentally tough, which was crazy to see at such a young age."

In the regular season of their grade 9 year, Grand River was in a close game with rivals Cameron Heights Collegiate when Jamal drove down the court, side-stepped to his right foot, and hit a fadeaway three at the buzzer to win. Then a couple weeks later in the city semifinals against the same team, Jamal came up with a steal and hit a three off the same right foot from practically the same spot at the buzzer to beat them again, leading the junior team to the city title.

"Early on in high school, we called him 'Glitch,'" Iliev says. "Because like in a video game, it looked like a glitch when he was hitting shots."

Jamal started playing for the Kitchener Wolverines OBA program while jumping up to the senior team at high school as a tenth grader, dominating the Kitchener-Waterloo basketball scene as he got better, more athletic, stronger, and added to his game each year. The only problem was that Kitchener had a limited basketball infrastructure. "There wasn't as much of a basketball culture as there is now," Iliev says. "You kind of learn how to play the game from tribal knowledge" that was passed down from former players and coaches like Roger. And it soon became clear that Jamal had outgrown his hometown and was going to need to move on in order to reach the lofty goals he set for himself since he saw his idol, Vince Carter, at a Raptors open practice at the University of Waterloo when he was five. "I remember screaming and him looking up and pointing at me," Murray said. "He was my favourite player growing up, and I was so excited."

One day, CIA Bounce coach Rono Miller went to Kitchener to visit a cousin and saw Jamal play. He was so impressed that he told four fellow CIA Bounce coaches that Jamal was so talented, "he could be on this team," Miller says. However, three of the coaches started laughing, and one said, "No kid from Kitchener is making this team."

But program co-founder and coach Mike George was always looking for talent, even if it came from a most obscure place. And after Jamal's stock rose with a dominant performance at the annual Jane and Finch tournament in Toronto a few years later, George saw Jamal play and immediately realized that he could start for CIA Bounce.

Jamal was deciding between playing AAU for Grassroots or CIA Bounce when George challenged Roger to a game. "If I beat you in one-on-one, the kid has to play with us," George says. But the outcome of the game will never be known. "He's gonna tell you he won, and I'm gonna say I won." Either way, George developed a relationship with Roger and recruited Jamal to CIA Bounce, where he joined a stacked team with Brooks, Jalen Poyser, and Kyle Alexander.

After showcasing his shot-making prowess in front of rows of NCAA coaches on the EYBL Circuit, Jamal had his pick of the litter of American prep schools for his final two years of high school. But instead of following in a long line of Canadians who had left home for the States, Jamal chose to do something unprecedented — something that would change the trajectory of Canadian basketball forever: he stayed home.

"When you stay in Canada, you just have to work harder to get noticed," Murray said. "Going to the US is what everyone else is doing. There always has to be an outlier. I guess that's me."

•

Jesse Tipping grew up in Orangeville, Ontario, a small town of about 30,000 an hour northwest of Toronto. It was the 1980s, and like most of his friends in town, he played hockey before discovering basketball during his teenage years.

Tipping decided to pursue an NCAA scholarship in basketball. The problem was that janitorial and teacher strikes halted the public school's athletic programs in back-to-back years when he was in high school. And because almost all gyms in Canada exist inside government-owned schools rather than private facilities, he had nowhere to play. Meanwhile, if Tipping transferred to a different public school, he would have had to redshirt for a year.

Tipping eventually transferred to a couple of private schools around the GTA before playing basketball at Brock University and the University of Waterloo. "Along that whole journey, I realized that our system in Canada is broken," Tipping says. "If there's a kid who wants to get a Division I scholarship, there is no pathway that he or she can start on that allows you to move up." Unless, of course, you followed the "Russell Doctrine" and left the country to pursue basketball down south as early as grade 9, with so many kids leaving for American prep schools by 2010 that many worried if it had gone beyond a pipeline and become a full-out talent drain.

"That really killed our talent pool," said Tariq Sbiet, who runs the basketball recruiting service North Pole Hoops (NPH). "As guys were leaving, we weren't really giving ourselves a chance for [the Canadian basketball] industry to elevate."

After getting his degree in kinesiology, Tipping moved back to Orangeville and started the Athlete Institute in 2010, a strength and conditioning program to train elite young Canadian athletes based out of a private sports and recreation facility that his family built with money they made in the trucking industry. All of Tipping's siblings went to IMG Academy for basketball, so he understood how the best prep schools operated, eventually creating Orangeville Prep in 2012, a high school basketball team based out of Athlete Institute. "I knew that I had a facility here that I could use," he says. "I just needed to build the programming and the pathway to allow a kid to come here, get everything that they need, and then be able to get a Division I scholarship and move on."

Initially, Tipping received a lot of pushback, as the Canadian basketball establishment wasn't sold on the prep model. OFSAA, the governing body of high school sports in Ontario, was against anything not considered amateur sport, such as recruiting players from all over the country or allowing them to transfer schools without red shirting. As a result, they refused to allow prep teams to compete in its competitions. Meanwhile, club and AAU coaches were hesitant to send their kids to a program they were unfamiliar with that had no history of sending kids to the NCAA, especially given the history of fly-by-night diploma mills disguised as prep schools.

"They all said it'll never work," Tipping said. "All the best players will always go to the States first."

Orangeville Prep had gyms and weight room facilities that could stand up to any NCAA college while the team attended school at nearby Orangeville District Secondary and lived at the Rosebud Motel in Orangeville, where *Schitt's Creek* was filmed. Still, it was initially difficult for Tipping to recruit Canada's best players.

However, Tipping hired CIA Bounce co-founder Tony McIntyre as the director of basketball operations and CIA Bounce head coach Larry Blunt to coach the team ahead of its second season, when Canada's top AAU program started sending some of its best athletes to Orangeville — allowing kids and parents to benefit from staying close to home. "I saw what I went through, how much money I spent, how much time I missed out on raising my kids," McIntyre says about sending his sons to American prep schools. "Allowing Canadian kids to go home on weekends and be a part of their families" was Orangeville's goal.

The CIA Bounce connection helped Orangeville Prep add a number of high-level prospects ahead of its second season, but none came with more notoriety than Murray, who had the confidence to bet on himself, stay close to his family, and still achieve his dreams of getting to the NCAA. "He's one of the first players that kind of didn't take the typical route of 'Hey, automatically it's the US or nothing,'" Tipping says. "That was the strong willpower and the belief that Roger had and the ability to stay connected and a part of Jamal's development and life."

"It was a chance to stay home," Jamal said. "For my father to see me play, and to get a good education."

Roger would make the hour-long drive from Kitchener to Orangeville three or four times a week to train Jamal after practice, maintaining a steady presence in his life. And the rest of the athletes got better as a result, seeing the work Jamal was putting in on top of an already intensive schedule that had them waking up at 6 a.m. to lift weights before school, practise for three hours after school, and go back to residence for dinner and study hall before any extra training.

"He was just always there," Poyser says. "Even if it's a snowstorm, it doesn't matter what it is, you'll see Roger at the end of practice working out with Jamal. So, he always kept Jamal sharp."

"He's working out at like 11 at night," teammate Kyle Alexander says. "You're just seeing this work ethic being put in from these guys who are really good. And it just prepares your mind mentally for what's to come."

After his first season at Orangeville, Jamal played at the 2014 Nike Hoop Summit for Roy Rana, the head coach of the World Team representing the best prospects outside of the United States. "After that game, I realized: All these great players got nothing on me," Murray said. "Because I'm always going to have the mental edge."

In the fall, top-ranked Sudanese big men Thon and Makur Maker joined Murray at Orangeville Prep because their American visas expired and they had to leave the country. It created one of the best prep teams in history, with Orangeville dominating American competition while NCAA coaches lined up across their gym floor to watch practices. In fact, all 12 of the athletes from that team got Division I scholarships.

Putting so many top-ranked prospects on the same team had the added benefit of creating an ultra-competitive environment where they were always having to prove themselves and see who really was the best. "The hardest practices that I've had in my life," Keshaun Saunders, the youngest player on that team, says. "We were fighting. There were days where we would be in practice and it would get too competitive, and dudes would probably just leave the gym, square up, duke it out, and come back to practice."

But the group bonded over that competition, playing one-on-one late into the night or playing manhunt in the dark after leaving the gym, returning to their hotel rooms to laugh about the time Alexander fell off a cliff trying to run away. "Yeah, you miss it," Jamal says. "You're playing with the free spirit, just playing with your friends and guys that you're close with. And sleeping next door to each other.

"So, you grow and you learn a lot from each other, and you depend on each other at that age."

After the 2014–15 season, Jamal returned to the Nike Hoop Summit and won MVP, dropping 30 points for Rana and the World Team. He then reclassified to the class of 2015 and chose to attend the University of Kentucky after sorting through a host of offers from the best NCAA programs. "Jamal was always special in the sense that he knew that he bet on himself," Tipping says. "He just was such a competitor that he knew that he could do it from anywhere."

Seven players from Orangeville Prep have gone on to play in the NBA including Jamal, Thon Maker, Alexander, Lu Dort, Oshae Brissett, and Ignas Brazdeikis — by far a Canadian prep school record — while over a hundred athletes have gotten Division I scholarships from the school. And it all started with Murray, who put Orangeville Prep on the map by believing in himself enough to stay home and do things his way.

"I mean, sure, you could call it [a risk]," Jamal says. "But I had so much confidence in my game and what I can do, and I didn't really need to worry about what-ifs. I just go out there and play and everything will take care of itself."

•

Orangeville Prep won a lot of games in the Grind Session and other American tournaments. But in order to sustain success with a schedule that wasn't too travel intensive or cost-prohibitive, they needed to find competition within Canada.

Because OFSAA refused to create an additional division for prep schools, high schools like Eastern Commerce, Father Henry Carr, St. Marcellinus, and Orangeville decided to start the Ontario Scholastic Basketball Association (OSBA) in 2016, catering exclusively to Canadian prep schools and run in conjunction with Ontario Basketball.

"I knew that it was going to be sort of the start of an evolution of change for the prep scene of Canadian basketball," Tipping says.

During its peak from 2016 until 2020, the OSBA was considered a top-three prep league in North America, with several boys' and girls' teams that were all stacked with talent. When it started, about 70 percent of Canadian NCAA players were coming out of American prep schools. Now, that number has been flipped on its head. The OSBA fell off in recent years and has been surpassed by new leagues founded by ground-breaking media companies such as On Point Basketball — who runs the Platinum Circuit — and NPH — who runs the National Preparatory Association (NPA), which is now the top prep league in Canada.

When the COVID pandemic shut down high school sports in 2020, more and more prep schools started popping up throughout Ontario and other parts of Canada because they were allowed to continue operating as "elite amateur sports" — accommodating the thousands of students who left public schools to chase their dreams of playing pro basketball. Now, there are more than 50 prep schools in the GTA and almost a hundred in Canada. However, several of these new prep schools are money grabs that charge students tens of thousands of dollars despite not being very good for basketball or academics. "There's too many prep schools, and a lot of them are very weak," Canadian basketball scout Wes Brown says. "The kids are desperate these days for Division I. And everyone's selling the dream."

In fact, many Canadians are no longer able to find well-coached public school teams as the landscape shifts towards prep.

Despite the recent issues, these prep schools have produced countless athletes that have gone on to play in U Sports, the NCAA, and the pros, including current Toronto Raptor A.J. Lawson, who was inspired by Murray to stay in Canada. "Seeing Jamal go to Kentucky and seeing them being draft picks and all that definitely gave me hope," says Lawson, who attended GTA Prep and played in the NPA before going to South Carolina.

Meanwhile, Tipping and McIntyre created the BioSteel All-Canadian Game in 2015, providing a platform for the best Canadian players to showcase themselves to fans, coaches, and the media, similar to the prestigious McDonald's All-American Games. It built off the previous success of Wayne Dawkins's All-Canada Classic, which ran from 2001–2012, but differentiated itself with the funding of a major Canadian sponsor — something that wasn't possible when Dawkins and Russell were helping Canadian basketball get off the ground in the early 2000s.

The emergence of elite Canadian prep schools and showcase tournaments has created an infrastructure where it is no longer necessary to go to the United States for high school — to live alone as early as grade 9 and deal with culture shock, strange food, and predatory coaches in an unfamiliar environment. "If you stay in Canada, I feel like you'll be fine," Lawson says. "The scouts are gonna find talent. They're always looking for talent. I feel like they're coming to Canada a lot more than they were 10 years ago."

The original group of athletes who attended Orangeville Prep took a risk by staying home. But they are to thank for the burgeoning Canadian prep scene, blazing a trail for the next generation. And no one had a bigger impact than Murray, who left Orangeville Prep in 2015 and started every game as a freshman at Kentucky, averaging 20 points, 5 rebounds, and 2 assists while shooting 41 percent from three. He was selected seventh overall by the Denver Nuggets in the 2016 NBA Draft.

At 28 years old, Murray was already one of the most accomplished Canadian basketball players ever, with a bronze medal at the Under-16 FIBA Americas in 2013, a silver in the Pan Am Games in 2015, and an NBA Championship in 2023, when he averaged 26-6-7 on 47/40/93 shooting splits throughout the playoffs to help the Nuggets win its first ever championship. In 2025, he owned the Canadian records for the most points in an NBA regular season (55) and playoff game (50), establishing himself as a bona fide big game performer with an impressive list of game-winners and almost $400 million in career earnings.

"Jamal embraces the moment," Nuggets head coach Michael Malone said. "Some people run away from those moments. He looks for them."

"After everything I've done to get here," Murray said, "this is easy."

Whenever he gets the chance, Murray returns home to Ontario to witness the burgeoning high school basketball scene that he helped give birth to. "It's really cool to see the growth," he says. "At first, people didn't know who we were, and now we're well-known in America.

"So, it's nice to be a pioneer in that sense."

CHAPTER 20

THE PARIS OLYMPICS

GREGORY SHEAMUS, GETTY IMAGES

Evan Fournier and Victor Wembanyama celebrate after hitting a big shot against Team Canada during the 2024 Paris Olympics.

"It's a terrible feeling. Obviously, I think for me personally, I might have overlooked the opportunity a little bit. Like, once the game was over, I realized it's another four years before we get this opportunity. That's a long fucking time."

— SHAI GILGEOUS-ALEXANDER

LeBron James sat on the couch of his Southern California home as he watched Gilgeous-Alexander and Brooks combine to score 70 points against America's B team in the bronze medal game of the 2023 World Cup. That's when an idea began to formulate inside the head of the greatest player of his generation. James started to recruit some of America's best players, including Steph Curry and Kevin Durant, for the 2024 Olympics, starting a group chat that would be come to be named "The Avengers."

The Paris Olympics would end up being the greatest international basketball tournament of all time, with a record 51 NBA players spread across 12 rosters, including all of the best Americans as well as Greece's Giannis Antetokounmpo, Serbia's Nikola Jokic, and France's Victor Wembanyama.

That injection of talent didn't make things any easier for Team Canada, which was in uncharted territory after qualifying for its first Olympics since 2000 — with several key decisions to make before the Games even began, including which 12 players to roster.

Canada originally committed to prioritize roster spots for the 14 players that were listed on the three-year summer core. "Our commitment for those players is really simple," Barrett said when they announced the summer core in 2022. "[If] you've committed, you're going to be in here [on the team]" for future World Cups and Olympics. "If you look at this list and the guys on it are able-bodied and ready to go, there won't be any more room," Barrett added. "Players that could not [commit] . . .

we'll move on from them and we'll maybe look at them again in the next quad."

The core idea was necessary to get a historically hard to pin down group of athletes to commit to a long-term project. However, Canada Basketball went back on its word ahead of Paris 2024, handing out training camp invitations to NBA players who did not commit to the core including Trey Lyles, Andrew Nembhard, and Andrew Wiggins, who ultimately turned down the opportunity to play.

The idea was to inject the roster with NBA talent and to bolster its 13th-ranked defense from the World Cup, creating a deeper bench along with more ball-handlers to spell rest for the team's top players. "We are going to this competition in Paris to win," Barrett said. "And as a result of that, we have to create the strongest possible roster that we could to get that job done."

But not everyone took the decision to eschew loyalty in favour of talent well. "I took the honour of playing for [my] country very seriously and did it many times over the years," said former captain Cory Joseph, who did not receive a training camp invitation despite being on the summer core and showing up to training camps in 2022 and 2023. His 50 games and 529 points rank 15th and 9th all time, respectively. "For me it's a little disheartening to be like, 'Wow, I wasn't even given an opportunity to compete for whatever position?'"

The Olympic roster was made up of eight holdovers from the 2023 World Cup (Gilgeous-Alexander, Brooks, RJ, Powell, Olynyk, Ejim, Alexander-Walker, Dort) and four new players (Murray, Nembhard, Lyles, Khem Birch). Eight of the twelve players grew up playing in the OBA, while only Lyles and Olynyk were from the West Coast — showing how far the balance of power had swung since the turn of the century.

The team had an intensive eight-day training camp in Toronto's OVO Athletic Centre while staying at the nearby five-star Ace Hotel, practising twice a day with a level of focus that only an Olympic year could demand. "It was definitely a feeling of it didn't need to be explained, the magnitude of the moment that we were participating in," Powell says. "I think everybody showed up on day one understanding that this was a very unique situation."

Gilgeous-Alexander had become a clear leader, waking up early and driving in from Hamilton to be the first one at practice each morning. After working with Mitchell at the national training centre all spring, he came into camp as the best conditioned athlete there — a key characteristic in FIBA, which has fewer whistles and stoppages than the NBA. He led by example with how hard he played, how much fun he was always having, and how well connected he was with everyone on the team.

"It would have been easy for Shai to be like, 'This is my team. This is the way that I'm going about it. This is how we need to do things,' and he did when it needed to be done," Ejim says. "But I think at the same time, he allowed people like me, he allowed people like Kelly [Olynyk] and Dwight [Powell], older, veteran guys, to still have a prominent voice, to have our inputs.

"And I think it takes a special type of character in a person to understand when it's okay for others to lead and when it's his time to lead. He allowed people that grace."

Brooks, Dort, and Powell were responsible for bringing a different level of intensity to the drills, playing hard even in non-contact 5-on-0 shooting drills, raising the level of their teammates as a result. Brooks's competitiveness came out once scrimmages began, at one point trash talking RJ by saying, "Your dad paid the refs," after the fellow Missisauga native got a favourable foul call. Later, after arguing with the refs about a non-call, Brooks's teammates tried to calm him down and he responded, "What are they gonna do, fine me?"

■

Coach Jordi Fernandez and his assistant coaches Nate Bjorkgren and Nate Mitchell wanted the Canadians to play a fast, frenzied style that relied on speed and skill rather than size. The idea was to take advantage of the wealth of two-way perimeter players on the roster and insulate its lack of reliable big men on defense by pressuring the ball high up the court to speed up opposing offenses.

He preached the need for hard work and constant improvement, challenging them to be the best defensive team in the world after calling them out for giving up 118 points to Team USA a year before.

"[We can] be disruptive, in passing lanes, ball pressure. Make it kinda tough to enter [the post]," Gilgeous-Alexander said. It was a similar style that Canada played the previous summer, only even smaller and faster, causing turnovers and pushing the ball in transition at every opportunity. In fact, Fernandez added a full-court element to almost every drill. "It was still the number one thing," Bell-Haynes, one of the final cuts, says. "You don't have a lot of time to build . . . The chemistry is still growing. And the easiest way to get good shots and good possessions is to play fast and catch defenses off guard."

After an exhibition game against Team USA in Las Vegas; another week of training camp in Blan, France; and a series of exhibition games against France, Puerto Rico, and Brazil in Orleans, France, Canada traveled three hours north of Paris to the city of Lille for the group stage of the Olympics. The players were disappointed to learn that they would be staying in a dorm-like mini-village while Team USA was staying in a five-star hotel in Paris and France was staying at a private facility in the countryside. America and France spend about four times what Canada Basketball does yearly, showing that while the program had come far in terms of resources, they still had work to do.

Canada missed the Olympic opening ceremonies in order to prepare for its opening contest against Antetokounmpo and Greece, where Fernandez started Gilgeous-Alexander, RJ, Brooks, Powell, and Dort, who's job was to provide pressure on opposing point guard Nick Calathes while Brooks could stick to Antetokounmpo. The trio of Gilgeous-Alexander, RJ, and Brooks picked up right where they left off, scoring 58 points in the one-sided game, which Canada won 86–79. Dort, meanwhile, was a +26 in 18 minutes after holding Calathes to just 3 points, 5 assists, and 3 turnovers. As a result, the coaches decided to stick with him in the starting lineup and Murray coming off the bench moving forward.

Canada built a defensive identity as the tournament went along, with Dort and Brooks shutting down primary ball-handlers like Josh Giddey for Australia and Lorenzo Brown for Spain, as Canada's ball-pressure sped up opposing offenses and led to turnovers that fed its own offense, leading the tournament in points off turnovers during the group stage with 67. Meanwhile, Gilgeous-Alexander, RJ, and Brooks continued their scoring run from the previous summer as they combined to score more than 60 percent of Canada's points in the group stage. Nembhard came off the bench to drop 18 points in the final game against Spain, while Lyles, Olynyk, Powell, and Birch all had moments where they looked like key pieces of Canada's team.

Murray, however, struggled to find his rhythm as he slowly ramped up his minutes each game, coming off the bench for the first time since 2017 and playing off the ball more than he was used to in the NBA.

"We got a great group of selfless guys, though," Murray said. "Our captain Kelly [Olynyk] is coming off the bench, an NBA champion is coming off the bench, and the starting unit is rolling . . . Everyone's embraced their role."

•

Canada went a perfect 3–0 in what was originally dubbed the "Group of Death," beating 14th-ranked Greece, 4th-ranked Australia, and 2nd-ranked Spain. Its reward was a quarter-final round matchup against the host nation, France. And despite the fact that Canada had beaten France by 30 points at the 2023 World Cup and again in back-to-back exhibition games in France a week before the Games, the circumstances had changed and the stakes had risen.

The Olympic knockout stage moved from a converted soccer stadium in Lille to Bercy Arena in Paris, where 21,000 French fans towered over the court to support their home nation with faces painted blue and white, flags flung, drums beating, and chants like "*Allez les bleus*" being sung throughout the entire game. "That was probably one of the craziest FIBA environments that I've been in," Powell says.

France got off to a slow start to the tournament, going 2-1 in the group stage after losing to Germany and needing overtime to beat 26th-ranked Japan; veteran leaders Evan Fournier and captain Nicolas Batum called out the team for its lack of intensity. Meanwhile, head coach Vincent Collet preached the need to play with passion and desperation in the days leading up to the quarter-final matchup against Canada, rarely talking about X's and O's. "Playing in [front of] our home crowd, the Olympics, it happens once in a lifetime," French player Frank Ntilikina said. "This is a special moment for us and especially tonight. When we play Canada, we felt like, 'Let's give it all on the court, let's not regret anything.'"

A little adversity proved to be exactly what the French squad needed, as they responded to being called out by their veteran leaders and coach, feeding off the crowd to get off to a quick start against Canada. France took a 23–10 lead after one quarter behind 10 quick points from point guard Isaia Cordinier and dominant interior defense from 20-year-old, 7'4" French phenom Wembanyama, who single-handedly forced the Canadians to rethink their shot selection after they started the game 2-of-13 from the field. "The crowd was amazing," Fournier said. "People that were here, they gave us everything."

But it wasn't just the crowd that had Canada playing from behind from the opening minutes. After playing Canada multiple times in the last year, Collet made a bold move to shake up his starting lineup and game plan, taking two of his program's most veteran players, Fournier and Rudy Gobert, out of the starting lineup in favour of overseas pros Cordinier and Guerschon Yabusele, who combined to score 42 points in the game.

"The main reason [for both starting lineup changes] was the lineup from Canada," Collet said. "They always start the game with Dillon Brooks at position four, and they play small ball."

France's strategy was to take advantage of Canada's lack of size and switch-heavy defensive scheme by relentlessly attacking the paint, feeding big men Wembanyama, Yabusele, and Mathias Lessort in the post and bullying the smaller Canadians inside. Canada had no answers early, either fouling or double-teaming the post, which led to open kickout threes from France. "They changed a little bit of the way that they played, and the emphasis in where they played," Ejim says. "And I think they adapted well to our aggressiveness and our switching on defense . . . They figured out a way to kind of slow us down and play towards their strengths."

Canada had their opportunities to score against the Frenchmen, but they struggled to shoot the ball until Gilgeous-Alexander made his first basket of the game with 5:45 left in the half, after which he looked up to the heavens as if to say thank you. Canada made a small comeback in the second quarter but the French continued to beat up on them inside, shooting 25 free throws to just 8 for Canada while getting Brooks and RJ into foul trouble in the first half.

"Can you please call it?" Fernandez asked the referees before heading to the locker room at halftime. "I'm playing for my life."

Canada knew that they were going to have obstacles pertaining to the crowd and the referees favouring the home squad in France, telling the players before the game not to react to calls. In fact, Olynyk complained about a no-call during one of the team's scrimmages in the days leading up to the Games, and Fernandez stopped practice to deliver a message to his team. "You think we are gonna get any fucking calls in France?" he said.

With the team trailing 45–29, Canada's locker room was quiet at half. Instead of players calling each other out for a lack of discipline or poor shot selection, nobody said a word. It appeared as if the young team had taken on coach Fernandez's personality as a professional, competitive, no-nonsense group — one who was not necessarily comfortable stepping on each other's toes like France and some of the more established nations were.

Fernandez asked, "How do we get back into this game?"

"Defense," Gilgeous-Alexander said.

"Right now, it comes down to win this quarter, stay together," Fernandez responded. "Nobody said that this shit would be easy. So let's go and fight for it!"

Canada started the third quarter strong, as players fought harder to pressure the ball and to deny the entry into the post, while Gilgeous-Alexander hit a string of jumpers to get it within 12, 54–46, with 3:39 left in the third. And Canada kept it in that range until RJ came out and scored the first five points of the fourth quarter, going on a 10–4 run to pull Canada within six, 61–55, with Gilgeous-Alexander at the free throw line with a chance to cut further into the lead. But Canada's leader uncharacteristically missed both free throws, showing signs of fatigue after having to dig the team out of an early hole.

Despite the controversial decision to go outside of the summer core to inject the team with more talent and ball-handlers, Canada's supporting cast struggled to pick up the slack. Brooks started the game 0-of-7 from the field and finished with two points; Olynyk and Nembhard both went scoreless; Powell and Birch struggled to protect the paint and rebound; while Dort and RJ were productive offensively, combining for 24 points.

However, both got into foul trouble after struggling to contain bigger forwards in the post, limiting their playing time.

"Everybody around the world is getting better," RJ says. "And FIBA is also just a different game. Going over there, the European players, they have the advantage. That's their game that they play."

France reopened the lead by once again using their size to attack the glass, with 10 offensive rebounds and 15 second-chance points in the game. But Canada made another run after all its starters returned late in the fourth quarter, cutting the lead to five, 65–60, with 4:09 remaining, when France called a timeout.

Despite coming off the bench for the first time all tournament, Fournier found a rhythm as the game went along. He came out of the timeout to ice the game, hitting two deep three-pointers in the final minutes, including a dagger from near half court as the shot clock expired and he turned to the crowd and waved his hand near his ear encouraging the rabid fans to get even louder.

France won 82–73 and sent Canada home with a fifth-place finish.

"They were better than us, played harder than us, and we saw it from the jump," said Gilgeous-Alexander, who led all scorers with 27 points. "We obviously tried to make our run in the second half. It wasn't enough, but that's what happens when you let teams get off to a good start."

While the officiating clearly played a role in Canada's demise, as France shot a tournament-record 42 free throws compared to 25 for Canada, the reality was that similar to how it felt 24 years ago against France, Canada simply didn't play its best basketball when it mattered most. And the French team was a more together group that exploited Canada's size disadvantage. The Canadians, meanwhile, weren't versatile enough to adapt from a small-ball, transition-based game and figure out another way to win — lacking a traditional centre to create matchup problems like Team USA's Joel Embiid or 7'4" Chinese-Canadian Zach Edey, who won back-to-back national player of the year awards at Purdue before being drafted ninth overall by Memphis in 2024, which held him out of the Olympics.

"For us, it's always been playing with pace, touches in the paint, and reverse the basketball," Fernandez said about what he called Canada's most "selfish" game of the tournament offensively. "That's how we got good shots, and that's what we've done for the most part, but not in the game that you had to win to stay in the tournament."

Canada was supposed to have the best backcourt in the world, but while Gilgeous-Alexander continued to build off his historic performance at the 2023 World Cup, Murray didn't even start a single game for Canada, finishing with 7 points on 3-of-13 shooting, 1 assist, and 3 turnovers against France. He scored a total of 24 points in the 4-game tournament.

After a long NBA season during which his body got banged up and then a personal matter that forced him to miss part of training camp and two exhibition games, Murray came into camp with bumps and bruises. He never had the time to get in a rhythm or build chemistry with his teammates — participating in just one full scrimmage before the Games despite not playing international basketball since 2015. "He came back. Was a little banged up, missed part of the preparation," Fernandez says. "We played with Lu, played very well, and I made the decision to bring Jamal off the bench."

"It's an adjustment, for sure," Murray said about coming off the bench. "But that's a question for higher-ups."

The team struggled to integrate most of the new players, who as a whole did not perform nearly as well as the ones who played in 2023. But Murray's struggles were particularly notable, as he never found a rhythm despite playing a tournament-high 24 minutes against France, closing out the game at the expense of Nembhard and Alexander-Walker. "But he threw caution to the wind and said, 'No, I want to do this for my country,'" Barrett said. "I would say there was just some ups and downs there and just trying to make sure we can acclimate him."

Canada never got the balance right, and its offense got bogged down as a result of playing lineups that had little familiarity or established hierarchy. "You might see that where there was a lot of chemistry between those guys [in 2023] and now they are trying to get deeper and to improve. And this is not easy," Spanish head coach Sergio Scariolo says. "It's challenging when you put a player like Jamal Murray coming off the bench with a certain status, which is basically getting into Shai's team.

"But I think the most difficult step was this one, the first one. Because once that step has been made, then definitely you know what you have.

You might like it, not like it, accept it, be willing to repeat it or not, but you know what it is. And there is no more surprise in the following situations."

As the Canadians filtered into their locker room following the loss, Fernandez told his team that while nobody wanted it to end this early, it was not going to be their final Olympics together; he told them to remember this feeling so that the next time they are in a position to play a game of this magnitude, they will be inspired to be better.

"Yeah. It's a terrible feeling," Gilgeous-Alexander said when prodded to speak. "Obviously, I think for me personally, I might have overlooked the opportunity a little bit. Like, once the game was over, I realized it's another four years before we get this opportunity. That's a long fucking time.

"So for me — and I advise the rest of you to remember what this feels like — this opportunity is what it is because it only comes around every four years, and we got to be ready. So, come 2028, let's be the best we can be."

As the Canadian team huddled up with their arms around each other one last time that summer, captain Olynyk had a final message for the group. "Stay together," he said. "We'll be back."

OUTRO

O CANADA!

As much as the Canadian basketball infrastructure has grown to include some of the best programs and players in the world, one key ingredient has been missing for most of the country's history: a professional league.

The first NBA game ever was held in Toronto's Maple Leaf Gardens in 1946 between the Toronto Huskies and New York Knickerbockers, who won 68–66. But Toronto's economy was reeling from a post-wartime austerity and the team couldn't sell enough tickets to survive, folding after just one season. "The fans just weren't ready for basketball," Canadian player Hank Biasatti said.

In the ensuing decades, more than 40 amateur and pro franchises have come and gone in Canada, with professional leagues like the Continental Basketball Association (CBA) in the 1980s, the American Basketball Association (ABA) in the early 2000s, and the Premier Basketball League (PBL) in the 2010s all trying to make inroads before the teams went bankrupt or the leagues folded. "It's been the business plan," Otis Hailey, who coached five franchises in Canada, said. "People do not know how to market pro basketball in Canada."

However, some owners of the former Canadian PBL franchises decided to band together and create their own domestic league, the National Basketball League of Canada (NBLC), in 2011. But with lackluster ownership groups, rosters dominated by Americans, and a failure to market the league in hockey-first towns, the NBLC never gained a foothold outside of the East Coast and London, Ontario, which won six of the league's 10 championships before the league folded in 2023. "A lot of people with great intentions, and sometimes with not-so-great intentions, have tried to create a professional basketball league in Canada," sports management executive John Lashway says. "And they never took off."

Richard Petko wanted to change that. After growing up in Toronto around Jane and Eglinton, Petko made his living in real estate and moved to Mississauga, where he was a season ticket holder of the NBLC's Mississauga Power. Despite being one of a handful of season ticket holders and seeing less than 100 fans at most home games, he understood the potential of Canadian basketball and purchased an expansion franchise, the Niagara River Lions, for $300,000, to play in the brand-new Meridian Centre in St. Catharines starting in 2015.

But at his first board meeting, Petko discovered that the NBLC was a shoestring business with no long-term vision. In fact, the league didn't have any employees to run marketing, scheduling, and events, which was instead managed by the owners. "We're making literally all these trivial decisions," Petko says. "So when I came back from that meeting, I was like, 'Oh my God. What did I get myself into?'"

As a Slovakian-Canadian who grew up visiting his native country every summer, Petko understood that while Canada historically aligned itself with the American basketball infrastructure, the rest of the world played in FIBA-sanctioned domestic leagues. He figured that if a country as small as Slovakia, with a population of five million, could have a successful league, so too could Canada. So, Petko did something unprecedented in Canadian sport and put his money where his mouth was, launching the Canadian Elite Basketball League in 2019. "Canadians don't care because we don't have kind of a national back," Petko says. "There's literally no pride here, in a sense that way, whereas you go to all these countries in Europe or anywhere, they actually take pride in that they have a league, that they have their local things. And that was kind of what it was about with the CEBL."

A small group of businesspeople and basketball gurus came up with a bold plan to play in the spring and summers when they could get the best players and access venues without having to compete with hockey. They elected to play FIBA rules with about 70 percent of the league being Canadian and a target score ending that made most games finish on a buzzer-beater.

The original six teams were located in Niagara, Edmonton, Guelph, Hamilton, Saskatoon, and Abbotsford — based almost entirely on the availability of venues — but the league has since expanded to 10 franchises, many of which are in big metropolitan hubs like Montreal, Vancouver, Calgary, and Scarborough. Petko owned the original six teams before selling them off for $3 to $4 million a piece after the league rapidly expanded. "No one was crazy enough to be alongside Rich to do this," CEBL Commissioner Morreale says. "Because . . . the history of basketball in this country was littered with tons of things that went wrong."

The CEBL has been a game changer for Canadian players and coaches, providing them with an opportunity to play at home in front of friends and family for the first time ever. "As I get older, and the more you play in Europe, the more you miss home," Phil Scrubb says. "I would have loved to just live in Canada and play basketball."

Fortunately, things are trending in that direction, as team salary caps rise each summer from about $6,000 per game in 2019 to $10,000 in 2025, allowing the top players to make as much as $50,000 in one summer. As a result, the calibre of player continues to improve, to the point where the CEBL is considered a top-10 league in the world with a style of play that blends the best of Canadian athleticism and above-the-rim finishing with FIBA-centric ball-movement and execution.

Plus, the platform has given Canadian players an opportunity to showcase themselves in a FIBA environment that is easy to translate to other professional leagues and international play. Athletes like A.J. Lawson and Jackson Rowe have gone from the CEBL to the NBA, while Trae Bell-Haynes, Prince Oduro, and others have used the CEBL to get better contracts overseas. "I played for the River Lions with [head coach Victor Raso], and he really helped me develop my jump shot," Bell-Haynes says. "That kind of gave me confidence to then go to Germany and have the best season of my career."

"Everything that's been happening for me, it all stemmed from me coming to CEBL," Oduro says. "Getting on the senior men's national team again came from the CEBL." In fact, the CEBL has become a pipeline for the senior men's national team, which fills its rosters for the winter qualification windows primarily with CEBL players. "It keeps more players in the game longer so that they can develop more," Barrett said. "In the end, all that does is create a better product for us."

Countless former players have been able to stay in the game through the league, with Rock Anderson and Jevohn Shepherd joining front offices and Joel Anthony joining the ownership group of the Montreal Alliance — enabling former players to invest back into their communities.

That matters when you consider that the money in professional basketball is growing, with modern stars like Murray and Gilgeous-Alexander set to make more than a billion dollars combined in their NBA careers — money that could be invested back into Canadian basketball through local programs, facilities, and eventually professional teams.

"We were the missing link, I think, in Canada Basketball's master plan," Raso said. "We needed a professional league in Canada. And the CEBL now is that."

■

Canada has come a long way since Maurizio Gherardini walked into a Canada Basketball board meeting and wrote "revolution" on the whiteboard 20 years ago — back when Canadian players couldn't get jobs overseas, let alone in the NBA.

As older players learned from their experiences and passed down knowledge to their children, each generation of Canadians had a slightly easier time moving up the basketball ranks. With a record number of NBA players, a developmental infrastructure that includes club programs teaching kids fundamentals, prep schools keeping athletes in Canada, and a rapidly growing pro league, Canada is by all measures a premier basketball country.

That doesn't mean the system is perfect. By learning from our neighbours to the south, Canadian basketball has become ensnared by many of the same capitalistic defects that come as a result of bad-faith actors trying to get a piece of a sports market valued at $30-billion in Canada. With the ability to create a program or become a coach without any association or oversight from the provincial or national bodies, it is a Wild West of poorly structured programs and selfish coaches competing against each other to pull athletes in different directions instead of working in unity for the betterment of Canadian basketball.

Plus, as good as the top AAU and prep schools are for showcasing elite talent, kids who just want to play basketball for fun are falling to the wayside as the costs of rep basketball rise to thousands of dollars a season. "There's a whole section of our population that can't afford that experience," says Claude Nembhard, the president of Ontario Basketball.

The new Canadian basketball model also focuses on early specialization, creating professional standards from increasingly young ages, which can suck the joy out of the game. "What used to be driven by someone's hunger to improve, to figure it out and work to get better, becomes a job for a lot of these kids," said Nash, who learned the game by playing pickup with his best friends in Victoria. "[They are now] essentially trading their enjoyment and motivation for a calculated approach." It's no wonder that worldwide, 70 percent of kids quit youth sport by the time they are 13.

Canada would be wise to err closer to the European development model in the coming years, where the national and provincial bodies regulate the basketball ecosystem by collaborating with grassroots organizers to create standards for coaching, refereeing, and player development. It would also help to have more youth clubs that prioritize development, team success, and stability instead of the AAU model that prioritizes exposure at the cost of stability.

"The real problem is the transient nature of players in North America," says Roy Rana. "The reason why I think Europe's doing a really good job of developing players is that, for the most part, they're in pretty well a similar structure — there isn't that movement of school to school, team to team. There's a little bit of consistency in what they're being taught and what they're being asked to express.

"We have a lot of players playing basketball just to find the best way to the next step, and not necessarily to help their teams win."

The senior men's national team had as much turnover as anyone in recent years, with more than 80 players and seven head coaches in the past six years, including head coach Jordi Fernandez's surprising departure in early 2025. Canada Basketball chose not to renew Fernandez's contract after clashing with Barrett over decision-making power during the Olympics — something Barrett has been known to do with previous coaches Rana and Triano.

Canada Basketball also valued the opportunity to scour the world for top-flight coaches in the aftermath of their disappointing Olympic run, eventually hiring former national team player Gordon Herbert to coach Team Canada through the 2028 Olympics.

Herbert has had stints coaching Canada before, working as an assistant under Triano and Nurse, finishing as the runner-up for the head coaching job twice before proving that the third time is a charm in 2025. "I'm incredibly honoured and excited for the opportunity to coach my home country," Herbert said.

The Penticton, BC native played ice hockey as a kid but grew quickly and started playing basketball when he was 14, inspired by his mother — a former player at UBC.

After winning MVP of a Gonzaga University basketball camp, Herbert left Canada for North Idaho Junior College, chasing his dreams of playing in the NCAA. He landed a scholarship at the University of Idaho in 1977, when he also attended training camp for the Canadian national team, coached by Jack Donahue. There were 40 players at camp and Herbert was the first one cut. However, after leading the Vandals to a program-best 27-3 record and a trip to the NCAA Sweet 16 as a senior, the 6'6" forward returned to tryouts and made the team in 1982, representing Canada at the Olympics two years later. "It was my goal to play for the Canadian national team," Herbert says. "That was what I really played for."

A 30-year coaching journey has taken Herbert from Finland to Austria to North America to Germany — where he won gold with the German men's national team at the 2023 World Cup.

After finally landing his dream job, the challenge for Herbert will be to keep the core group of Canadian NBA players together through the 2028 Los Angeles Games, when Gilgeous-Alexander, Murray, RJ, Dort, Brooks, Alexander-Walker, Nembhard, and Edey will be in the prime of their careers, flanked by an exciting group of young players. They cannot allow the politics of playing time, hierarchy, or ego get in the way of a potential gold medal and the next "where were you when?" moment in Canadian sport history — not after how much the previous generations have sacrificed to lay the groundwork for the national team to thrive.

"Having been in the program for as long as I have, I'm very proud of where we are, and I'm very proud of where we've come from," Dwight Powell says after Canada won its first ever World Cup medal and qualified for its first Olympics in 24 years, boosting the country's world ranking from 21st in 2020 to 5th in 2025. "I would look at this as the beginning.

"We have an amazing pool of guys and we've set a new standard, a new bar that we can all aim at, and we understand what it takes to get there."

■

On June 22, 2025, moments after leading the 68-win Oklahoma City Thunder to the franchise's first NBA Championship, Shai Gilgeous-Alexander sat atop the press podium. With champagne running down his shirt and a pair of gold signature Converse sneakers slung over his shoulders, the 26-year-old point guard from Hamilton couldn't help but smile.

"As a kid, you dream," he said. "Every kid dreams. But you don't ever really know if it's going to come true."

Gilgeous-Alexander made history by becoming the fourth player to win a scoring title, regular-season MVP, and finals MVP in the same season, averaging 30 points, 5 rebounds, 7 assists, and 2 steals in the 2024–25 NBA playoffs. A couple days later, at the championship parade, Gilgeous-Alexander ran around the streets with a giant Canadian flag after proving that — until further notice — the best player in the world hails from Canada.

"This isn't just a win for me," he said. "This is a win for my family. This is a win for my friends. This is a win for everybody that was in my corner growing up." It was also a win for Canada — one of the many reasons to be optimistic about the future of Canadian basketball and the national team.

But the stakes could not be higher heading into the next Olympic quadrennial. It took 24 years for Nash to pass the baton to a superstar of Gilgeous-Alexander's quality, who holds the weight of the nation on his shoulders leading up to the 2028 Los Angeles Games. After him, who knows how long it will be until the next generational superstar comes along to guide Canada towards international basketball glory?

Fortunately, there's one thing you can count on: inside school and community centre gyms across the country, young boys and girls are falling in love with the sounds of basketballs bouncing and sneakers screeching on the hardwood floor; the smells of body odor mixed with Gatorade and popcorn filling the air; the competition, trash talk, intensity, intimacy, and beauty that only basketball can bring.

Those kids are training diligently to reach the pinnacle of their sport — to make it to the NBA and to lead Team Canada to Olympic glory.

And instead of envying Mike, Kobe, or Lebron like their predecessors did — instead of watching Carter, Iverson, or Nash — today's kids are inspired by Jamal, Andrew, RJ, Dillon and, of course, Shai.

They are modeling their games after the first group of Canadians to truly make a name for themselves on basketball's biggest stage: The Golden Generation.

ACKNOWLEDGEMENTS

I fell in love with basketball at Oakwood Collegiate Institute. After school, my friends and I would sit in our tiny gym shoulder-to shoulder and watch the best team in the city. We were proud of it, stomping our feet and cheering "O.C.I. until I die," taunting opponents, cracking jokes, and occasionally following the team to rival schools.

Basketball was unlike any other sport I had grown up with because, as a spectator at least, you can see, hear, and feel everything: The ability to embarrass an opponent at any given moment, the jaw-dropping plays that get a whole crowd on its feet, and the mano a mano factor that can immediately turn a team sport into a one-on-one battle.

There was something about the intimacy of the sport that entranced me. And while I didn't know it at the time, young people like me were falling in love with the game in public school and community centre gyms across the country for similar reasons.

I quickly became hooked on the NBA and started following the Raptors. My friends Alex and Mel would put Michael Jordan highlights on repeat and we would watch them in Alex's living room, occasionally listening to *The Lowe Post*. In university, I started covering the Raptors for a blog called *Raptors Republic* (*RR*), witnessing the team's run to the NBA Championship in 2019. But as I began attending NBA games and interviewing NBA players, I noticed that more and more Canadians were not only reaching the best league on Earth, but dominating it. And I wanted to understand why. That question is the driving force behind this book.

There have been several editors who helped me on this journey, but I owe a specific shoutout to Chris Toman, who gave me my first real break at *VICE Sports*; and *RR* co-founder Zarar Siddiqi, who gave me the creative freedom to practise my craft for years and $500 to travel to Victoria, BC, in the summer of 2021 to cover the Canadian senior men's basketball team. Despite staying in a shoebox hostel with no air conditioning during a heat wave and watching Team Canada lose to the Czech Republic in the semifinal, it was the best experience of my career because it helped me realize exactly what — and who — I wanted to cover.

I owe a great deal of gratitude to the Canadian basketball community — and specifically the Torontonian basketball community — for creating an open space and embracing me. From Kareem Griffin offering me a volunteer assistant coaching position with the Seneca College women's team, to my fellow diehards like Libaan Osman and Wes Brown who are always happy to go to games with me, to the players and coaches that opened up to me for this book, I am forever grateful to you. Two years ago, when I started pitching this idea to publishers, I didn't know what the final product would look like because I wasn't sure who would be willing to talk to me. But almost everyone that I reached out to spoke to me on the record, including countless NBA players who didn't have to.

It has been an incredibly welcoming community, and I hope I did your stories justice with this book.

I do owe an apology to the people of Quebec. While I originally wanted to include more of the country's history, I realized that I did not have the space to include the long, rich history of Quebec basketball within these pages. But the province is on the come-up, with more and more NBA players coming out of Quebec (and specifically Montreal North). Your stories deserve to be told soon. Ditto for the Canadian women who have historically been underfunded and underreported.

Thank you to Michael Holmes and everyone at ECW Press for believing in this project and signing me to my first book deal. It has been a dream come true working with you all on this project. I am also grateful to the Ontario Arts Council and Saskatchewan Arts Board for their generous grants.

To my editors, Alex, Susan, Tina, and Holly, thank you so much for helping turn this project from an assortment of stories into a book. Alex, you have answered every question of mine since I cold-called you many years ago, and your guidance in getting this project off the ground was invaluable.

Last but not least, to my best friends, thank you for keeping me in check and slapping me upside the head if I ever get too big for my britches. To my parents, Harvey and Ariela, and my brother, Josh, thank you for always lending me your support and unconditional love.

ACKNOWLEDGEMENTS

They say it takes a village and, throughout the process of writing my first book, I came to understand the wisdom of that saying — I couldn't have done this without you all.

APPENDIX

TEAM CANADA MEN'S ALL-TIME RECORDS

(Current as of 2025. Including Pan Am Games up to 1987. Not including FISU World University Games.)

* incomplete data
^ active player

	Name	Official FIBA Games
1	Steve Nash	74
2	Eli Pasquale	73
3	Jay Triano	66
4	Gerald Kazanowski	63
5	Jermaine Anderson	61
6	Michael Meeks	60
7	Sherman Hamilton	60
8	Rowan Barrett	58
9	Levon Kendall	56
10	Phil Scrubb^	55
11	Joel Anthony	54
12	Aaron Doornekamp	53
13	Greg Wiltjer	52
14	Brady Heslip	50
15	Cory Joseph^	50
16	Tony Simms	49
17	Peter Guarasci	47
18	Melvin Ejim^	47
19	Howard Kelsey	46
20	Martin Keane	45
21	Kelly Olynyk^	45
22	Jesse Young	44
23	Andy Rautins	44
24	Romel Raffin	43
25	Dwight Walton	43
26	Shawn Swords	42
27	Jamie Russell	41
28	Will Njoku	41

	Name	Official FIBA Points
1	Jay Triano	1032
2	Steve Nash	923
3	Rowan Barrett	754
4	Eli Pasquale	619
5	Tony Simms	613
6	Gerald Kazanowski	607
7	Michael Meeks	572
8	Leo Rautins	554
9	Cory Joseph^	529
10	Jamie Russell	503
11	Sherman Hamilton	485
12	Carl English	485
13	Brady Heslip	462
14	Phil Tollestrup*	456
15	Phil Scrubb^	451
16	Kelly Olynyk^	435
17	Greg Wiltjer	430
18	Jermaine Anderson	423
19	Fred Ingaldson	411
20	Todd MacColloch	389
21	Denham Brown	386
22	Bill Robinson*	385
23	Peter Guarasci	380
24	Levon Kendall	378
25	Andy Rautins	366
26	Joey Vickery	361
27	Shai Gilgeous-Alexander^	359
28	Andrew Nicholson	358
29	Joel Anthony	356
30	Martin Keane	345
31	Melvin Ejim^	339

Created by Nick Ruzich (in collaboration with the The National Basketball Teams Alumni Association).

INTERVIEWS AND SOURCES

Over 100 original interviews were conducted for this project, with a focus on members of the Canadian men's national team from 2000 to 2024. Of the 12-man roster from Team Canada's 2024 Olympic team, 10 players responded to interview requests and agreed to participate in the project: Shai Gilgeous-Alexander, Jamal Murray, Dillon Brooks, RJ Barrett, Andrew Nembhard, Nickeil Alexander-Walker, Lu Dort, Kelly Olynyk, Dwight Powell, and Melvin Ejim. The majority of the interviews took place during a period from February 2024 to March 2025.

Credit is also due to my colleagues in the sports-writing business whose work has informed this book with helpful insights and archival quotations.

The majority of research was conducted from Sportsnet, *The Globe and Mail*, and the *Toronto Star*, relying largely on the work of long-time Canadian basketball reporters Michael Grange (Sportsnet and *The Globe and Mail*) and Doug Smith (*Toronto Star*).

I also leaned on the work of Bruce Arthur, Brian Daly, Cleve Dheensaw, Myles Dichter, Dave Feschuck, Mike Ganter, Eric Koreen, Josh Lewenberg, Blake Murphy, Libaan Osman, Jeff Rud, Nick Ruzich, Tariq Sbiet, Steve Simmons, Jay Triano, Ryan Wolstat, Alex Wong, and several other Canadian journalists and colleagues.

Below is a list of books that were critical in the research process and used throughout the book:

- *Canada's Other Game: Basketball from Naismith to Nash* (Brian Daly).
- *How Basketball Can Save the World: 13 Guiding Principles for Reimagining What's Possible* (David Hollander).
- *Jamaal Magloire: A Biography* (David Goldstein).
- *Open Look: Canadian Basketball and Me* (Jay Triano and Michael Grange).

- *Prehistoric: The Audacious and Improbable Origin Story of the Toronto Raptors* (Alex Wong).
- *Raptors 25th Anniversary* (Damien Cox and Andrew Podnieks).
- *Rapture: Fifteen Teams, Four Countries, One NBA Championship, and How to Find a Way to Win — Damn Near Anywhere* (Nick Nurse and Michael Sokolove).
- *Steve Nash: The Making of an MVP* (Jeff Rud).
- *Steve Nash: The Unlikely Ascent of a Superstar* (Dave Feschuk and Michael Grange).

Additional external sources used throughout the book:

- *Alaska Highway News*
- Associated Press
- *Austin American-Statesman*
- Basketball.ca
- *Basketball Sphere*
- *The Bill Simmons Podcast*
- *Bleacher Report*
- *Calgary Harold*
- Canada Basketball
- Canadian Press
- *Canton Rep*
- CBC.ca
- CBC's *The Fifth Estate*
- *Chatham Daily News*
- Coachcal.com
- *Court of Gold* documentary (Netflix)
- CP24
- *Denver Post*
- *Denver Gazette*
- ESPN.com
- FIBA broadcast
- Global Wellness Institute
- *Globe and Mail*
- *GQ*

- *Guelph Mercury*
- *The Hamilton Spectator*
- *Hoops Hype*
- *Inside the Thunder*
- *Interview*
- Journeyofanelite1.com
- Kentucky.com
- *LA Times*
- Luka Doncic Foundation report
- *Macleans*
- maxpreps.com
- *Mind the Game* podcast
- Mississauga.com
- *Mississauga News*
- *National Post*
- NBA.com
- NBA TV Canada XL
- NBA Youtube
- *The New Yorker*
- *New York Times*
- Niagara radio
- *North Pole Hoops*
- *Orange County Register*
- *Ottawa Citizen*
- *The Province* (BC)
- *Raptors Republic*
- *The Record*
- *The Ringer*
- Sharenews.com
- *SLAM* magazine
- *Sports Illustrated*
- Sportsnet.ca
- Sportsnet Radio The Fan 590
- Sportsnet Youtube
- Steve Nash's Naismith Memorial Basketball Hall of Fame speech
- *Telegram*

- *Toronto Life*
- *Toronto Star*
- *Toronto Sun*
- TSN.ca
- TVO.ca
- *USA Today*
- *Vancouver Sun*
- *Victoria Times Columnist*
- Vision 2020 document (Canada Basketball)
- X&Os podcast

AURORA SHIELDS

Oren Weisfeld is a freelance sports journalist based in Toronto. He covers Canadian basketball, the NBA, and the intersection of sports and politics/culture. Oren's work appears in several internationally esteemed publications including *The Guardian*, *Toronto Star*, *VICE*, *SLAM*, CBC, *Complex*, Sportsnet, and Yahoo!.

After years of covering the NBA, Oren shifted his focus to highlight the growth of Canadian basketball in 2020 and has made it his mission to spotlight as many Canadian ballers as possible. This book is the culmination of that process.

Entertainment. Writing. Culture.

ECW is a proudly independent, Canadian-owned book publisher. We know great writing can improve people's lives, and we're passionate about sharing original, exciting, and insightful writing across genres.

Thanks for reading along!

We want our books not just to sustain our imaginations but to help construct a healthier, more just world, and so we've become a certified B Corporation, meaning we meet a high standard of social and environmental responsibility — and we're going to keep aiming higher. We believe books can drive change, but the way we make them can too.

Being a B Corp means that the act of publishing this book should be a force for good — for the planet, for our communities, and for the people that worked to make this book. For example, everyone who worked on this book was paid at least a living wage. You can learn more at the Ontario Living Wage Network.

This book is also available as a Global Certified Accessible™ (GCA) ebook. ECW Press's ebooks are screen reader friendly and are built to meet the needs of those who are unable to read standard print due to blindness, low vision, dyslexia, or a physical disability.

This book is printed on FSC®-certified paper. It contains recycled materials and other controlled sources, is processed chlorine free, and is manufactured using biogas energy.

FSC www.fsc.org MIX Paper | Supporting responsible forestry FSC® C103567

ECW's office is situated on land that was the traditional territory of many nations, including the Wendat, the Anishinaabeg, Haudenosaunee, Chippewa, Métis, and current treaty holders the Mississaugas of the Credit. In the 1880s, the land was developed as part of a growing community around St. Matthew's Anglican and other churches. Starting in the 1950s, our neighbourhood was transformed by immigrants fleeing the Vietnam War and Chinese Canadians dispossessed by the building of Nathan Phillips Square and the subsequent rise in real estate value in other Chinatowns. We are grateful to those who cared for the land before us and are proud to be working amidst this mix of cultures.

ecwpress.com